WITHDRAWN

Life and Love

D1566031

Life and Love:

Positive Strategies for Autistic Adults

Zosia Zaks

Foreword by
Temple Grandin

APC
Autism Asperger Publishing Co.
P.O. Box 23173
Shawnee Mission, Kansas 66283-0173
www.asperger.net

Education Resource Center
University of Delaware
Newark, DE 19716-2940

TS3670

P SPS
Z 139
2006

APC

© 2006 Autism Asperger Publishing Co.
P.O. Box 23173
Shawnee Mission, Kansas 66283-0173
www.asperger.net

All rights reserved. No part of the material protected by this copyright notice may be reproduced or used in any form or by any means, electronic or mechanical, including photocopying, recording, or by any information storage and retrieval system, without the prior written permission of the copyright owner.

Publisher's Cataloging-in-Publication

Zaks, Zosia.

Life and love : positive strategies for autistic adults / Zosia Zaks ; foreword by Temple Grandin. -- 1st ed. -- Shawnee Mission, KS : Autism Asperger Pub. Co., 2006.

p. ; cm.
ISBN-13: 978-1-931282-93-2
ISBN-10: 1-931282-93-5
LCCN: 2006925998
Includes bibliographical references and index.

1. Zaks, Zosia. 2. Autism. 3. Developmentally disabled–Life skills guides. 4. People with mental disabilities–Life skills guides. 5. Life skills–Handbooks, manuals, etc. 6. Social skills–Handbooks, manuals, etc. 7. Self-reliant living. I. Title.

RC553.A88 Z34 2006 2006925998
616.85/882--dc22 0606

Cover photo by Gena Zaks.
Designed in Palatino and Futura.

Printed in the United States of America.

DEDICATION

This book is dedicated to my father, Arthur Zaks. He told me once that it was in fifth grade when he noticed the gulf between him and his peers. He said it was as if he couldn't figure out how they knew what to say and what to do to be among each other. He was sure he could find a book that would explain how, or have the rules in it, and when he found the book he would save it and give it to his children so they wouldn't have the same problem.

Well, Dad, I know you never found that book, but now we can write ourselves into our own book. Thank you for always understanding and loving me.

■ ■ ■

FOREWORD

This book will provide many insights and much practical advice that will help individuals on the autism spectrum to achieve independence and live more comfortable and satisfying lives. Zosia Zaks, a person with autism, provides step-by-step inside views and "how to" information on many topics such as dealing with sensory issues, renting an apartment, getting along with family and friends, succeeding at work, appropriate subjects for conversation with casual acquaintances such as the letter carrier, and much more.

I can really relate to her tips on making categories to organize housekeeping tasks. Putting things into categories is how I think, and I also use it as a way of organizing my stuff. To form concepts, I sort the image in my visually thinking mind into categories.

Playing the game of "20 Questions" helped me to learn how to make up new categories that would be subcategories of bigger categories. In "20 Questions," one person thinks of a thing such as "dinner plate" and the other person tries to guess what the thing is by asking 20, or fewer, questions. All the answers have to be either yes/no or one word. Dr. Nancy Minshew, an autism researcher, has discovered that individuals on the autism spectrum often have a difficult time thinking up new categories. Learning how to organize categories is the beginning of learning how to think in a more flexible manner.

Learning how to think by creating categories makes many tasks easier. Shopping is easier if the list is broken down into categories such as toiletries, underwear, or breakfast food. When I think about these categories, I see the goods in the store. When I pack for a trip, I also think in categories such as medicines, toiletries, good shirts, underwear, stuff such as wallet, glasses, comb, etc. Thinking in categories makes tasks comprehensible and divides the tasks up into chunks that are not overwhelming.

Zosia has already successfully used the many tips in her book in her own life, including the world of employment. There are many similarities to my own career path. Both of us like to have several different jobs. This helps to prevent getting entrenched in workplace politics and provides more flexibility – if one job/project doesn't work out, there's always another. I work part time as an associate professor and she works a variety of rotating jobs as a heavy equipment operator. My part-time position as a university professor has made it possible for me to avoid almost all of the socially complicated faculty meetings. I just concentrate on doing a good job of teaching my classes and mentoring students.

Thinking in categories makes tasks comprehensible and divides the tasks up into chunks that are not overwhelming.

Both Zosia and I have a freelance business that started slowly. I have been designing livestock handling facilities for thirty years. When I started my business it took a few years for it to make enough money to support me. Zosia is having a similar experience with a jewelry business she and her partner, Gena, started. Gena makes the jewelry and Zosia does all the business functions such as shipping and receiving, accounting, and running the webpage. Gradual progress in a freelance business helps to prevent it from becoming overwhelming.

Another area of this book that related to my own experiences is that Zosia and I have both traveled extensively. I have traveled to most places around the world giving talks on autism as well as consulting related to my livestock business, and Zosia traveled for five years doing many different jobs. This experience of being with people in many different places has been invaluable. For many of us, extensive travel will not be possible, but varied experiences can be found in other ways, for example, by having a hobby, joining a club or doing volunteer work.

By experiencing lots of different places and constantly meeting new people, which is not my favorite thing, I have learned to keep my mouth shut and to recognize that no matter where you go, you have to put up with certain things or people, whether you like it or not. This is a lesson that is not always easy for us on the spectrum to learn. One time I was mentoring some management trainees at one of my best plant clients. The trainees were complaining about stupid engineering mistakes. I told them, "Stupid things happen in all companies. Good companies have fewer stupid things than bad companies. This is a good company." To relate this statement back to the concept of categories – one of the ideas that attracted me so much to this book – this means that a good company has fewer incidents that will go into the "stupid" category and more incidents to put in the "smart" category.

Temple Grandin
Author of *Thinking in Pictures* and *Developing Talents*

Table of Contents

INTRODUCTION

My purpose in writing this book is to make life better and more enjoyable for my fellow members of the broadly defined autistic community. I wrote it specifically for adults who are autistic, high-functioning autistic, or diagnosed with Asperger Syndrome. The chapters will help you deal with everything from sensory issues, disclosure, and surviving at work to getting along better with your spouse or close friend. Certainly, friends and family can understand us better by reading the book, but the book is for us.

I also wrote the book with the goal in mind of making those of us who are autistic more visible in society. When we can do all the things we want to do, when we can achieve our goals, when we can reach our potential, the world will see all the gifts our way of living and loving can offer. We shouldn't feel ashamed for needing to navigate the world in our own way. When we can create methods and strategies for doing everything from shopping to dating, the world benefits as much as we do because we model for the world creative and new concepts of what it means to live, what it means to love, and what it means to have courage.

I do not distinguish between autism, high-functioning autism, or Asperger Syndrome in this book. I refer to the autism spectrum. Currently, academic and scientific circles are struggling to sort out these different definitions. Some clinical differences must exist because if we put everyone autistic into a room, we would see a wide range of characteristics – some of us are verbal, some are not; some are career professionals, others are unable to work; many of us are single by choice or not; others are married and have children. What a nonverbal autistic person who has trouble with self-care and vocational tasks faces is very different from what an autistic person who has no academic or vocational trouble might experience. This in turn can make a big difference to therapists, educators, other professionals, and parents who work or live with individuals on the spectrum – which is why, I think, the debate to classify the different kinds of autism continues.

However, I feel – and I am certain that I am not alone in feeling this way – that although we are a diverse community, we face many of the same core challenges, feelings, and hopes. In other words, we are autistic individuals. The differences among us cannot always be correlated

I choose to avoid categories, envisioning instead branches of the same tree, and focus on how we as autistic people – wherever we are on the spectrum – can maximize our potential to contribute to life and to enjoy and experience all that life has to offer.

to which category of autism we "technically" fall into. Similarly, being diagnosed with one type of autism or another cannot be correlated to one specific set of challenges, behaviors, or predictable outcomes. I choose to avoid categories, envisioning instead branches of the same tree, and focus on how we as autistic people – wherever we are on the spectrum – can maximize our potential to contribute to life and to enjoy and experience all that life has to offer.

A quick note on language: I do not use person-first language. I use "autistic people" instead of "people with autism" because autism and personhood are ultimately synonymous. Autism isn't something distant from our identity. Autism pervades the totality of who we are and is inseparable. Also, I realize that the words autistic and autism should be capitalized when referring to the title of a community or when deferring to an individual's preference, the same way people capitalize Deaf when referring to the Deaf Community. But for simplicity's sake, I've kept all references lower case.

Another quick note on some of the people you may hear about throughout the text: My domestic partner Gena and I were officially married by Mayor Jason West of New Paltz on February 27, 2004, in a groundbreaking act that we hope will change society for the better. This book is not a political one. I refer to Gena as my wife in life and in my writing. I mention this so the reader is not confused. Our close-knit family of daughters, parents, sisters, grandparents, aunts, uncles, in-laws, cousins, and close friends is also occasionally mentioned when pertinent.

I have many people to thank for helping me along the way; otherwise, this book would never have come into fruition. I would like to extend a special thank you to Stephen Shore, who encouraged me to put what I had to say in writing. Thanks are due to my editor, Kirsten McBride, whose suggestions strengthened and unified my writing into a cohesive book. Thank you to Dr. Grandin for writing the foreword, for invaluable suggestions, and for providing me through her writing with my very first understandings of autism and how my mind works. And thank you to Jim Sinclair for helping me clarify my thoughts on the language of autism. I also want to thank staff members at the Boynton Beach public library for patiently helping me locate reference material, and to the Dan Marino Autism Center in Weston and CARD of Boca Raton for allowing me to use their resource libraries.

I would like to thank my mother, Mary Zaks. I would not have been able to write this book without her support, nor would I have grown up with a sense of confidence if it hadn't been for her guidance and tolerance. And I would like to thank my wife, Gena, for taking the cover photo and for all the nights she stayed up late editing, listening, and demonstrating or explaining the NT view of things, in addition to her sense of partnership, her willingness to see autistic strengths and to bridge gaps between autistic and non-autistic people positively, and to view autism with hope as a optimistic journey into another way of being. Thank you also to my daughters, Ruby and Eislyn, for your smiles, your love, and all the joy you bring to my life. And thank you to my brave cat, Zero, for your sweet companionship and for keeping me company as I typed.

It would be impossible to thank all the other people by name who have touched my life in some way, directly or indirectly influencing the writing on the pages of this book. Trusting that you know who you are, I say thank you to each of you as well.

– Z.Z.

■ ■ ■

PART 1:
LIFE

In this part of the book, I describe and suggest concrete ways to deal with some of the issues and problems faced by those of us on the spectrum.

The first chapter deals with a feature of autism – sensory issues – that sometimes poses a challenge. The other chapters in this section do not cover features of autism per se, but address challenges in daily life that may result from being autistic. For example, difficulty maintaining a home or shopping are not problems endemic to autism but because of sensory issues, trouble decoding social rules and norms, or needing visual clues to organize activities and possessions, these and other common everyday tasks can be tough to manage or to complete.

I tried to include a range of everyday events that most people, on and off the spectrum, run into frequently, such as caring for living spaces or traveling. Unfortunately, I could not cover every possible task of daily living. I hope what has been included is useful for you and that you will extrapolate the suggestions and techniques to other areas of your life as needed.

■ ■ ■

Chapter 1

Coping With Sensory Issues

Sensory issues pose a challenge for many people on the spectrum. Indeed, some say sensory differences were the first clues they had that they might be autistic. For young children, sensory issues may be a primary challenge at school or at home; for adults sensory issues may be a big problem at work or while trying to socialize.

So what exactly are sensory issues? Sensory issues may be thought of as difficulties interacting or dealing with the environment posed by the way the autistic brain handles sensory information.

The body processes light, sound, smells, touch, and taste to gain information about the world. The brain interprets these sensory signals collected by the body's five main sense organs to construct and respond to the environment in a process called sensory integration. Most people on the autism spectrum correctly identify sensory signals; however, because of disruptions in sensory integration, we may be overwhelmed by sensations that are considered pleasurable or neutral by others. Conversely, an autistic person may be underwhelmed by some sensations and seek extra input to bring the sensation to a comfortable level.

After first explaining in greater detail how the vast majority of those of us on the spectrum process sensory information, I will describe how sensory issues manifest and what steps may be taken to address the corresponding challenges.

My senses seem to work on a quota system. I only have a set amount of energy or capacity to deal with incoming sensory information. I refer to this as my finite number of Sensory Processing Units.

How Autistic Sensory Processing Works

Sensory Processing in Action

Based on my personal experiences, I will attempt to demonstrate autistic sensory processing in action. My senses seem to work on a quota system. I only have a set amount of energy or capacity to deal with incoming sensory information. I refer to this as my finite number of Sensory Processing Units. If most of my Sensory Processing Units are dealing with one type of input, fewer units are available for processing other types of input. Vice versa, if units are not needed by one sense organ, more units are available to tackle other stimulatory sensations that might be intolerable under different circumstances. For example, if I am in a dark room, I can tolerate more auditory chaos because my eyes are not busy. If I am in a quiet library, I can tolerate the bright lights slightly longer than usual because my ears aren't dealing with a lot of noise.

Sensory Overwhelm and Other Sensory Problems

Using my quota system metaphor as a backdrop, it is now easier to see where sensory problems might take root. Since each sense organ and the sensory system as a whole has a finite number of Sensory Processing Units, what happens when those units are completely used up?

Basically, I can't tolerate receiving any more sensory information. At this point, I am not able to continue conversing, answering questions, or socializing, since these activities require further sensory processing and integration. I need time to calm my nervous system. Usually, this means retreating to a quiet, dark spot where I will not be interrupted. Even kind

> **Sensory Quota System: An Illustration**
>
> Say my brain has only 100 Sensory Processing Units. If it takes 95 units to decipher the sounds of a conversation, decode the conversational signals that indicate turns and innuendo, pick up the contextual clues that impart social meaning, and modulate my voice, I have just five units remaining to use for other sensory sources. Since looking at someone's face, decoding facial expressions, and coping with the pain of the fluorescent lights requires (hypothetically) at least 75 units, in this case I would not have enough Sensory Processing Units to look at the other person, or even open my eyes, while we conversed. This helps explain why most autistic people are unable to look at someone in the eyes while also talking, a characteristic behavior of autism spectrum disorders.

and gentle suggestions like "Would you like some help?" continue the sensory depletion rather than helping matters. It's best to leave me alone. The faster I can retreat somewhere to recharge without further sensory bombardment, the faster I'll be able to gather myself and rejoin whatever is happening. This is what autistic people call a sensory meltdown or being "overstimulated."

Other sensory problems include scrambling and sensory cross-firing. Some on the spectrum report difficulty sorting the multitude of incoming sensory signals into meaningful chunks of information that can be interpreted and acted upon. Others on the spectrum report "hearing" colors or "seeing" music. In my own experience, these cross-fires are not hallucinations. It is as if the nerves that control one sense organ send the signals down the wrong highway. Auditory information is processed by the sight nerves. Or colors and images wind up on the sound pathway. Scrambling and cross-firing can cause confusion, anxiety, or frustration and can also lead to sensory overwhelm.

Soothing and calming techniques. Certain types of stimulation can be soothing when an autistic person has reached sensory maximum. For example, rocking back and forth, touching an item with a certain texture, or concentrating on an area of special interest can be comforting and can bring an autistic person back to sensory equilibrium. We may also "space out" briefly, move our bodies, make gestures in repetitive ways, hyper-focus or "stim" on a toy or object, or play word or number games to displace some of the tension involved in handling sensory input, even if we are not having a sensory emergency.

Now I will endeavor, sense by sense, to present common sensory challenges and practical ways to manage sensory issues. These suggestions can help prevent the uncomfortable plunge into sensory overwhelm. By easing the load on the sensory system, the impact of other sensory problems such as scrambling and cross-fires may also be reduced.

Tastes and Food Textures

Many autistic people, especially autistic children, have severe reactions to the tastes and textures of common foods. Taste reactions vary from person to person: One person gags from just the thought of a crunchy carrot. Another person can tolerate only crisp vegetables. Some can't tolerate strong flavors. Others won't eat anything that isn't heavily spiced. An adverse reaction to the taste and texture of water has caused some of us to become extremely dehydrated. As a result of these sensitivities, the types and amounts of foods and drinks we can tolerate may be quite slim.

If you have trouble getting yourself to eat or drink, try picking a few nutritious substances and just concentrate on them. In other words, if you can get yourself to eat one vegetable or fruit, one source of protein, and one carbohydrate, that's a good start. You can build more foods into your diet as you go along or if you discover a nutritional deficiency.

Sometimes it is easier to eat alone in a quiet place. The overwhelming noises of a cafeteria or restaurant can make it impossible for me to tolerate the taste and texture of anything. If you really can't get yourself to eat or drink, try eating or drinking something that is your favorite color. You can dye water your favorite color, too, if that helps you drink it. Do you have a favorite character from a movie or TV show? Or do you love cats? Even though such items are geared for children, buy yourself a plate or a cup featuring this character or crackers in the shape of your favorite animal. Sometimes having a personal connection to food and to serving pieces eases the transition into the act of eating.

If your diet is extremely limited, it is important to monitor nutrition and hydration levels. You can keep a chart or diary of how many drinks and how much food you are taking in each day and then compare your records to nutritional guidelines for someone your age and weight. Ask your doctor for the latest nutritional guidelines. It is also a good idea to ask your doctor to help you determine if you are drinking and eating enough because nutritional information can be confusing.

Because our diets tend to be limited, we sometimes need additional nutritional supplements such as multivitamins. If you can't tolerate or swallow supplements, you can crush them onto your favorite foods. Some supplements can be purchased as powders that you can mix into drinks. Again, your doctor should help you determine what nutrients you may be lacking and what supplements, if any, you need to take.

Smells

Moving on to the sense of smell but remaining on the topic of food for a moment, special accommodations may be necessary around mealtimes due to olfactory issues. Ever since I was a little girl, the smell of cooking meat has made me throw up. I cannot be in the house if meat is being cooked, nor can I sit at a table while others eat meat. I literally had to leave the house and stake up in the backyard whenever my mother stuck meat in the oven. I couldn't get away from the horrible smell fast enough. Some on the spectrum have reported the same problem with melted cheese, broccoli, fruit, fried food – an autistic person can react negatively to any food smell.

Other types of smells such as perfume and scented products can be troubling, too, especially in confined spaces. At church, for example, you might find yourself constantly needing to change your seat because someone plops down next to you drenched in scents that make your stomach turn or your throat close up. At school or work, you may be able to talk your teacher or boss into making the area a designated perfume-free zone. But some people are resistant to this idea because they enjoy their perfume. Or they may be willing to forgo perfume, but may still want to spray air fresheners or use heavily scented shampoo.

If scents are unavoidable and make you sick, try wearing a special filtration mask such as those used by cyclists to eliminate car fume smells when they ride in traffic. The brand of mask I have used successfully is Respro (see the Resources section on page 359 for more information). Check large sports equipment stores and allergy product stores, or do an Internet search to find out where you can order a filtration mask online. I have used such a filter in subways, at work, at synagogue, in the park, and even at home.

Some autistic people experience the reverse: They are hyposensitive to smell and only notice very strong odors. This sometimes results in personal hygiene problems. To be on the safe side, schedule a shower each day and make sure you wear fresh clothing. If you enjoy scented personal care products, scented candles, and scented air sprays, check first if you live with other people to make sure the smells won't make them ill as even people not on the spectrum are sometimes bothered by these fragrances. And if you are going on a date, it is polite to ask the other person if she or he would be bothered by perfume or cologne. If the answer is yes, don't wear it. Even one drop can make someone sensitive feel sick.

Sight

Autistic people often have sensitivities to light. Regular lights that do not cause other people stress can sting or hurt an autistic person's eyes, cause a severe headache, or induce nausea. Fluorescent tubes, halogens, and incandescent bulbs without lampshades are usually cited as the worst culprits, even imparting a sensation of suffocation or dizziness. Some of us can't tolerate the flashing lights of the television or movies. Your vision may measure within the normal range at the eye doctor's, and yet you may still have a problem with painful eyes. Sensory challenges with light cannot be detected by a test the same way your vision can be tested. All you have to go by is how awful your eyes feel.

If you have to sit under fluorescent squares of light all day at school or work and you have a sensory reaction, ask about alternatives. Perhaps you could have a spot near a window, allowing you to rely mainly on natural light. Wearing sunglasses or a big hat indoors can help in situations where annoying lights can't be avoided. But it can be awkward if you have to wear dark shades in class or on the job. Discuss your sensory issues with whomever is in charge and try to come up with alternatives together.

Those with an uncomfortable sensitivity to sun can use hats and umbrellas outside. Heavy window blinds are useful for reducing sun glare spilling into the home, classroom, or office. Some shades are better than others at blocking sunlight – ask your hardware store for the blockage percentage rating of different shades you might buy. If you can't change the shades in your windows because you are renting or you aren't allowed by your school or workplace, see if you can hang dark fabrics on curtain rods or strings and have them rest over the shades.

Also, light contrast seems to aggravate light sensitivity. For example, I absolutely can't go into a supermarket at night. The glare of the white lights against the dark night sears my eyes. It feels like my forehead will rip into two. It is also terribly painful for me to walk from inside to the outdoors on a bright sunny day. Besides the pain in and behind my eyes, it takes my pupils a lot longer than other people's to adjust to the new quantity of light.

Some describe not so much a problem with light per se, as difficulty with multiple visual distractions. The plethora of differently shaped

Autistic people do not like to be surprised by what many others consider friendly touching. Even shaking hands can cause us stress as we struggle to adjust to the pressure and texture of different hands.

and differently colored objects in a room can make an autistic person dizzy or anxious. Try putting stuff behind cabinet doors or under a solid colored blanket. Grouping objects by size or color can also help. When you go out, wearing a baseball cap and skier's sunglasses can reduce the visual bombardment on the street and in public places.

Touch

Tactile sensitivities pose challenges for many autistic people, too. What to someone not on the spectrum is a pleasurable touch – a hug, a kiss on the cheek – is often an autistic nightmare, creating an uncomfortable zinging sensation throughout the skin and muscles. Beards, wet lips, and unexpected touches can create tactile emergencies – overwhelming our nervous system and causing us to cringe or flee. Autistic people do not like to be surprised by what many others consider friendly touching. Even shaking hands can cause us stress as we struggle to adjust to the pressure and texture of different hands.

Touch is an area where some of us are both *hypersensitive* (over-sensitive) and *hyposensitive* (under-sensitive). We can't stand, for example, the light touch of someone else's jacket wiping across our skin on the bus, but we like firm tactile pressure to relieve stress. Some of us like to sleep against a hard wall, or cover our bodies with heavy pillows while zoning out on the couch. Some of us can't stand hugs and kisses, but enjoy a firm, steady hand placed on an arm or a leg instead. If this is true in your case, you can compromise with your loved ones, allowing them to display their affection for you alternatively. Just ask them to place a hand somewhere that won't startle you, instead of approaching you with hugs, kisses, and touches that are going to make you jump.

Tactile sensitivities also surface when it comes to clothing, and again are expressed as a hypersensitivity or hyposensitivity. Some autistic people can't tolerate any fabric that is scratchy, stiff, bumpy, ribbed, or "hard" like denim. We may not be able to tolerate squeezing our feet into sneakers or boots, preferring sandals or bare feet. The lightest touch can be irritating or anxiety provoking. If a piece of clothing is even slightly off – a sock that just doesn't fit on the foot, a shirt that cuts too close to the neck – an autistic person can experience great sensory distress.

On the other hand, some of us need and prefer scratchy wool clothing, thick fabrics, or heavy shoes. We may not notice that a sock is falling off our foot, or that a shirt is too tight, due to a tactile hyposensitivity. Still others have a mix of hyposensitivity and hypersensitivity. For example, an autistic person may find it impossible to tolerate tight nylon stockings, but crave thick wool ones. If you find an article of clothing that is tolerable, buy as many as you can and save the extras for the future.

Issues with touch can surface in other surprising ways, too. Some autistic people absolutely can't stand the slimy feel of soap on the skin, affecting personal hygiene. Others can't stand going from dry to wet and from wet back to dry, causing difficulty if it is time to shower, swim, or go out if it is raining. Because changing sensations can be difficult or uncomfortable, an autistic person might not take off a sweater even if it is hot in the room. To remove the sweater would change the sensation on the skin from the feel of the cloth to the feel of the air and that can be very overwhelming.

In order to avoid overheating or freezing, it may be necessary to rely on external rules instead of your own inner sense of the temperature. It can be easier to follow rules than to adjust to nuances in temperature or environment that we may have trouble noticing anyway. If changing your clothes around and adjusting to fluctuations in climate throughout the day is difficult for you or causes you stress, making some rules to go by can be comforting. For example, maybe your rules would require you to take an umbrella if it is raining, to wear a sweater and hat if it is under 50 degrees, to wear short sleeves if it is over 80 degrees, or to take off your jacket if you are sweating.

Sound

Auditory issues are another major source of challenges for autistic people. Certain sounds produce great anxiety. Even "natural" sounds like laughter or thunder can make an autistic person feel sick or throw up. If someone has an extreme sensitivity to the sounds of forks and knives screeching against plates, mealtimes may be problematic, requiring the autistic person to eat alone. Cacophonous music, clapping, laugh tracks on TV, fireworks, ticking clocks, and smoke alarms appear to be among the top offenders.

The most obvious answer is to get away from the noise. But that is not always possible. Sometimes listening to acceptable music on a walkman can drown out the din. Others choose to wear ear plugs. If an intolerable noise suddenly occurs, an autistic person may need to bolt from the scene until measures are taken to reduce or eliminate the source of distress.

Sometimes people on the spectrum are hyposensitive to sounds. For example, if we are extremely focused on something we consider vitally important, we may not register our names being called or an alarm ringing. If you have a problem registering sounds, it is wise to let others know. Your office co-workers can make sure you follow them out of the building in the event of a fire, for example. Similarly, if the situation is explained in advance, those you live and work with won't take it personally if they call for you and you don't answer. With your help, they can devise some other method for getting your attention that registers without startling you.

Strategies for Navigating in the World

Sensory Emergency Kits

Everywhere I go, I carry a Sensory Emergency Kit. This kit contains the items I need to handle a sensory emergency should one arise. Most items fit in my jacket pockets – even the walkman I use to drown out unpleasant noises. You can also carry your items in a special backpack or in your purse.

Everyone's Sensory Emergency Kit will be different. Think about your senses, what bothers you, and how you could cope. In general, your Sensory Emergency Kit will probably contain the items on the following list. You may think of other items to add, or you may not need some of these items. The important point is to make sure you create your kit and then take it with you everywhere you go.

Sensory Emergency Kit Items: Sample List

Sunglasses to shade your eyes from lights

Walkman, ear plugs, or noise cancellation ear phones to drown out sounds

Personal filtration mask to filter out smells

Snacks/drinks in case you are away from home and can't find any tolerable food or drink

Gum or candy in case you try a new food or drink and the taste is horribly unpleasant

Distraction items such as little games, toys, puzzles, or a pad of paper and a pen to soothe or calm yourself if you are very anxious, or have to wait a long time

Tactile items such as something interesting to hold, squish, or roll in your hands if tactile stimulation soothes you

Extra clothing if you are hypersensitive to air conditioning or have other temperature issues

Honesty As the Best Policy

The best way to navigate sensory problems, in addition to always being prepared with your Sensory Emergency Kit, is to be honest with yourself and with others. Because I have extreme sensitivities to the smells and sounds of most foods, restaurants and mealtimes are a major source of trauma for me. Knowing this about myself, I eat alone at home and avoid restaurant situations as much as possible. I don't make dinner meetings with business colleagues, for example, though I will meet for coffee or a soda. And when I was dating, I almost never made plans to meet over dinner.

My family loves restaurants. Every occasion in life is a reason to try a new place, it seems. When I was first getting to know my wife's family, we had to prepare them somehow for my issues. This was humiliating to me. The last thing you want to tell your new in-laws is that you can't stand the sounds, sights, and smells of dinner at their favorite Mexican cafe. But I have discovered that honesty is best. They have all been briefed that I will take breaks during the meal, I won't sit through the main course, I will probably be wearing my sunglasses, and that none of this is a statement about them or their company.

Every one of them has been supportive. They go out of their way to find quiet restaurants or to reserve private rooms and quiet tables. They make reservations for odd times of the day when it's less crowded. One time when we were out to dinner, my grandmother-in-law was about to order the rack of lamb. Then she looked over at me and caught herself. She said, "Oh no – that'll be no good for Zosia. I'll take the fish special." It was the sweetest gesture on her part. I'll never forget it.

At first I was very uncomfortable explaining all of my sensory limitations to people, but I've realized through trial and error that telling people is usually better than not telling. People have a strange way of assuming things that are usually far worse. For example, I was invited by someone at my synagogue to join an informal and impromptu gathering of people my age one Saturday night after Havdala, a sunset ceremony that takes place at the end of Shabbat, the Jewish holy day. The sounds of everyone's laughter were hurting my ears. I needed a break, so I went out onto the terrace and watched the stars for a while. When I went back in, the raucous joking that had been taking place was over and people had settled into quieter conversations. I had a good time. But later that night, the hostess came up to me and said, "I'm sorry you had a bad time." She thought I didn't like the other guests because I had stepped outside for a break! When I explained to her that I have sound sensitivities, my actions made a lot more sense to her and she didn't take it personally.

Keeping It Brief

I've also learned that you usually do not need to launch into a full explanation of autism or disclose your disability if you don't want to. A few key phrases seem to do the trick. For example, if you need to flip on your sunglasses, just say something like: "I have an extreme sensitivity to light. You might think it's weird for me to wear sunglasses in your home, but they help reduce the pain in my eyes." Or, if you are invited to a restaurant: "I know you'd like to take me out to your favorite restaurant. But restaurants are hard environments for me to relax in because I have a lot of sensitivities to sound." One or two sentences are usually enough to get the message across.

Two Other Senses: Vestibular and Proprioceptive

Human beings have at least two other senses: vestibular and proprioceptive. The vestibular sense is based inside the inner ear and gives the body a sense of balance. The proprioceptive sense is based inside the brain and muscles, and gives the body a sense of where it is in space, how body parts are moving, and where the body is in relationship to outside objects.

You may be so uncoordinated that you drop things and make accidental messes constantly. Try my "10-second rule" – if you drop your fork, count to 10 before leaning over to pick it up.

The Vestibular Balancing Act

If your vestibular sense is hyper, you may have trouble balancing or have a tendency to fall. Activities requiring a lot of motion may make you queasy. If this is the case, be sure to wear sturdy shoes, place most of the objects in your home at arm's reach so you don't have to reach over your head or down toward the floor to retrieve things, and take safety precautions when the environment is dangerous. For example, buy a waterproof chair and sit down when you take a shower.

On the other hand, if your vestibular sense is hypo, you may not be able to stop moving because your body overcompensates with excess motor stimulation. You may be so uncoordinated that you drop things and make accidental messes constantly. Try my "10-second rule" – if you drop your fork, count to 10 before leaning over to pick it up. This gives you a few seconds to process carefully where the fork is, where the floor is, where the table is, and where you are, so you can pick up the fork without knocking over other things or falling out of your seat.

Proprioception and Daily Life

The proprioceptive sense guides spatial relationships. A sensitivity in this area, hyper or hypo, can result in challenges in many areas of life. Getting dressed, brushing your teeth, picking up the phone, carrying a package, picking things off the grocery store shelf, positioning yourself next to a stranger in line at the movies, adjusting to a new seat, getting onto an escalator – every one of these activities is controlled in part by the proprioceptive sense.

If you have to move objects, an imbalance in the proprioceptive sense can cause you to grab them too quickly or too slowly or to knock into other objects in the process. You may not have a good sense of how objects should be arranged in physical space either. Some have the most trouble with small objects and fine-motor coordination, others with large objects and large-motor coordination; some have trouble with both. For example, you may find it tiresome and challenging to manipulate and arrange the various objects in the bathroom or on your desk, but heavy or big objects may not be a problem because, due to their large size, you have a much better sense of how much space they take up, what size they are in relation to your body, and what you have to do to interact with the objects. Or your experiences may be the opposite.

To address challenges caused by imbalances in the proprioceptive sense, try some of the techniques listed below.

- **Practice reaching and grabbing**
  If you misfire when you reach for objects, if you grab too hard or not hard enough, if your speed is off, practice helps. For example, if you have no idea how much pressure to use to pick up your toothbrush, how hard you have to squeeze it to keep it from dropping out of your fingers, or how far to move it to reach your mouth, this can make brushing your teeth a fatiguing, messy enterprise.

  One day when you aren't tired or stressed out, put the toothbrush on the kitchen table. Try reaching for it at different speeds and with different amounts of pressure. Bring it to your mouth fast. Bring it to your mouth slowly. Which works better? Do you have to squeeze the toothbrush as hard as a rock to keep it safely in your fingers? Or can you squeeze it with a little less force? When you find the right combination, practice until you can use the toothbrush with less effort. You can practice with large or small objects, whichever causes you difficulty.

- **Break down tasks**
  You can also break actions into steps that are easier to follow. For example, if you're always knocking into the front door because it isn't clear to you how to open it and then move your body through it with the right "amount" and types of motion, break the process down into smaller chunks. First, approach the door slowly and wait until your feet are squarely in front of it. Next, turn the handle or push. Try different amounts of force until you find the perfect amount. Practice several times until you can feel inside your hands and your arms how much "turn" or how much "push" is required.

Next, step through the door and plant both feet on the other side. Only after you have moved all the way through the entrance should you turn around to close the door behind you, if necessary (some doors shut automatically once you're through). Write or draw the steps if you need visual clues.

Break Down Your Tasks: Entering the Front Door

1. Stop in front of the door.
2. Make sure your feet are planted firmly on the ground.
3. Use your hands to open the door with the right amount of turn or push.
4. Watch the door as it opens.
5. When the door is fully open, step through the entrance way.
6. Stop on the other side of the door.
7. Make sure your feet are planted firmly on the ground again.
8. Turn slightly to close the door (if the door doesn't close automatically).
9. Use your hands to close the door with the right amount of twist or pull.
10. Watch the door as it closes.
11. When the door is fully closed, turn your body and head to face forward.
12. After making sure your entire body is facing forward, begin walking.

- **Measure it out**

  Another technique that can help you relate physically to the objects in your environment is to size out everything with a tape measure. This way, you will be able to "see" literally that only eight inches exist between the chair and the wall in the dining room. After measuring these eight inches and visually seeing how much space eight inches take up, you may be able to maneuver your chair more easily. Is your microwave at eye level or at arm's reach? Do you have a foot of space between your bed and your nightstand or less? Pulling out a measuring tape and having fun measuring all the distances in your house can help you gain an understanding of how much space you have to maneuver yourself and your objects.

- **Have a family member or friend demonstrate appropriate body distances**

  If you have trouble knowing where to position your body in relationship to other people's bodies, demonstrating spatial distances may be useful. You'll need a family member or friend to help you. Don't be embarrassed. It's better to figure out how far or how close to stand next to other people than to knock into others by accident or send out the wrong signal by positioning yourself in the wrong way.

  Get several giant pieces of strong white poster board and some magic markers. Stand on the poster board and have your helper draw a circle around your feet demonstrating the proper person-to-person distance for whatever situations come up frequently in your life. For example, you can draw circles for standing on line at the movies, sitting next to someone at a restaurant, standing next to a date, standing next to a complete stranger, asking a police officer for directions, or asking your teacher or boss a question. While standing in the middle of the circle, gain a sense of how far the other person should be. Your helper should stand at the edge of the circle she just drew for an additional visual clue.

  Notice if your circles for different situations are a full arm's length away, a little closer, or a little farther. Mark down next to each circle "stranger," "date," or "teacher" and then compare. You'll see that you stand next to a date much closer than to a complete stranger. Keep your poster boards for future reference. If you are going out

Despite the challenges described in this chapter, many of us on the spectrum take pleasure in the positive attributes of how we perceive, collect, organize, and absorb sensory information.

and anticipate a specific situation, you can practice just before leaving to refresh your memory.

- **Use photographs**
  Lastly, you can use photographs to help you learn how to position yourself. For example, if you have trouble getting comfortable, have someone take a picture of you sitting at your desk or on your couch. Then analyze the photo: Do you look comfortable? Are you slouched or crunched up? Are you squished into a tiny area when you could spread out a little bit more?

  If you notice that indeed you do look uncomfortable, practice rearranging your position and your posture and then consciously try to notice how it feels to be comfortable. Mirrors can be useful in the same way if you are able to determine the position and comfort level of your body. But if you aren't sure what to do with your body to increase comfort or improve posture, or if you can't even tell if you are uncomfortable, stick to photos. Ask family and friends to analyze the picture with you and ask them to demonstrate better ways of sitting and lounging. They may have to literally move your limbs or press on your shoulders to help you into a new position.

Conclusion

It is important to note that on the plus side, despite the challenges described in this chapter, many of us on the spectrum take pleasure in the positive attributes of how we perceive, collect, organize, and absorb sensory information. The sensory situation is not completely bleak. A tiny scrape of a fork on a plate can pierce my ears, but I love going to hear Melissa Etheridge rock the house in concert. The sound pours through me and transports me into the world of her music. Lights can sting my eyes, but I love the millions of colors in the produce aisle of the grocery store. I can get lost in the beauty of the colors and forget to keep my mind on the shopping. In short, sensory stimulation can be both a challenge and very enjoyable.

The context of sensory input is very important, too. Overwhelming, discordant, piercing sounds in a stressful, chaotic environment can shake me up terribly. But listening to a CD of stirring, soul-encompassing Beethoven or Led Zeppelin in my favorite pajamas relaxing on the couch can lift my spirits. My relationship to a sound, a sight, a smell, a taste, or a touch can influence my positive or negative experience of it.

I've learned that getting to know myself and what I can tolerate is critical for being able to navigate the world around me. Keeping an open and creative mind is important: Maybe a restaurant won't do, but a picnic would be fine. Maybe just turning off the lights would enable you to have that serious talk with someone. Sharing my reality with people is far better than leaving them guessing. Armed with your Sensory Emergency Kit and prepared to explain your experiences to others, you'll be able to navigate the world with less stress. Loved ones, especially, are almost always willing to make accommodations, if only they knew what was going on for you.

■ ■ ■

Chapter 2

Maintaining a Home

This chapter looks at and addresses some of the blocks autistic people might experience when trying to maintain a healthy, safe, and organized home. While not everyone on the autism spectrum has trouble getting and staying organized, many of us have a tough time creating a comfortable place to live. Strategies are described for maintaining sanitary conditions, tackling mess, prioritizing tasks, organizing possessions and managing time. With the goal in mind of boosting confidence in the ability to live independently, these strategies, tips, and new skills may foster competence in daily living.

Major Road Blocks: What Makes It So Hard?

Some autistic people have difficulty managing all the tasks that go into maintaining a home. What has to be done first? Where do you begin? What are the steps involved in cleaning a tub? Which chores are mandatory? Which are optional? And how do you schedule your time so everything is completed thoroughly without sacrificing other life activities?

Autistic people may also have trouble sorting different objects in the home. For example, we may not realize that the enormous pile of "stuff" on the bed can be broken down into separate piles of clothes, books, papers, and trash, and therefore managed more easily. It may be difficult to sort and control things that arrive in the home, with newspapers winding up all over the place and packages left by the door for weeks.

External pressures from society to make our homes look a certain way may make us feel so awful about our living quarters that we give up trying. We feel as though we cannot possibly keep pace with the images and messages from magazines and TV that decree what a home should be like.

It may not be obvious where to store items either. Where do you put your shoes? Is there a rule that states where shoes go? Lastly, it may not be obvious that you are supposed to do something with objects. If an autistic person does not want to continue wearing his shoes, the tendency is to just take them off. It does not naturally occur to many people on the spectrum that removing shoes also requires picking them up, transporting them to a set location, and then placing them carefully in the assigned spot.

Social stressors may impede home organization. Because of social isolation, some autistic people may not feel motivated to care for their homes. Why bother, if you have few or no visitors? The living space may be so out of control that it seems too overwhelming to tackle the mess. If no one else is coming over anyway, why go through the hassle?

External pressures from society to make our homes look a certain way may make us feel so awful about our living quarters that we give up trying. We feel as though we cannot possibly keep pace with the images and messages from magazines and TV that decree what a home should be like. Additionally, well-meaning non-autistic friends and relatives can inadvertently put pressure on us or assume we are lazy when, in fact, we may be having serious trouble caring for our living quarters, further fueling a sense of frustration.

Before I discuss specific strategies and methods for organizing the home environment, it is important to assess how you feel about where you live. Do you feel bad that your home isn't like everyone else's? Has the house or apartment gotten so out of control that you feel it would be impossible to begin? Depression and anxiety can be triggered or magnified when you don't feel comfortable in your own home. If you are feeling terrible about the condition of your place, you may want to talk to somebody you trust about your feelings. If you have no one to talk to, or your feelings are overwhelming, seek out professional help.

First Things First: Chore Priorities

Sanitation

The first priority at home is sanitation. Your home may be considered hazardous if it is unsanitary to an extreme degree. Examples include trash overflowing all over your yard, rotting food piling up in your kitchen, or living with too many animals and/or allowing animals to make messes everywhere. Family members and neighbors can alert local authorities to deplorable living conditions such as these because unsanitary conditions in your home pose a problem for others around you as well: Filth attracts bugs, mice, and rats, which in turn spread disease. Filth is also usually malodorous. Your local board of health or other local agencies that monitor home conditions and animal safety may have the right to force you to clean up, to condemn your property, to reduce the number of animals living with you, or to make you move out. Before you do anything else, you must make sure your home is sanitary. A basic level of sanitation is your number one goal.

With this in mind, your first chore should be removing trash. Garbage includes left-over food, packaging materials like food cans and bottles and boxes, papers you no longer need, items that have broken, and items you no longer use. You need a garbage bin or receptacle in each room of your home, including the bathroom. When garbage bins are full, you bring them to a central location such as the garage or the front porch and there, dump the contents into a central trash bag or can. The central bag or can is stored somewhere secure like the garage until trash collection day. On trash collection day, you bring the central bag or can to the curb.

If you are renting, be sure to ask your landlord where to store your trash until trash day and where on the curb it should be placed on trash day. If you live in a city or an apartment building, you may just dump your household bins right into a hallway trash chute. Even in this case, double-check with the landlord or superintendent to make sure you understand the trash rules. For example, certain items such as newspapers are not allowed in apartment building trash chutes because they can catch on fire.

Just taking care of your garbage involves many steps. If your community recycles glass, paper, plastic, and metal, you have to add a few steps to your list. If managing your garbage is overwhelming you, use the tips outlined later in this chapter for sorting items, breaking down tasks, scheduling chores, and using visual aids as prompts and guides. If your living space is overflowing with trash, you may need to ask somebody to help you put it in large bags and bring it to the curb or wherever appropriate. Don't be embarrassed. Your priority is to create sanitary conditions for yourself and those who live near you.

If you live with animals, you need to clean up after them. Cats can use litter boxes indoors, but you must remove the waste and clean the box regularly. Throw out the box and get a new one if the box becomes stained or smells even after cleaning it. Dogs should not go to the bathroom indoors. Dogs need to be taken outside to specific designated areas. Then the waste needs to be put inside a plastic bag and disposed of in the trash properly. Do not let dogs go to the bathroom in your yard or your neighbor's yard (or a city park) and then just leave the waste. If you have other kinds of pets, consult your veterinarian for tips on properly handling their waste.

Steps for Managing Trash If You Live in a House

1. Place a bin in each room of the house/apartment.
2. When full, dump contents of individual smaller bins into a central trash bag or can.
3. Store the central bag or can somewhere safe.
4. Clean up after animals and dump waste in trash, if applicable.
5. Sort for recycling, if applicable.
6. On trash day, bring the central trash bag or can and/or recycling bin to the curb, or wherever appropriate.

Safety

The next big priority is maintaining basic safety conditions. Do you have wires hanging out of your ceiling fan? Are chunks of your plaster wall crumbling? Is paint peeling around the windowsill? Is mold spreading over your bathroom like an alien infestation?

Mold, paint dust, crumbling walls, dangerous electrical wires, broken windows, and broken floors are among the top safety problems in the home. You may ask, who cares? The answer is that faulty wiring is a major cause of house fires. You can trip on broken floor tiles, or get a splinter from damaged boards. Children and animals can fall out of broken windows. Mold and dust contribute to health problems like asthma and respiratory illness.

Take a short walk around your home once a month to check for serious safety violations. If you aren't sure if something is a problem, ask others. Again, it may seem overwhelming to you to keep track of your home's condition. The tools explained later in this chapter, like Monthly Easy Charts (see page 46), can make it easier. Besides being safer to live in, your home will also be more comfortable when basic safety is maintained. For example, you'll be able to walk around barefoot if your floors are safe and you'll be able to hang out in your basement and have fun down there if it isn't dripping with mold.

Body Care

Your next priority is creating clean spaces to take care of your body. On the most basic level, you need a clean place to shower (or take a bath if you prefer), a clean place to use the bathroom, and a clean place to make and eat food. If you can't take a shower because you can't differentiate the soap from the scum, how are you going to wash your body? And if the toaster is so greasy it is in danger of catching on fire, how can you heat up your dinner?

You have to shower and eat every day, so after removing your garbage and making sure your house is free of major safety violations, keeping clean places to shower and to eat is third on your list.

Everyday Objects

Organizing your objects – and keeping them clean – comes after sanitation, safety, and body care. The "Everyday Objects" category includes chores like washing and sorting your clothing and changing the sheets on your bed regularly. This category also includes vacuuming carpets and dusting furniture. You may have papers to sort or mail to deal with, too. And you have to put away objects you buy at the store.

Taking care of the objects in your home is important, but you won't die or get sick if the material things in your house do not get taken care of frequently. Your couch will get dusty if you only vacuum once a month, but if you don't take out your trash, fix safety violations, eat, and shower, you can jeopardize your living situation or your health as discussed above.

Optional Activities

Last but not least come all the things you can do, if you so choose, to make your home cozy and beautiful. For example, you may want to paint your walls a pretty color. You may want to hang wind chimes on your front porch or by your window. Some people enjoy planting flowers in the front yard or growing indoor plants. You may want to install a new, fancy bathtub with a spa-jet feature in your bathroom. But you do not have to do these things to survive.

Five Main Areas of Home Care Tasks in Order of Priority

- Sanitation – remove your garbage, recycling, and pet waste
- Safety – fix major hazards
- Body care – maintain a place to shower and a place to eat
- Everyday objects – clean rooms and furniture, organize possessions
- Optional activities – decorate, upgrade, enjoy home-related hobbies

Sorting: A Basic Skill

Sorting is an important skill. Everything from trash to clothing to paper has to be sorted. Keep in mind the five-part priority list just described as I discuss sorting. As you begin to sort, do not worry about what you will do with the stuff when you are done. Just concentrate on sorting everything into piles to start. Remember, everyone's piles will be different, based on what you own. Therefore, the examples given are hypothetical.

Sorting by Type or Location

Put all the trash in one pile. Put all your clothes into a second pile. Put newspapers into a third pile. Put all your comic books into a fourth pile. Go around the house gathering all the stuff lying around and begin separating it by category.

Another way of sorting that is easier for some involves making a pile of all the objects belonging to certain rooms. Make a pile of all the objects that belong in the kitchen. Make another pile of all the objects that belong in the closet. Make a third pile of everything that belongs in the bedroom or the basement. Keep plowing through your junk with all of the rooms in your house in mind.

Micro-Sorting by Adjective

Once you've got all the stuff lying around the house sorted into piles – whether by type or location – micro-sort according to adjective. For example, if you've gone from room to room and collected all the clothing in the house into one giant clothing pile, now micro-sort it into Clean Clothes/Dirty Clothes. The goal is to micro-sort your big piles into smaller ones based on a more detailed description.

Another example: After you collect all the papers and mail that have accumulated throughout the house into one giant paper pile, micro-sort it into File/Recycle. Note that in the previous example, clothing was micro-sorted according to its condition – clean or dirty. In this example, paper is sorted according to what should happen with it. You won't always micro-sort by adjective per se. What you are doing is breaking down big overwhelming piles of objects into smaller chunks based on condition or function that will be easier to manage.

If you have a ton of stuff all over the house and you don't know where to begin, go down the list of Home Care Priorities on page 32.

To clarify this last point, here is a third example: Say you go around the house and sort by location, collecting everything that belongs in the kitchen. You wind up with a big pile of lost cups, old plates, a few spoons that fell behind the couch, a spatula you left in the back yard, a basket of apples your grandmother sent over last week that is still in the living room, and some candy that was in your bedroom.

What should you do with this big pile? Micro-sort it into two sub-piles according to a tangible quality, things that go into the dishwasher – cups, plates, spoons, the spatula – and things that don't go in the dishwasher – apples, candy. It is now clear how to proceed. Load the dishwasher, add soap, and turn it on. Put the apples in the fridge, candy in the cupboard. These two tasks aren't difficult and don't take much time, but are not obvious when you are staring at an unsorted mound of junk.

Sorting Tips

Here are some additional tips for sorting.

- **Go in order of chore priorities**
  If you have a ton of stuff all over the house and you don't know where to begin, go down the list of priorities outlined earlier on page 32. For example, start with the trash. Take a day to collect all the trash in your home. Don't worry about any other objects. Just go room to room, pick out the garbage, put everything that is trash into a bag, and throw it out.
- **Make lists**
  If you like making lists, make one of all the kinds of things lying around – cups, shoes, notebooks, newspapers, mail, toys, computer disks. Check off your list of items as you go along or paste a star sticker next to each item as you finish compiling it to give yourself a sense of accomplishment. You

can also motivate yourself with a reward if you manage to check off all the items on the list.

- **Don't try to do all your piles in one day**
  Sorting doesn't happen once, and then you are done. Sorting stuff into piles is something you will do on a regular basis. Don't be too hard on yourself. Making piles and then micro-sorting them is an ongoing task. If you can't get to each type of item this week, pick one or two to do now and leave a few for next week.

- ***Make a junk box***
  Stick everything that defies categorization into a junk box. If you come across a confusing item, throw it into the junk box for now. Later, when you are ready, you can take one or two items out and decide what to do with them at your own pace. But at least the junk box items will be off the floor and out of your way in the meantime.

- ***Use visual aids***
  Make signs for your categories and piles. Everyone has different problem areas. Perhaps you go through a lot of clothes each week and they wind up all over the place. Or perhaps you get home delivery of the newspaper each morning and don't know where to put all the loose sections after reading them. Decide which items are the hardest for you to keep sorted. Then draw yourself visual reminders. You can also cut out pictures of dirty clothes/clean clothes, or trash/not trash, if it would help you to match your items to the pictures.

Sorting and then micro-sorting enables you to determine what to do with all the things you own and use. Again, refer to the priorities list if you don't know where to start. Garbage is always first. Then do piles that contain things you need, such as clothing. You have to put something on each morning, so clothing is an important pile to sort. While papers, books, comics, magazines, toys, videos, pens, and computer disks might be messy, you don't need these things to survive, so leave these piles for last.

If necessary, you can write out a plan of action in advance. Jot down some ideas about what you want to do with your piles. If it seems too overwhelming to decide what to do, pick just one pile and focus on it solely. Don't worry about tackling all of your piles in one night. You will continue making piles and taking action throughout your life.

Preventing Pile Build-Up in the Future: Zone Maps and Absolute Spots

Zone Maps

Making a Zone Map will help you keep your objects in the right places over time. Take out a sheet of paper and draw a sketch of the rooms in your home. You can do this by hand with a pencil, or you can get fancy and use architectural software on your computer – it doesn't matter. Now make different zones based on what you do at home. Generally, you will have at least a Kitchen Zone, a Bedroom Zone, and a Bathroom Zone. You may also have a Hanging Out Zone, a TV Zone, a Home Office Zone, or a Video Game Zone, depending on where you live and what you like to do.

Next, determine rules and boundaries for each zone. For example, perhaps you decide that clothing is not allowed in the Kitchen Zone. If you come home from work and you are too tired to hang up your clothes, at least they will go into the Clothing Zone near the bedroom closet. Maybe you will decide that mail goes right into the Home Office Zone. That way, even if you can't deal with opening the mail immediately, it won't mysteriously migrate all over the house.

Ask yourself: What belongs in each zone? What things definitely do not belong in certain zones? For example, it is probably a good idea to ban food from your Computer Zone. All food items, including cups, should probably stay in the Kitchen Zone, though you can make an exception to take a glass of water into your bedroom at night. Post your Zone Map somewhere obvious. This way, you can easily check the map for guidance, especially as objects such as newspapers, backpacks, groceries, mail, and purchases like video games come into the home.

Example of a Zone Map

The map includes applicable zone rules and an Absolute Spot for keys.

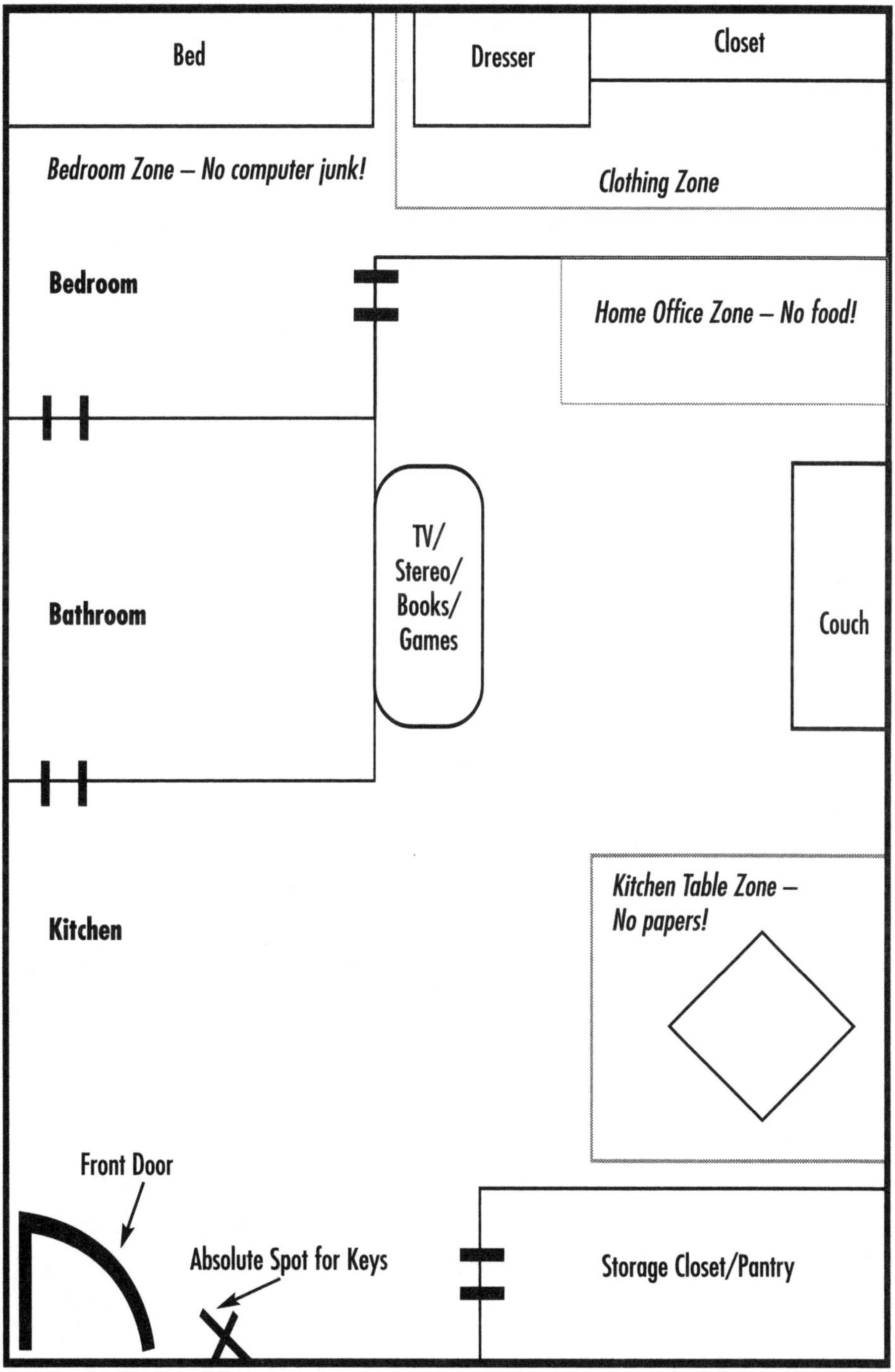

You can mark your Absolute Spots on your Zone Map. Your Zone Map and Absolute Spots provide a geographic method of organizing your possessions and will help prevent build-up of random junk all over the place.

Absolute Spots

Determine Absolute Spots for the most important objects in your life. Maybe this is your keys. Maybe it is your shoes or your briefcase, your lunchbox, the dog food, soap, or your shaver. Everyone has different "most important" objects. You may have several "most important" objects. After you make your list of the most important objects in your life, decide on an Absolute Spot for each. This means that from now until eternity, you will always put an object in its associated Absolute Spot no matter what, even if you are tired, overwhelmed, busy, or preoccupied.

If necessary, mark the Absolute Spots around your apartment with visual aids. For example, if you decide the Absolute Spot for your keys is a hook next to the front door, put a picture of keys there as a visual prompt. If you decide your shoes always go in a certain spot by the hall closet, tape a picture of a shoe onto the floor so you can see every day where your sneakers should be. If you constantly lose the can opener for the dog food, hang a picture of your pet near the dog supply cabinet to mark an Absolute Spot for it. If you can never find your wallet, pick one spot on your dresser and put a sticker there to remind you that this is where your wallet now lives.

You can mark your Absolute Spots on your Zone Map. Your Zone Map and Absolute Spots provide a geographic method of organizing your possessions and will help prevent build-up of random junk all over the place. Using a Zone Map and Absolute Spots will enable you to find things and will remind you where to put things. Even so, over time the stuff in your house may spread out again. This is why every now and then you'll have to go through the house, make piles, sort, micro-sort, and then perhaps revise your Zone Map and Absolute Spots accordingly.

Hot Spots

If you reflect for a moment, you may realize that it is only certain areas of your home that are causing you trouble. I call these areas "Hot Spots." Perhaps you have a very specific clutter problem because of the kind of work you do or because of a hobby. For example, maybe the problem in your bedroom is your magazine collection, which has sprawled out all over the place. Just fixing up the magazines can make your bedroom feel 100% better. Maybe the problem is that coats and mittens and hats wind up all over the kitchen. Just nailing a few hooks for them or putting a box for winter accessories near the front door can make the kitchen a lot more organized. Or if you are a video game expert and your game cartridges have taken over the living room, maybe you need to designate one shelf where all your cartridges can stay.

If you notice that you have a Hot Spot, or several Hot Spots, be sure to mark them on your Zone Map so that they do not flare out of control. Using the video game example above, you can mark on your Zone Map the exact Absolute Spot in the living room where all of your video game cartridges will go – perhaps on a neat shelf or in a nice box. You know in advance that your video game collection is a problem and has a tendency to spread through the living room, but now you have your Zone Map to guide you. If you ever see a video game lying around the house, anywhere, move it to the Video Game Absolute Spot immediately. Do not wait one second. You'll be surprised how much more organized your house and your possessions will be.

Cleaning Up: Managing Chores

Once you've got your house in sanitary condition, you have sorted most of your stuff into piles, and you've started to figure out what to do with your piles, you can begin to tackle the next big chunk of taking care of your home – cleaning.

This part of the chapter deals with daily and weekly chores. The key to getting chores done is to know how to do them and when to do them. For example, you know you have to mop the kitchen floor. But when? How often?

"Mop the floor" may not be specific enough. What happens first? You don't just get the mop and start mopping. You have to get a bucket of water, you have to add floor soap to the bucket, and you have to prepare in advance a sink or tub for ringing out the mop. What order do you go in? You also have to remember to dump the mop water when you are done and stay off the floor until it dries. And this is just one chore!

The "How" of It: Breaking Down Chores Into Chunks

To prevent chores from feeling overwhelming, break them down into logical steps. If you discover that every time you are supposed to do a certain chore you give up in frustration or can't get started, try making a list of the parts involved. You can even check off the parts as you go along.

If you can't figure out all the steps involved in a certain task, ask someone to help you write out the steps. If you have nobody to ask for help, try watching somebody do the task. For example, ask the janitor at work if you can watch him mop the floor of the cafeteria if you have no other inconspicuous opportunity to observe him casually from a distance. He may think your question is strange, so prepare an explanation in advance. For example, you can say, "Do you mind if I watch you mop for a few moments? I'm trying to figure out better techniques for taking care of my home." Take notes. Mental notes are better than writing notes on paper because most people consider it rude if you stand there writing down what they are doing. But if you are going to write notes, ask permission. What steps does he go through? You can then do the same steps in your home.

Also notice what you need to complete the task successfully: You'll need a mop, a bucket, floor soap, and a sink or a tub to wring out the mop. If you can't fig-

Mop the Kitchen Floor

1. Remove any items from your sink or tub where you will be rinsing out the mop.
2. Get a bucket.
3. Fill the bucket with hot water and floor soap.
4. Get the mop.
5. Dip the mop into the bucket.
6. Swish the mop back and forth across the floor in parallel rows.
7. If the mop gets dirty before your rows are done, rinse it out in the sink or tub. Then dip it in the soapy bucket and continue.
8. When you are done with your rows, squeeze the mop out in the sink or tub and rinse it.
9. Run the clean wet mop over the floor to rinse off the floor soap.
10. When you are done rinsing the floor, squeeze all the water out of the mop into the bucket.
11. Empty the bucket.
12. Put the mop away.
13. Walk away.
14. Don't come back until the floor is dry.

ure out what items you need for a certain chore, have someone brainstorm with you. Or again, watch someone doing the chore and see what tools, equipment, soap products, or other items are required.

The "When" of It: Daily? Weekly? Monthly?

Maybe you have a good idea of how to mop the floor, clean the tub, do a load of laundry, or dust the living room. But when? Do you do every single chore every day? Or only once a week? Do you mop the kitchen floor only when you drop something like a bottle of ketchup?

Unfortunately, no strict rules exist for this area of life. People usually clean each item or area of the house once a week and then do extra cleaning if an accident happens. For example, you will probably mop the kitchen floor once a week. But, if you spill something, you'll need to mop it up right away. Leaving a spill on the floor creates an unsanitary condition and is also a safety hazard.

It may seem impossible to get everything done each week. This is a normal feeling that most people experience. Again, learning to prioritize is a key skill. Refer to the *First Things First: Chore Priorities* section at the beginning of this chapter or study the list below. You may have to adjust this list according to your unique situation, but generally speaking, this is a good order to keep in mind for prioritizing your chores.

Cleaning Priority List

1. Garbage
2. Bathroom: tub/shower/sink/floor/toilet
3. Kitchen: counters/floor/fridge/microwave/stove/dishes/utensils/pots
4. Laundry: clothes, sheets, blankets, towels
5. Vacuum carpets/sweep and mop floors
6. Dust/wipe/clean surfaces (TV, windows, desks, mirrors, doors)
7. Clean heavy furniture (couches, bookshelves)
8. Continue sorting items into piles
9. Special projects (mow the yard, shovel snow)
10. Optional projects

Some chores need your attention every day, but other chores need to be done only monthly or seasonally, such as raking leaves. If you are having serious trouble determining what to do first, follow the list on page 42 or have someone help you make up your own list. Remember, if an accident happens, you will have to "bump" other chores and take care of surprise problems like spills first before returning to your usual schedule.

Weekly Easy Charts: Spreading out the Work

If you come home from work and try to clean the kitchen, water the plants, put clothes away, vacuum, wash the toilet, take a shower, and open your mail, you will be overwhelmed, and chances are nothing will get done. Sometimes it seems like you have way too many things to do to keep your house in order, but making and then sticking to a Weekly Easy Chart will help you pace tasks. Each task will get done, but tasks don't have to get done all at once.

The Weekly Easy Chart is like a chore calendar. Each day of the week is listed on a piece of paper. Then, chores are assigned to each day. The chart can be further divided into morning chores and evening chores. As you go through your week, refer to your Weekly Easy Chart and simply do what is listed for that day. For example, if you come home from work on Tuesday and your Weekly Easy Chart says all you have to do is water the plants and sweep the kitchen floor before bed, that's not too bad. You can even check the tasks off as you do them.

To make your own Weekly Easy Chart, first write a list of everything that has to get done in your house each week. Divide the chores into tasks you have to do every day and tasks that have to happen only once a week. Don't worry about tasks that have to happen less often – monthly chores are covered in the next section. If it is too confusing to figure out all the chores that must get done in your house, think about the things that you do as you go through your day. Most people have to do the dishes, take out the trash, sweep, mop or vacuum, water plants, feed pets, do the laundry. If you are stuck, ask someone to brainstorm with you.

After you have made your list, draw a Weekly Easy Chart or print one out on the computer. Then fill it in each morning and each evening with one or two tasks to do from your list. If visual aids help you, use different colors for different chores or for different days. You can also draw what has to be done or cut out a picture of the chore and paste it to your Weekly Easy Chart.

After you have made your list, draw a Weekly Easy Chart or print one out on the computer. Then fill it in each morning and each evening with one or two tasks to do from your list.

Do not assign yourself many chores on a day you know you are very busy. If you have your Star Gazing Hobby Group on Thursday nights, for example, Thursday night is not a good night to do the laundry. If Monday morning is super-hectic with the start of the work week, don't assign yourself the vacuuming. Give yourself at least one evening and one morning off. You may still have to feed the dog on Saturday morning, but you can take the rest of Saturday off to rest and relax.

Remember to schedule time to go through the house and make piles if you have a problem with objects accumulating around the house. With a regular time to make piles and go through them, the piles won't build up. And remember to be specific. If your chart says to clean the kitchen Friday morning, what does that mean? It could mean just wiping the kitchen counters. Or it could mean wiping the counters, cleaning the sink, mopping the floor, organizing the pots, and cleaning the microwave. So be specific.

What if you have too many chores on your list and you can't fit all of them onto your Weekly Easy Chart? You may have to decide what tasks are absolutely critical and must go on the chart versus tasks you may be able to do less often. If you can't figure this out, ask someone to help you. You can also try putting only one chore a day onto your Weekly Easy Chart at the beginning and adding chores as you clarify which ones are most important.

One of the benefits of using a Weekly Easy Chart is reduced anxiety: Because you have your chart to refer to, you can relax knowing that most of the household chores will get taken care of at some point. If you miss vacuuming one Sunday because you go to a special Sponge Bob convention, you know the vacuuming will get done next Sunday. Skipping a week won't cause your house to fall apart.

The benefits of using a Weekly Easy Chart accumu-

Sample Weekly Easy Chart

	Monday	Tuesday	Wednesday	Thursday	Friday	Saturday	Sunday
AM	Water Plants	Take Trash to the Curb Sweep Kitchen	Vacuum Bedroom	Water Plants Take Recycling to the Curb	Clean Bathroom Mop Kitchen Floor	*Free Morning*	Vacuum Living Room Dust Furniture
PM	Do Left-Over Laundry Gather Trash for Collection Tomorrow	Tidy up Bedroom Sort Papers	Clean Bathroom Gather Recycling for Collection Tomorrow	Clean Kitchen	*Free Night*	Sort Piles/Check Zones	Do Laundry

Note: Some days have fewer chores to accommodate personal activities. Note also that time is set aside for sorting piles and checking zones.

NOTE: If you have great difficulty with time management, you can place other tasks of daily living onto your Weekly Easy Chart. For example, you can add showering, shaving, dressing, going to school or work, and shopping for food. Especially if you live alone, it can be hard to maintain the "rhythm of life" – you may forget to eat dinner each night or to go to bed at a reasonable hour. Referring to your Weekly Easy Chart can remind you of the things you need to do to take care of yourself, not just your home.

late over time. After following your Weekly Easy Chart for a week, your house may still be a mess. Don't give up – give yourself a chance. You won't see a difference overnight, but by doing one or two tasks each day, you will feel more in control of your environment.

Also, be open to revision. After using your Weekly Easy Chart for a few weeks, you may discover that you really need to sweep the floor three times a week, not just two – or that you only need to vacuum upstairs once a week. Or maybe you gave yourself way too many things to do on Tuesday, but almost nothing on Wednesday. You may also realize you forgot to put a certain chore onto the chart. The nice thing about these charts is that you can change them as you go along.

Monthly Easy Charts

Some chores, like cleaning out the refrigerator, mowing the lawn, washing windows, or paying bills do not have to happen daily or weekly, so it doesn't make sense to put them on your Weekly Easy Chart. Instead, you can create a Monthly Easy Chart. Again, make a list of all the chores that have to happen on an infrequent basis. Then assign a specific date for each chore.

For example, if you have to clean the fridge once a month, you might pick the 14th of the month to do this task. Whether it is the 14th of March or the 14th of July, whether the 14th happens to fall on a Monday or a Thursday, the fridge gets cleaned. It doesn't matter what date you pick. What is important is that each chore is assigned a date so you will remember to do it.

Get a blank calendar with squares marked 1 to 31. Then fill in the chores. Again, you can draw a chore or glue on a picture if visual cues help. Hang your Monthly Easy Chart where you can see it and

Sample Monthly Easy Chart

Monday	Tuesday	Wednesday	Thursday	Friday	Saturday	Sunday
1	2	3	 4 Refill prescriptions	5	6	7
 8 Pay bills	9	10	11	12	13	 14 Clean refrigerator
15	16	17	18	19	20	21
22	23	 24 Buy toilet paper	25	26	27	 28 Pay bills
29	30					

When you like where you live and when you can relax at home, you'll feel better about yourself, too.

refer to it. Like Weekly Easy Charts, you can rest assured that all tasks will be completed on their assigned dates, reducing anxiety. For example, if you decide to sort your mail and pay bills on the 8th and 28th of each month, you don't have to panic the rest of the time. As with Weekly Easy Charts, your Monthly Easy Chart may need revision and refinement over time.

Asking for Help: Another Important Skill

You can ask your relatives and friends to help you take care of your home. If you are staring at that mound of junk that takes up half the downstairs with no idea how to start sorting it, ask someone to look at it with you and help you decide on categories. If you find that one of your main problems is that you have nowhere to put all of your comic books, you can ask someone to help you find a nice shelf or storage box. If you find the perfect storage box but can't afford to buy it, ask for it on your birthday or a holiday.

Lots of people enjoy organizing domestic spaces and shopping for the home. If this is challenging for you, ask a friend to pick up a few cleaning supplies the next time she's buying them for herself anyway. If you have no idea what color pillows would go with your new couch, ask a friend what she thinks. Friends and relatives are usually willing to help you if you can articulate for them what is difficult for you. We all have strengths and weaknesses. It is nothing to be ashamed of if shopping, sorting, prioritizing, or decorating are hard chores for you. Friends and relatives like helping you out because they care about you. Don't be afraid – all you have to do is ask.

Setting Your Own Standards

Remember that we are under some degree of pressure to keep our homes a certain way. You may feel bad if your apartment does not look like apartments on TV or in magazines. You may be embarrassed if everyone else seems to have a perfect home.

As long as your home is sanitary and safe, your piles of stuff are under control, and your chores are getting done, you don't have anything to worry about. It is O.K. to have a Zone Map on the wall, visual aids to help you complete tasks, a Weekly Easy Chart to keep your chores on schedule, and Absolute Spots marked around the house. Our homes may look different with visual prompts everywhere, but these tips and tools can help you create the home you've always wanted. You may need help prioritizing or shopping for supplies, or you may decide that after dealing with trash, piles, chores, and self-care, decorating takes too much energy. That's O.K., too. We can have homes that are comfortable for us to live in, even if they are different. We can be proud of where we live, even if we must create our own autistic ways of keeping house.

Conclusion

Getting and staying organized isn't easy. Keeping your house clean isn't easy either. But the benefits are great. Over time, your ability to deal with all that goes into maintaining a home will increase. The tasks will become less overwhelming and more manageable. Instead of worrying about your home, or wondering how on earth you'll get any of it done, you'll have more time to do the things you enjoy. When you like where you live and when you can relax at home, you'll feel better about yourself, too. Having a home, taking care of it, and being proud of where you live contribute to a strong and healthy sense of self.

■ ■ ■

Chapter 3

Living on Your Own

Some of us live alone. Some of us live with others by choice or because we have to. Most of us will, at some point, live independently – with or without housemates. When deciding where to live, you will have to consider the benefits and drawbacks of each type of housing option. This chapter was originally part of Chapter 2: *Maintaining a Home*, but upon further reflection, the issue of living independently seemed to warrant its own chapter. Our society is extremely mobile, and it is probable that you will live in a variety of situations throughout your life. Knowing the pros and cons of each arrangement will help you make the best decisions possible.

Living at Home

If you are living at home with your parents, you are probably very comfortable with your arrangement. Chances are your parents still reside in the home you lived in as a child, in which case your environment will be extremely familiar. Sometimes family members will help you obtain and maintain employment, take care of you when you are sick, or give you a big financial break by providing you with free food and utilities. Also, living with your parents can prevent or circumvent feelings of loneliness. Someone will probably be at home on the weekends and in the evenings to keep you company. You can share chores like grocery shopping, cleaning, or maintaining the yard.

But if you are living in your family's house, you will have to follow your parents' rules and be sensitive to their needs. How are you going to feel

You have to weigh the benefits of living with your parents against the chance to have your own life, assuming you are ready for independence. It may cost more to live on your own, and it may get lonely sometimes, but most adults prefer having their own home.

if your mother gets mad at you for coming home at 3:00 a.m.? Do you want to have to explain where you were? What if your parents put restrictions on you that you don't like, such as no TV after 11:00 p.m. because it makes too much noise for them? Most adults prefer to come and go as they please and to make up their own rules. If you are living with your parents in their home, you are automatically agreeing to abide by the rules they choose.

You have to weigh the benefits of living with your parents against the chance to have your own life, assuming you are ready for independence. It may cost more to live on your own, and it may get lonely sometimes, but most adults prefer having their own home. If you aren't ready to leave your parents' house, that's O.K. But as you grow up and get older, finish school and find a job, it may be time to start considering where and how you will find your own place to live.

Living Independently

Finding a Place to Rent

If you are ready to live on your own, it's time to find your own living quarters. Most people start out renting a place to live. This means that you do not own the space. You pay money each month to stay. Sometimes you pay rent to an individual such as the owner of the property. In this case, the owner is referred to as a *landlord.* Sometimes, an entire company owns the space or a real estate agency acts on behalf of the owner.

Usually before moving in, you sign an agreement called a *lease.* The lease states how much you will pay each month, what date the money is due (almost always the first of the month), where or to whom you should send your rent payment, and what will happen if you damage the property or you do not pay your rent. If you don't pay your rent on time, you will be evicted (forced to leave). In some states or cities, the landlord is required to give you a period of time to come up with the payment before you are permanently evicted. Any exceptions to outright eviction upon non-payment should be specified in your lease. Read the lease thoroughly before you sign it and make sure you understand all the rules, including whether or not you are permitted to have animals live with you. Don't sign a lease that prohibits pets if you have one or want to get one soon. Find another apartment.

It is important to read your lease because the document also indicates how long you are entitled to stay. For example, a yearly lease means that in one year, both you and the owner have the right to reconsider the arrangement. At the one-year mark, the owner can rent the apartment to someone else if he chooses. The owner can also increase the amount of rent. Therefore, you retain the right to move somewhere else at the one-year mark. The lease should specify under what conditions you may be excused from the lease early, such as bankruptcy, a dire emergency, or a disaster that makes the place unlivable. However, upon signing a yearly lease, you are considered legally obligated to pay for the whole year.

Sometimes you can sign a lease for less than one year. The most common short-term lease is called a *month-to-month lease*. The advantage of a month-to-month lease is that at any time, as long as you give the owner 30 days' notice, you can leave. You won't owe any more rent. This can be great if you want to try out a neighborhood to see if you like it before committing to a year-long lease. The disadvantage is that the owner has the same privilege: As long as he gives you 30 days' notice, he can ask you to leave. You may have to move on short notice.

Other Costs of Renting a Place to Live

When you rent a place to live, you have other fees besides the monthly rent to consider. When you first find the apartment, before you even sign the lease, you may be required to put down a *deposit*. This shows the owner you are serious about renting. The deposit "holds" the apartment for you until all the paperwork is signed. Before you hand over a deposit, find out if you can get it back if you choose not to rent at the last minute. Usually, your deposit is not refundable, so make sure you really want to live there before you pay. Your deposit should be credited toward other payments or ripped up upon signing the lease.

Next, upon signing a lease, you have to give the owner a *security deposit*. This is not the same as the initial deposit you give to hold the place. This is an amount of money that the owner keeps in a bank account in case you fail to pay him or seriously damage his property. Usually the security deposit is equal to one or two months' rent. Your security deposit should be returned to you when you move out, assuming you have followed all the rules of your lease.

You also have to pay a *broker's fee* if an agent from a real estate company helped you find the apartment. Brokers usually collect a percentage of the yearly rent. For example, if your broker gets a 4% commission and your monthly rent is $1,000, then you must pay the broker 4% of $12,000. When you see an advertisement for a place to live and you call for more information, be sure to ask if you will be dealing with a broker and what the broker's fee will be. You can try to find a place without a broker. Some owners rent directly to the public. But in some locations, brokers seem to know about the better apartments.

Renting a place to live is not cheap. It may take you many months to save up enough money to move into your own place. You have other expenses to plan for, too. Find out if your monthly rent payment includes utilities such as electricity, natural gas for your stove, heat, hot water, and cable TV. Some monthly rent payments include some or all of these utilities; others include none. If your monthly rent payment does not include any utilities, you will be responsible for activating the services and then paying your own utility bills each month. Some utility companies require a deposit from you before services are activated, especially if you have never paid utility bills before.

Do you have furniture? How much will it cost to buy a bed, a sofa, a TV, kitchen items, and whatever else you will need to live comfortably? It is important to begin planning financially to live on your own as soon as you think you are ready.

Typical Costs Associated With Renting a Place

- Monthly rent
- Deposit
- Security deposit
- Broker's fee
- Utilities (may also involve a deposit)
- Cable TV
- Furniture and other items for the house
- Renter's insurance (optional)

Lastly, discuss with someone you trust whether or not you need *renter's insurance*. Renter's insurance protects you in case your living space and/or your possessions are destroyed in a flood, a fire, a building collapse, a robbery, or some other tragedy. Though these incidences are rare, it is usually a good idea to get such a policy. In the event that your home becomes unlivable or you lose all of your clothing, your computer, your dishes, your TV, or your furniture, what would you do? Renter's insurance provides you with an emergency place to stay – such as a hotel – and gives you money to replace all of your items.

Deciding What Type of Place to Rent

In addition to the financial costs involved in finding your own place, you need to consider where you want to live. Do you want to be in the middle of a city? City life can be exciting and full of opportunity. Also, cities usually have public transportation. But cities can be loud and crowded. Sometimes certain parts of a city are not safe to live in. Most apartments in cities are small and expensive.

If you rent an apartment or house in a suburban or rural area, you'll have more room and a lot less noise. But how will you get around? Will you need a car to get to work or the supermarket? Will you feel isolated? You may also have more home maintenance responsibilities than in a city. Most city dwellers don't have to mow the lawn or put their garbage on the curb on trash day.

Living With Roommates

After thinking about where you want to live and how you will pay your rent and other expenses, your next major decision may be whether or not to have roommates.

Advantages

Having one or more roommates has some advantages. For example, you and your roommate(s) can split costs like the broker's fee or the security deposit and share the costs of utilities or cable TV, lessening your overall financial burden and allowing you to move into your own place sooner.

Generally, roommates share household responsibilities and help each other by providing companionship and assistance. For example, say your roommate notices your bedroom is a disaster area because you don't have a shelf for your books. If your roommate likes to shop, she may volunteer to take you to the store to pick out a bookcase.

In order to live with other people, you need to be able to communicate and compromise with them. You have to solve problems together. If you can cooperate, communicate, and compromise, living with one or more roommates can be a healthy and mutually rewarding experience.

Disadvantages

Despite many potential advantages, having a roommate poses a whole set of unique problems. If you live with others, you have to share decisions about *everything*. You'll have to discuss with your roommate or roommates where to put things and what furniture to have in the house. You'll have to come to an agreement about chores: Who does which chores? What if somebody slacks off? What if someone spills soda all over the couch and doesn't clean it up, but you want to sit there and watch TV? Will you get stuck cleaning up the soda?

You also have to deal with different personalities and preferences. What if you like it quiet, but your roommate likes to blast rock music? What if you want tofu for dinner, but your roommate eats only junk food? What if your roommate gets mad at you because you always leave toothpaste all over the sink? How would you feel if your roommate recycled your favorite magazine by accident?

Deciding on Rules and Dealing With Serious Problems

If you are going to have one or more roommates, come to some basic agreements and rules about chores, noise, messes, visitors, parties, decorating, food, pets, and any other issues that are important to you *before* moving in and write them down. Don't move in with someone who likes to party every single night if you need peace and quiet. Don't move in with someone who expects her boyfriend to visit every weekend if you don't like company. Don't move in with someone who is looking forward to getting a dog if you are allergic to dogs. Also decide in advance if everyone should have his or her own telephone. Having your own is usually a good idea; otherwise, you may have fights over the phone bill.

Other problems with roommates can arise after moving in, so be prepared. What if one roommate stops paying rent? Will you be able to ask her to move out or will you feel too shy to do so? What if you can't pay your rent? Do you have a back-up plan? Will you be responsible enough to explain to your roommates that you are having financial trouble and to cooperate with them to come to some agreement? What if a roommate seemed great when you first moved in together but then turns into a nightmare, eating all of your food, running up high bills by leaving the heater on full blast, dumping messes everywhere, borrowing your things without asking, or even stealing your things?

Problems with roommates can become serious. You have to be emotionally ready to deal with the drama, to stand up for your rights without being rude, to admit your own mistakes and shortcomings

Problems with roommates can become serious. You have to be emotionally ready to deal with the drama, to stand up for your rights without being rude, to admit your own mistakes and shortcomings and fix them promptly, and to face change as necessary.

and fix them promptly, and to face change as necessary. This might seem overwhelming to you. Many people live with roommates and love the experience. You can enjoy living with roommates, too. Just be prepared – it isn't always easy.

Being an Autistic Roommate

You also have to decide whether or not to disclose your diagnosis to your roommates. It probably isn't necessary unless your roommates also become your friends. But it may be necessary if your autism-related behaviors and challenges are obvious. It is better for them to know the real reasons why you do the things you do than for them to guess. (See Chapter 13: *Disclosing Your Diagnosis* for more on the issue of disclosure.)

Remember that your roommates may have strengths that you don't have. But you have strengths to share with them. Autistic people can be very good at creating household systems and routines that ensure a sense of stability and calm. Many autistic people like making charts and lists. You could make a Weekly Easy Chart for everyone in the house, for example, or you could create a flowchart on the computer outlining the recycling process in your neighborhood. Some autistic people also have the patience to do jobs others can't stand or find too boring. If you can work with your housemates to resolve issues, share chores, and help each other, being autistic shouldn't prevent you from being a great roommate.

Finding Roommates

If you would like to live with other people, how do you find roommates? You could rent a place, pay the security deposit and any other fees, and then find roommates to fill all the bedrooms by posting signs or by advertising locally. The advantage here is that you alone are on the lease. If you later decide to live by yourself, or you don't like the first set of roommates, you can set a time frame by which your roommates have to leave.

The disadvantage is that you have to put up all the money at the beginning. Also, read your lease carefully. Your lease may prohibit you from turning around and renting out the bedrooms to others. This is called *subletting,* and it is illegal in some areas. Remember, too, that if you agree to let your roommates rent a space from you for a year, it is not kind to kick them out early. In some areas, your agreements with your roommates are binding – that is, a roommate has the right to stay until the end of the initially agreed-upon period.

If subletting is not allowed, or you want to share all the costs from the beginning, you could advertise for roommates in advance. When you find people to be roommates with, all of you can sign the lease on a place you already located, or the group can look for a space together. The advantage to this situation is that all of you are on the lease. Each person is legally responsible for a portion of the rent.

If you don't have a lot of money, or can't find a group to rent with, sometimes you can find someone who is looking for a roommate and join that person in his or her apartment. Look for notices around college campuses and food stores. You must be aware, though, that often someone looking for a roommate is, indeed, subletting to you. That means you are not on the lease. As mentioned above, this is sometimes legal but not usually. People rent spaces in their apartments to others because they can't afford to pay all of the rent by themselves. In some areas, subletting is so common that landlords overlook the practice and almost nobody ever gets into trouble. If you are comfortable with a subletting arrangement, legal or illegal, both of you should sign a written agreement, with a copy for each, stating how long you will be allowed to stay and what all the other rules and responsibilities will be.

If this is your first time living with other people independently, it is a good idea to start with roommates you already know. Perhaps someone from college or from your neighborhood wants to rent a place and needs a roommate, too. See if your siblings know anybody who needs a roommate. While it is possible to rent a place with new people, remember they are strangers. Interview them and meet with them to make sure you all agree to the rules of the house and have plans for dealing with problems that may come up before you sign any agreements.

NOTE: In roommate cases involving crimes, sexual abuse, or drugs, you do not owe any further money. You are entitled to a refund of your portion of the security deposit, if any, and a prorated refund of the current month's rent, since you can't use the place. You may have to initiate legal action to recoup your money. Do not attempt to make this decision on your own. Talk to someone you trust or seek advice from a local law clinic, tenant's rights group, housing court, or community center.

Safety Precautions

Because you may not know your roommates, or may not know them well, you must be cautious. If possible, have someone you trust meet your future roommates before you sign any agreements or move in to get a second opinion. Find out a few facts about your potential roommate or roommates and verify them. For example, if the person says he goes to a certain college, call the college and find out. If the person says he has a certain job, call the company and ask if someone by that name works there. Don't spy. Just make sure somehow that the person is who he says he is. If you are a woman, it is best to live with other women. If you are going to live in a mixed-sex household, agree in advance who will use which bathrooms, or if there is only one bathroom, ask how your privacy will be ensured.

You have the right to privacy in your room and in the bathroom. You also have the right to feel safe moving around the house and doing all the things you need to do to take care of yourself. If you don't feel safe, if your roommates constantly invade your privacy or make you feel extremely uncomfortable, or if you experience any degree of sexual attention that you do not want, it's time to move. In a case like this, inform your roommates that the arrangement is not working for you and that you need to move out. If you feel so unsafe that you do not even want to go back into the home to retrieve your things and make the announcement, find someone to do this for you. You still have to meet your financial obligations. Your roommates will expect you to carry your portion of the rent and expenses until they can find a new roommate.

If any of your roommates commits a crime, sexually harasses or date rapes you, or brings drugs or illegal substances into the house, leave immediately! Don't go back. This type of situation is very dangerous. Because of the nature and severity of such situations, you will need someone to help you. If you've been attacked or if your possessions have been stolen, alert the police.

This is the worst type of situation that can happen with roommates and is very rare, so don't read this and be too scared to live with others. The point is you need to realize that sometimes things can go wrong. When this happens, you'll have to move out quickly even if abrupt change is difficult for you. That's why it is crucial to have some kind of back-up plan. Always save a little money and ask a friend or relative in advance if you can stay in the event of just such an emergency until you find a new place to live.

Living by Yourself

Advantages and Disadvantages

When you live by yourself, the obvious advantage is that you do not have to deal with anybody else. You can decide what atmosphere you want in the home, you don't have to wade through other people's messes, you can do your chores at your own pace, and you can make your own decisions. Having total control over your environment can provide relief. If the thought of even just having to say hello to somebody else makes you extremely anxious, living by yourself is probably the right choice for you.

One disadvantage to living alone is that it may be hard to maintain the rhythm of life. If you live with others, you can eat when they do, you can go to bed when they do, you can put your shoes where they put theirs. Roommates may help you "stay in touch" with the world around you, but all alone you may forget to eat or sleep or shower. A Weekly Easy Chart for personal care and daily life can be as useful as one for chores if you find yourself unable to create a healthy daily routine (see page 43).

Also, if you are living alone, you'll have to do all the chores, even the ones you hate. If you are having a hard time getting motivated to organize your house because no one is bugging you to clean up, remind yourself that you'll feel a lot better if you can find the things you need and if you can get into your bed without tripping over a lot of junk. Try some of the tips suggested in Chapter 2: *Maintaining a Home*, if organizing and cleaning are difficult for you.

Because you are alone, you need to develop a plan to deal with emergencies. Nobody else is around to call 911. Make sure you have a working telephone. If you have problems with verbal communication, or if you lose your voice when under stress, make sure your local emergency personnel know this . . .

Because you are alone, you need to develop a plan to deal with emergencies. Nobody else is around to call 911. Make sure you have a working telephone. If you have problems with verbal communication, or if you lose your voice when under stress, make sure your local emergency personnel know this so that they will still come to your house if you dial 911 and then don't or can't say anything. Either call your local police precinct when you aren't under stress, or go over there with someone who can explain on your behalf, and tell them to "flag" your address and phone as the home of someone who is or may be nonverbal. If you have a special medical condition, consider buying a necklace device that you can press to alert your local 911 center in the event that you can't get to the phone or can't dial it. It's also up to you to know where the fire alarm is, how it works, and how to escape if you need to. Ask your landlord if the building has any special rules or regulations when it comes to emergencies that you need to follow. For example, you may be required to hang hurricane shutters over your windows if you live in a hurricane zone. Or if you live in a large apartment building, you may be required to meet across the street and check in so firefighters do not spend all night looking for you.

Dealing With Loneliness

If you find yourself very lonely, you have several options. Sometimes just getting out of the house and seeing a movie, going to the library, following up on a special interest, or visiting a museum will lift your spirits. Find out if there is a park or other recreational facilities near your house.

You can also try making friends. This might be daunting, but you don't need to be super-social to make some contact with the world. For example, you could join a club based on some area of special interest, take a martial arts class, or sign up for a workshop. These types of activities are fun. You don't have to talk to anyone else if it is too hard. But at least you'll be getting out of the house, and you'll be around other people.

Living With a Romantic Partner

While dating and romantic relationships are discussed thoroughly in Chapters 8 and 9, it is worth mentioning here that, indeed, you may want to live with someone you are romantically involved with at some point, a living arrangement that has its own set of pros and cons. On the one hand, a romantic partner is not a stranger or a roommate. On the other hand, a romantic partner is another person. So living with somebody you love still requires all the negotiation, compromise, and cooperation that living with roommates does.

Unless you are in a seriously committed relationship with your romantic partner, it is best not to live together. What do you think will happen if the two of you break up before your lease is over? Both of you may not have enough money to move out. In the meantime, what if you want to start dating new people? Not only will your new date feel uncomfortable visiting your house, your ex's feelings will probably be hurt, just as yours would be if s/he brought over someone new. Do you really want to see your ex having dinner with someone new at the kitchen table or kissing someone new on the couch? The emotions you have to deal with when you break up are hard enough. It is even harder if you still have to share a home. Don't hurry into a living arrangement with a lover until you are sure the two of you are seriously committed to each other and mature enough to handle sharing a life together.

Of course, even if you are living with a partner in a seriously committed relationship or you are married, you may experience a breakup that will require separating your living situation. The point is that when you are seriously committed or married, you should have the maturity to handle the situation tactfully. Most likely both parties will be in a lot of emotional pain and turmoil. You'll have to divide possessions, decide if one person gets to stay or if both have to move out, and separate your money if you've been sharing finances. This is complicated and difficult for both people and usually takes time. It is imperative that before you decide to live with a romantic partner, you take a good look at yourself and make sure you are ready for this huge responsibility.

If you are considering a group arrangement, remember that many group homes for the disabled were not designed to take into consideration the special needs of autistic people.

Supported Housing

If you are ready to live on your own, but you can't handle renting an apartment or sharing an apartment with roommates, you may be eligible for alternative housing options. For example, some cities and towns have special places for people with disabilities to live where the rent is subsidized or lowered to make housing more affordable. Sometimes, a city or town provides a home for a group of disabled people staffed by professionals who help you manage daily life and financial responsibilities, make sure you receive the special services or therapy that you require, and provide social or recreational activities. Unfortunately, our country has no national housing system for the disabled. Therefore, it is impossible for me to describe the options that might be available in your area. Calling local autism organizations and general disability groups is a good first step.

In order to get a subsidized living space, you will need to fill out paperwork and show proof of your disability or how it impacts your chance to work and earn a living. You may also be required to document your expenses or explain how and where you have been living up to this point in time. Then, you may have to wait a long time for your turn to move in. You will need a place to live in the meantime. The agency that handles subsidized or special housing for persons with disabilities in your area may or may not be able to help you while you wait. Be sure you understand what documents you need to apply for subsidized housing and how long you can expect to wait until a spot becomes available.

If you are considering a group arrangement, remember that many group homes for the disabled were not designed to take into consideration the special needs of autistic people. For example, you may be expected to take part in group activities or to socialize with members of the household. If socializing is difficult for you or makes you anxious, staff members may incorrectly determine you have a behavioral problem. Also, others in the house, including staff, may not understand sensory issues or other challenges specific to autism. They may not understand why, for example, you will not sit in the cafeteria for dinner or why you can't stand the TV and presume falsely that you are uncooperative or unfriendly. Before moving in, make sure you have a clear understanding of what is expected of you and whether or not you will need to explain your special needs or obtain exceptions.

Conclusion

The information in this chapter should help you make better decisions about where to live. It is important to make living decisions carefully. If you move in with roommates or a romantic partner and discover you're better off alone, you may not be able to get out of the situation so easily if you have signed a lease, if others are depending on you to contribute money to the household, or if you have nowhere else to go. Vice versa, if you decide to move into your own apartment and discover you hate being by yourself, you may not be able to get out of your lease early or it could take a while to find a suitable roommate.

It is possible to make different options work well. In order to discover what would be the best arrangement for you, it may be necessary to try several. Remember, though, that moving around a lot is difficult and costly. Be sure to discuss all the pros and cons with someone you trust. Get to know yourself, too. If you know what your needs are, if you know how you want to live, and if you have a good sense of your personality, you will find the right living situation – it just might take some time.

■ ■ ■

Chapter 4

Shopping

Why a chapter about shopping? you might wonder. Sensory bombardment, confusion about the social aspects of shopping, and executive functioning challenges can make shopping an autistic nightmare. But shopping, in our society, is a crucial skill. A person must buy just about everything she needs to take care of herself, including food, medicine, clothing, and the incidental items of life such as stamps, toothpaste, and light bulbs. This chapter describes shopping strategies that autistic people can use to conquer everyday shopping challenges.

Shopping for Food

Coping With Sensory Issues at the Supermarket

I once saw a documentary on food shopping and consumer behavior. The narrator explained that when shopping at the supermarket, a customer will screen out most of what he hears and sees to prevent becoming overwhelmed by so many details and so much choice. Otherwise, he wouldn't be able to focus on his main task: shopping for the list of items he wants. This is why advertisers have to work so hard to capture the consumer's attention.

I am sure this does not apply to autistic people. I notice every single detail, every single item, every single color, every single sign – in fact, if I'm not in a moment of sheer overwhelm, I happen to think the array of products in the supermarket is quite beautiful. However, most of the time, the supermarket *is* totally overwhelming. Not only do I need to know what I have to buy, I have to figure out where the items are located. Then I have to select them. Lastly, I have to stand in line and purchase them. All the steps involved require multiple skills and types of thinking that are not intrinsic to my brain.

In addition to preparing for any sensory issues that might come up, my second tactic involves planning out a shopping trip in advance before I begin shopping at a particular store.

On top of that, I have to process an amazing amount of sensory input. To deal with the supermarket, my first tactic is to come armed and ready to do sensory battle. I shop at a 24-hour store just around dawn because by then the glaring outdoor night lights that sting my eyes have been turned off, or at least do not contrast sharply with the dark of night. Also, the daytime crowds haven't arrived yet. I bring a walkman or earphones to drown out the background music, the screeches of supermarket carts, random chatting, and assorted store noises. I also bring heavy-duty professional sunglasses to drown out the glare of the bright indoor lights.

If smells are a problem, try a personal face mask filter (see page 359). If you have tactile sensitivities and are worried about bumping into other shoppers, locate a 24-hour supermarket and shop in the middle of the night or at other odd times when crowds are unlikely and you won't have to squish against people in line. Nighttime shopping is sometimes quieter, too.

Planning for Your Shopping Trip

In addition to preparing for any sensory issues that might come up, my second tactic involves planning out a shopping trip in advance before I begin shopping at a particular store. Even if you already shop at your local supermarket, these tips and suggestions can still help.

- **Learn the lay-out of the store first**
  Go to the store when you are not shopping, you are not tired, you are not suffering from sensory fatigue, and you have plenty of time to wander around. Leisurely locate the items you eat regularly. You might notice, for example, that orange juice is usually in the dairy section. Canned juices are usually in the soda aisle, not near the orange juice or fruit. Tofu and organic items are sometimes in a health food aisle; at other times

they are mixed in with everything else. Buns for burgers and hot-dogs are often under the meat counter instead of in the bread area. Supermarket organization does not always appear logical.

- **Take notes**
  Jot down notes you can refer to later so that when it is time to shop, you don't have to spend extra minutes wandering around looking for things. For example, if you will always need a certain type of soup, make a note of which aisle has canned goods.
- **Plan out a shopping schedule or route**
  For example, you might write out a shopping route that has you stop at aisle 3 first for your favorite cereal, then has you continue to aisle 7 for the canned soup, and lastly has you pick up a bagged salad at the fresh foods counter. A routine planned out in advance makes shopping easier.
- **Make a map**
  Draw a map that indicates where all of your favorite items reside. Your map can include your shopping route. Some supermarkets have floor plans already made. If so, take a copy and fill it in with your personal notes.

Knowing where your food items are located in the store and having a plan to collect them will reduce stress when it comes time to shop. Advance planning may also encourage healthier eating choices. If you are under stress, can't handle the supermarket environment, or don't understand where healthy items are located, you're likely to grab the first few items you see, most of which will probably be junk food.

Understanding the Social Rules of the Food Store

One other area of difficulty when it comes to food shopping is the social behaviors that people assume are obvious, but that most of us on the spectrum must learn. For example, you may not realize that if you can't find something you want, you can ask a clerk to help you find it. Along the same lines, it may not be obvious that you can ask for help finding a price, seeing if the store has more of an item in the stock room, or carrying something heavy. If you can't find a supermarket worker in the aisles to help you, go to the customer service counter and ask for help there.

In some parts of the supermarket, you have to take a ticket with a

NOTE: Sometimes, when the store isn't busy, the specialty counters will stop using tickets for a little while. If you are not sure whether you need a ticket, just ask.

number on it and wait for your number to be called. This usually happens at the meat counter, the deli counter, the seafood area, and sometimes at the baked goods or prepared foods area. These tickets are usually in a container on top of the counter or nearby. If you aren't sure if you need a ticket or where the ticket container is, ask somebody. Otherwise, you could stand there for a long time while everybody else gets help.

As you go up and down the aisles with your cart or basket, you may get stuck behind someone who is blocking the aisle and won't move. Don't try to ram your way through. Politely ask the person to move her cart to the side so you can pass. If this type of social exchange is too difficult, back up. Return in the direction you came from and go down the next aisle over, then up the other end of the blocked aisle. Or come back later when the aisle is free.

Deciding What Food to Buy

Some people on the autism spectrum are not sure what food to buy. All of us are bombarded by the media with information about popular fad diets and the government's latest version of the food groups and the food pyramid. The danger here is that you may interpret nutrition and diet information rigidly. Also, some people on the autism spectrum have food sensitivities and eat only one or two main items.

It is important to try to eat a variety of *types* of foods, even if the selections within each type are limited. For example, perhaps the only fruit you can stand is apple and the only vegetable you can eat is string beans. At least you are getting fruit and vegetable. Try to eat a little apple and some string beans every day. If you can't stand bread, pasta, or cereal because these items are too mushy, perhaps a healthy cracker would be acceptable for your carbohydrates. When you find the mix of items that are both tolerable and nutritious, be sure to include them on your shopping list.

NOTE: If you aren't sure how to pick out at least one or two fruits or vegetables, one or two items that contain adequate protein, and one or two items with whole grains, if you aren't sure what constitutes a balanced diet, or if your food sensitivities are severe, ask your doctor to help you explore your options. Your doctor can make sure you are getting enough nutrition and can guide you in selecting the best kinds and the right amounts of foods you need to stay healthy. Your body needs you, so take the time to ask your doctor or a certified nutritionist to help you figure out what you can handle eating that is also healthy.

Paying for Your Food

When you are done shopping, get your money ready in advance. Paying can be very tense. Other people in line expect you to pay quickly. If having to pay and then collect your bags in a coordinated and quick manner causes you anxiety, consider asking the manager to ring you up in a cashier lane that is marked "Closed." Most cashier lanes marked "Closed" still have a register ready to go that the manager can use at her discretion. Just tell her you have a disability and you can't move or think quickly. Explain that because of this disability, the regular line causes you to panic. If the manager can't ring you up separately, you'll have to go through the regular line like everyone else. Shopping at odd times like the middle of the night can be an effective alternative if cashier line anxiety is a problem for you. In the middle of the night, you can usually take your time counting your money and organizing your bags.

An Alternative: Food Delivery Services

Some people – mostly in cities – make use of supermarket delivery options. You either fax in your shopping list or order online. Then the food is delivered to your home for an additional fee besides the cost of your items. I have never had success with these types of services. The store always delivers the wrong products, which means I have to go back anyway.

Ultimately, conquering the supermarket is the real answer. Once you figure out methods to take care of yourself on a sensory level, and once you have your shopping plan developed and ready to go, shopping for food will be easier and less stressful.

Prescription medications can also sometimes be picked up at pharmacies inside the supermarket. See if your local supermarket has a pharmacy department and have your doctor send your prescriptions there.

Shopping for Medicine and Personal Care Items

Combine Shopping Trips

You can purchase most over-the-counter medicines and personal care items at large supermarkets. If you pick up items like soap, shampoo, Band-Aids™, cough medicine, and aspirin while you are shopping for food, that is one less trip to make. You can almost always get household items like laundry detergent, sponges, toilet paper, and cleaning products at supermarkets, too. Reducing the number of stores you have to go to is one way to reduce shopping anxiety.

Prescription medications can also sometimes be picked up at pharmacies inside the supermarket. See if your local supermarket has a pharmacy department and have your doctor send your prescriptions there. Write down the phone number of the pharmacy you decide to use and put it on your fridge. Before you leave the house, call the pharmacy and make sure your prescription is ready. You can save a lot of time and aggravation this way. Think of the sensory and physical fatigue involved if you have to go back twice because the doctor didn't call in the prescription yet, you are out of refills, the pharmacy is out of your medication, or the medication is still being prepared.

A special tip for when you go to the pharmacy: Study the counter for a moment. Sometimes the pharmacy has two different lines – one for dropping off your prescription if you are handing it in yourself and another for picking up your medicine when it is ready. Find out if the pharmacy has multiple lines and which one you should be waiting in. Don't be too shy to ask. It's better to ask than to stand there waiting, only to discover you've been in the wrong line the whole time.

Deciding What to Buy

If you are not sure what items you need to purchase, think of the activities you do every day: shower, go to the bathroom, clean the house, take out the trash. All of these activities require supplies. Listing your activities is one way to determine what you need to purchase in order to complete all the things you have to do.

Next, it is important to monitor when your supplies are low and you need to buy more. If you notice, for example, that you are running out of shampoo or paper towels, make a list of things you need and place it prominently on your fridge. The next time you go shopping, your list is ready. If you never notice when you need more of something, you could make a master list of all the basic things you need, such as toilet paper, shampoo, toothpaste, and trash bags. Then divide the items into things you need to buy monthly, every other month, quarterly, or yearly. Once a month, take your monthly list and buy some of everything on the list. Do this for your bi-monthly and quarterly lists also and you will never run out of something essential. For example, you may need to buy toilet paper and trash bags monthly, floor soap or laundry detergent every other month, a giant bag of cat litter every three months, and light bulbs yearly.

Sample Shopping Lists

Monthly	Bi-Monthly	Quarterly
Toilet paper	Dish detergent	Cat litter
Trash bags	Laundry detergent	Vacuum cleaner bags
Paper towels		

It is more difficult to determine what over-the-counter medicines to buy. We all hope to spend most of our time healthy, not sick. But it is a good idea to keep a stock of medical supplies in your house just in case. On the most basic level, you probably need Band-Aids for simple cuts, pain reliever for mild headaches and fevers, allergy tablets, and perhaps cold remedies in case you aren't feeling well (see Chapter 6 for more health care information).

NOTE: Remember, never take any medicine without reading the label and following the instructions carefully. If you are not sure what to take, how to take it, or what the right dose is, call your doctor first (see Chapter 6 for more health care information).

Think about all the things that go on with your body and develop a list of medicines that would be handy to have around the house on a regular basis. You can use the same monitoring system described for personal care and household items to make sure you don't run out of necessities.

Shopping for Clothes and Shoes

Shopping for clothing and footwear is one of the hardest things for me to do. I can't tell how I look in clothing. I can't tell if something fits. I can't tell if my feet feel good in a pair of shoes. I don't know what to pick out. I have no idea what is in fashion or not. Sometimes I don't even have a sense of how to determine what I would enjoy wearing. And I almost always can't stand the excruciating sensory bombardment that automatically seems to be part of the clothes shopping experience.

Clothing Catalogs: How to Use Them

Clothing catalogs revolutionized my life. It did not occur to me to shop for clothes by catalog until I saw my sister doing so. I watched her circle several pictures of clothing items, then call the number listed in the catalog and order with a credit card. I was fascinated. When she was done, I picked up the catalog to see for myself.

Over time, I worked out a trick: The models in clothing catalogs usually wear an entire outfit – shirt, pants, sometimes shoes, a jacket, or a hat. I find several pictures that I like, then call the company and ask for everything the model on page 32 is wearing in my favorite colors and size. If I am not sure what size would fit me, I ask the clerk. Usually she will ask me for specific measurements.

If she wants to know how many inches my waste is, I can easily use a tape measure to find out and tell her. While I wait for my order to arrive, I cut out the picture and paste it onto a poster board that hangs in my closet. When the clothing arrives in the mail, I know how to put it together and what goes with what. I literally copy the outfits I like.

This trick is great for work clothes, especially if you must conform to a corporate clothing standard. But you can also use this method for informal clothes like T-shirts and jeans. In addition to printed catalogs, you can use the Internet. Many clothing stores have websites that let you see the item on a model in different colors or in different outfit combinations before making your decision.

Despite the numerous advantages, shopping by mail or the Internet has one big disadvantage: If the clothing arrives and you don't like it after all, or it doesn't fit right, you have to mail it back and try again. Shopping for shoes by catalog or the Internet is also possible – just be patient. By ordering clothing and shoes, you can avoid going to a store for the rest of your life. For me at least, having to return the clothing or shoes by mail a few times until I get the exact fit is much easier than having to go to a store. Once you do shop by catalog or Internet successfully, record your sizes so next time you won't have to guess or measure all over again. And if you find a great pair of shoes or the perfect pair of pants, buy several and save some for the future.

Getting Help From an Avid Shopper

Many people not on the spectrum love to shop for clothing. They actually enjoy the experience! If you are lucky and happen to know somebody who loves to shop, ask this person to shop for you or with you. Chances are an avid shopper will be thrilled to shop on your behalf. She probably won't mind picking up a few shirts for you (or whatever you need) the next time she's out. Just be sure to let her know if you have any favorite colors or textures – or conversely, certain textures and colors to avoid – and your price range.

Sometimes people who love to shop will also volunteer to take you shopping. They are totally happy to go through the racks, pick things out, hold them up against you to see if they fit, help you try them on, deal with the cashier – they really enjoy all of this. Don't pass up such

If you must brave a clothing store on your own without assistance, you can ask one of the clerks to help you find what you are looking for quickly. Clerks in clothing stores usually know what they have in stock and what might fit you.

an opportunity if you have great difficulty shopping for clothes – you'll save yourself a lot of trouble.

Shopping for Clothes on Your Own

If you must brave a clothing store on your own without assistance, you can ask one of the clerks to help you find what you are looking for quickly. Clerks in clothing stores usually know what they have in stock and what might fit you. Just remember, though, that if you do not like what the clerk suggests, you can leave without buying it. It is polite to tell the clerk the item is not really your style before leaving. But if you can't handle talking or the social exchange is overwhelming you, it is alright to just step out of the store. You can also ask clerks to show you the layout of a store before you shop. If you have an idea of where the pants and shirts are in advance, you can avoid wandering around for hours looking for them.

Also, consider shopping at a big department or outlet store that has a little bit of everything. If you can shop for shoes, socks, pants, underwear, pajamas, a winter coat, and some T-shirts all in one location, that's a lot less of a hassle than having to go to seven different stores. You can probably get everything you need for an entire year in one afternoon at this type of store, unless something you need is out of season. It may be difficult, for example, to get a winter coat if you go shopping in July. And you'll have a hard time finding a bathing suit if you live in Maine and go shopping for one in December.

Shopping Online

When it comes to shopping for everything else, the Internet is a bonus for many of us on the spectrum. You can purchase almost anything online – from books to beds, toasters, and cat food. If you aren't used to shopping online but want to try, ask some of the people you know which online stores they recommend. Almost all physical stores now have an online version, so if you have a favorite shop, look it up on the Internet.

To shop online, you usually need a credit card. This is a barrier for some people and can be a real disadvantage. But if you have a checking account at a bank, ask the bank if you can have a card that doubles as an ATM card *and* an "instant" credit card. You'll see a credit card logo on it. One advantage to this type of card is that unlike a true credit card that lets you pay off the balances over time, your purchases are deducted from your checking account instantly. Therefore, if you do not have enough money in your account, you can't spend beyond your means and you won't go into debt. Another advantage is that you can use the card anywhere people use credit cards, including online.

The only disadvantage is that because the cards are so easy to use, you can use up all the money in your checking account and then not have enough for food, bills, or rent. When you are going shopping for extras like clothing, furniture, video games, household decorations, concert tickets, beach chairs, gifts – all the things you really don't need to survive – make a budget first and don't allow yourself to go over the limit.

If you don't want an ATM card with a credit card logo, or don't have good enough credit to obtain one, you can open a special account with an online payment service such as PayPal. These online payment services connect directly to your checking account. Just be careful: In addition to the cost of the item you are paying for, you may also be charged a per-transaction or monthly usage fee. Still, this may be an option for you if you want to shop online but have no other means to pay for Internet items.

If you order something online that is very heavy, such as furniture, you may have to pay special shipping or freight charges. Find out before you make the purchase what extra charges you will incur. Why would anyone pay extra to have a sofa delivered when you could go to a local

When you shop online, you can do so from the privacy of your own home at your own pace in a comfortable atmosphere.

store? Even if you shop locally, you're still going to have to get it into your house one way or another. In other words, it will still have to be delivered, often at an extra charge. You also have to go the store, which costs in terms of time, sensory bombardment, and store confusion. When you shop online, you can do so from the privacy of your own home at your own pace in a comfortable atmosphere. So even if Internet shipping charges are extra for large or heavy items, it may be worth it to you.

Again, if you can't shop online or you don't like online shopping, try shopping at stores that have a wide range of items so you can get everything on your list in one trip. Just like at the supermarket, you can go in advance, take notes about where all the things you want are located, and make a shopping plan. Then go back to shop when you aren't tired, fatigued by sensory overwhelm, hungry, or otherwise stressed out. You'll have a plan and all the sensory equipment you need.

Conclusion

Shopping is a major chore. At times, it can seem impossible to accomplish. The tips in this chapter can reduce the anxiety involved in buying the things you need to live. You can further reduce shopping anxiety by scheduling specific shopping trips on a Weekly Easy Chart. Also remember that society encourages us to consume a lot more than we truly need, so just focusing on the basics is often enough. And don't be afraid to ask for help! You'd be surprised to discover how many people actually love to shop and would be thrilled to help you.

■ ■ ■

Chapter 5

Transportation and Travel

During my early 20s, I spent just over five years living on the road. During my sojourn, I amassed a wealth of information about transportation systems and traveling. Traveling can be very challenging for those of us on the spectrum because of all the sensory distress, the disruption in routine, and the unfamiliarity of new places, new food, and new people. However, it is possible to use public transportation and to travel successfully by planning in advance and gaining a sense of what to expect.

This chapter is divided into sections according to types of transportation and methods of travel. Because food and sensory issues loom large in different ways depending on the mode of transit, these aspects of traveling are discussed within each category. Some general tips for all types of travel are included at the end.

Car Travel

When You Are the Driver: Rules of the Road

Whether you are driving a short or a long distance, operating a car is a huge responsibility. Your state government will not issue you a license until you pass both a written test and an actual driving test. The requirements of the tests and the age at which you can take them differ from state to state. Call your local department of motor vehicles to find out the rules.

Just because you obtained your license does not mean you can get on the road and do whatever you want. You have to follow all the rules

If you don't follow the rules, police and traffic agents can issue you fines, arrest you, confiscate your car, or revoke your license.

of the road, including wearing a seatbelt. If you don't follow the rules, police and traffic agents can issue you fines, arrest you, confiscate your car, or revoke your license. If you studied for and then passed the tests for your license, most of the rules of the road should be obvious or easy enough to figure out.

If you are ever confused by a road sign or you can't find a sign indicating the rules, proceed very cautiously until you are sure of what you are allowed to do. For example, if you don't know what the speed limit is on a certain road, go slowly until you see a speed limit sign. If you miss a turn, don't stop in the middle of the road or go in reverse. This is an upsetting situation, especially if you are late, but wait until you can turn around safely somewhere. This applies on the highway, too. If you miss an exit by accident or you can't switch lanes fast enough to get off, keep going to the next exit. Never back up on the highway, not even on the shoulder or emergency lane.

Car Trip Rules for Drivers

1. Follow all rules of the road, including wearing your seatbelt.
2. Require your passengers to wear seatbelts or to use car seats if necessary.
3. Never drive drunk or intoxicated.
4. Don't drive erratically or attempt stunts.
5. Don't tailgate.
6. Don't honk aggressively except to warn of danger.
7. Concentrate on driving only.
8. Pull over to make a phone call, have a snack, or read the map.
9. Restrain animals properly for their safety as well as yours.
10. Compromise with your passengers regarding temperature, radio volume, etc.

Courtesy Rules for Drivers

In addition to the rules of the road, you should also follow some basic courtesy rules. If a driver in front of you is going too slowly, don't tailgate, or drive up really close to the back of his car. This is dangerous and can also make the slower driver nervous. Instead, slow down until you have a chance to pass or the slow driver turns. Don't honk at the other driver aggressively, either, except to warn of danger. If you must honk at another driver to get him to move out of your way or for some other reason, just tap your horn a couple of times.

Don't drive in an uncontrolled manner. You share the road with many other drivers. Weaving around the street, going too fast, trying to make turns in a crazy way like in the movies, attempting stunts like revving your engine or jumping the curb, or showing off by sticking a hand out the window or taking your hands off the steering wheel are absolutely unacceptable driving behaviors under any and all circumstances and can get you and other people killed or seriously injured. It is also extremely dangerous and criminal to drive while drunk or under the influence of drugs. Drive safely or don't drive.

When you are driving a car, driving is all you should be doing. You can listen to the radio if you can still hear other cars and emergency vehicles. Don't talk on a cell phone, open packages of food, fix your hair, apply make-up, read a map, or flirt with other drivers or your passengers while driving. If you are hungry, lost, or tired, pull over. You can read the map and have a snack in peace at the next rest area or gas station, and if you can't stay awake, get off the road!

Making Rules for Your Passengers

If you are driving passengers, the following rules for them are important. Make all passengers wear a seatbelt. Refuse to drive anyone who won't wear one. All children under five need to be in a car seat in the back seat. Riders 12 and under should be in the back seat also. Dogs should use special dog seatbelts that attach to the belts already in the car, or should ride in a carrier. Cats should always be in carriers. Your passengers should not move around the vehicle while you are driving, nor should they do anything that might distract you. You have the right to request your passenger(s) stop any behavior that is causing you distress or breaking your concentration.

As the driver, you must be comfortable. Set the temperature of the car and decide if the radio is on or off. However, it is polite to consult your passengers and to take their needs into consideration. Ask if your passengers are too hot or too cold and adjust the temperature accordingly. Also make sure your choice of music and the volume level is not causing your passengers a problem.

You may have to compromise sometimes. For example, if you are giving your grandmother a ride to the airport, she probably won't like being subjected to loud heavy metal music. Or if you and a friend are going for a ride and she has severe allergies, you may have to switch on the air conditioner even though you prefer rolling down the window. And even if you don't want to stop, it is only fair to pull over if one of your passengers needs to use the bathroom, especially on long trips. You can ask once if it is possible to wait until your next planned stop, but if the answer is no, pull over at the next possible bathroom location. It should only take a few minutes.

When You Are the Passenger: Respecting the Driver

Being the passenger on a car trip can be fun. However, you need to remain respectful of the driver at all times. Besides following basic rules like wearing your seatbelt and refraining from moving around while the vehicle is in motion, try to be as helpful as possible. If you get lost, offer to read the map. If the driver is hungry or thirsty, offer to open packages or drinks and pass them to the driver carefully without disturbing the driver's concentration (if this is too hard, pull over to have a snack). Ask first before you eat, drink, or smoke in someone else's car.

Don't agitate or tease the driver. This behavior is not amusing and can cause an accident. Examples of unacceptable actions include flipping on the windshield wipers, constantly changing the radio station or temperature setting, adjusting windows or mirrors, setting off alarms or other noises, farting or burping profusely, picking fights and arguing, or flirting with the driver. This paragraph may sound funny. But it is absolutely not funny when accidents happen because the driver can't pay attention to the road.

Passenger Rules for Long-Distance Trips

If you are going to be the passenger on a long-distance car trip, be reasonable in your demands on the driver. Of course, if you have to use the bathroom, you'll need to ask the driver to stop. While it is fair to expect the driver to stop when you really need to use the bathroom, don't expect the driver to stop every few minutes or every time you want something. When you take a break to go to the bathroom, try to buy a snack or get whatever else you need at the same time. It is very difficult on the driver and considered rude if you announce with no warning that you must use the bathroom immediately. The driver may need a few minutes to slow down or find an appropriate place to pull over. So try to anticipate the need for a break in advance.

You can take over-the-counter medications that prevent nausea due to traveling if you are prone to getting car sick. If you do get carsick on a trip, announce your problem as soon as you notice the feeling. This way the driver can pull over safely until you feel better. If you get carsick with absolutely no warning and you have to throw up unexpectedly, try to throw up into a garbage bag. If you do make a mess, apologize and then clean up thoroughly when the driver stops the car at the next safe point. Clean yourself first, then the car.

Lastly, don't be afraid to ask the driver what his talking preferences are. Some drivers like to chat with passengers about easy subjects such as the weather or the towns you are driving through. Other drivers like to have long, complex discussions they may not have time for in their daily lives. Still others don't want to talk, or find that talking ruins their concentration. Or perhaps the driver would like to talk for a while but then have some quiet time or suddenly need to stop talking if traffic conditions worsen. Don't take this personally. The driver needs to do whatever is necessary to maintain his concentration.

Car Trip Rules for Passengers

1. Wear your seatbelt.
2. Respect the driver at all times.
3. Don't bother or distract the driver.
4. Don't move around the car.
5. Be helpful.
6. Ask the driver politely and with some warning if you need to stop.
7. Don't ask the driver to stop an unreasonable number of times.
8. Ask permission before eating, drinking, or smoking.
9. Apologize and clean up if you get carsick.
10. Ask the driver if she wants to talk or if she prefers quiet.

Public Transportation

Dealing With the Subway, Train, or Bus

If you do not have a car, if you are unable to operate a car for some reason, or if you do not know anybody who can give you a ride, you will have to use public transportation when you must go somewhere farther than walking distance. In most major cities, public transportation is generally widely available in all neighborhoods and throughout most of the day and night. In suburban or rural areas, it may be more difficult or even impossible to find transit when you need it, or you may have to walk far to catch it. Whether public transit is readily available or not, you almost always have to pay. Costs range considerably from location to location.

Taking public transportation may be extremely challenging if you have severe sensory issues. Use a Sensory Emergency Kit as described in Chapter 1: *Coping With Sensory Issues* to manage sensory stressors such as bleeps, screeches, passenger chatting, and harsh lighting. When I have to take the subway in New York, I always drown out the noises with a walkman and the lights with dark glasses.

Have your fare ready in advance. Scrambling for change in a hurry or not being able to board because you don't have the right amount of money can produce a lot of unnecessary anxiety and may cause you to miss your bus or train. Plan your route in advance so you know where you are going. If you are not sure where to get off, ask the bus driver or the subway clerk to advise you. If you get lost or confused, ask an official transit worker for help. It is better to ask a transit official or police officer than a fellow passenger. Some unscrupulous people, especially in cities, will take advantage of the fact that you don't know where you are or where you need to go and may mug you or worse.

Public Transit Tips

1. Bring a Sensory Emergency Kit.
2. Plan your route in advance.
3. Have your fare ready.
4. If you are confused or lost, ask a transit official or police officer for help.
5. Bring something to entertain or distract you when you have to wait or if there is a delay.

Alternative Public Transit for Disabled Persons

If the noises and other stressors of taking a bus, subway, or train make it impossible for you to use public transit, ask your local transit authority what alternatives are available for disabled people. For example, in New York City, vans will pick up temporarily or permanently disabled passengers at their homes and drop them off right at their various destination points. However, this is partially because many subway stops are not wheelchair accessible. If your city's transit system is highly accessible, alternatives such as van service may not be available. The only way to find out is to ask.

Your city may offer alternatives, but may not consider autism a qualifying disability.

Your city may offer alternatives, but may not consider autism a qualifying disability. If you are going to campaign your local government to include autism as a qualifying disability, be sure to provide officials with information about sensory issues, communication challenges, or whatever is impeding your ability to use the public transit system as it is.

Other Possibilities

If you truly cannot make use of the public transit system and your city does not offer alternatives, you will have to be very creative in order to get anywhere. If you need to get to a medical appointment, public assistance programs sometimes provide transportation or give vouchers for a taxi (see *Taxis*). If you want to get to a support meeting, consider asking the group leader if anyone coming from your neighborhood is willing to share a car ride or taxi with you. Similarly, your boss may be able to pair you with a co-worker who would be willing to give you a ride in turn for some money for gas or tolls.

Although I highly advise against this because the danger is enormous, I mention it only for the sake of presenting all options. If you are truly desperate, you may be able to find people to share rides with on websites like www.craigslist.org or www.commuterlink.com. Never, ever get into a car with a complete stranger. If you are going to engage in a ride-share situation with someone you don't know, ask the person for work and personal references. Agree in advance on how much you will contribute toward gas and tolls, where you will be picked up or dropped off, if anyone else will be in the car, and how much notice the driver will give you if arrangements change. Only look for ride-share situations if you have absolutely no other way of getting where you need to go. You are risking your life.

Taxis

Taxi Basics

Another option for getting around is going by taxi or cab. If you don't have a car and can't tolerate public transit, taxis can be useful. Unfortunately, in many rural and suburban areas, you often have to wait a very long time for a taxi, so call the taxi company early. Taxis can also be expensive. If you are going to use a taxi, make sure you understand how you will be charged before the driver takes off. Most taxis have a meter and you are charged a pre-determined amount per mile or per minute based on a formula of distance and time. Sometimes you are charged a flat rate based on location. Other times, you and the driver must negotiate and agree to a certain fare before the trip begins. Remember, it is also expected that you will pay extra for tolls if necessary and that you will tip the driver at least 10% for good service.

In some cities, you can flag a taxi down while standing on the sidewalk. Don't step into traffic just to get a taxi driver to stop. Stay on the curb. If you miss a taxi, you can catch the next one. Sometimes drivers in unmarked cars pull over, roll down the window, and offer you a ride. If the driver displays an official certificate allowing him to accept passengers and assigning him a cab license number, you could use this type of service. Be sure to agree on the fare first as described above. However, it is best to avoid these unmarked vehicles. The certificate could be fake or out of date. The driver could be a criminal posing as a taxi driver. And if you have a problem, you don't know which company to call to complain. Stick with taxis that clearly have a company name and phone number printed on the side of the car, or with taxis that clearly display their registration numbers with the local taxi commission of your city.

Sensory Issues and Taxis

Taxis can pose sensory complications, too. Many taxi drivers like to hang scented air fresheners from their rear view mirrors. If you are calling a taxi company to pick you up, request an unscented car. If you are flagging down a taxi on the street and you notice smells that bother you as you open the door, you have the right to refuse to get in. Tell the driver you can't breathe and hail a different taxi. If your taxi driver is listening to the radio, you have the right to request a silent trip (at least you do in

New York). If you ask the driver to turn off the radio and he does, but then slows down to increase your fare or drives poorly, report him to his supervisor and don't give him a tip. Always bring your Sensory Emergency Kit (see Chapter 1: *Coping With Sensory Issues*). Sensory emergencies from the bleeps from the taxi driver's CB radio, screeching brakes, unexpected smells, or other auditory assaults can occur. It is best to be prepared.

Long-Distance Buses and Trains

Public transit and taxi rides are usually of short duration, used to get around one city or one area. If you are going on vacation or visiting relatives, you may have to take a bus or train long distance. Though these days it is about the same price to fly and flying is much faster, Greyhound, among other bus companies, and Amtrak, the nation's rail company, do offer bus and train service around the United States.

Preparing for Your Comfort

Taking the train or bus for many hours can be uncomfortable on top of whatever sensory issues you may experience. So in addition to preparing for sensory emergencies, you will also need to plan for maximum comfort. Bring a pillow. You can usually fit a small one in your bag even if your luggage is stuffed. Bring a sweatshirt in case the train or bus is heavily air conditioned. And bring some form of entertainment. If you can read while traveling, bring books and magazines. If you can't read while moving, bring a walkman with some music CDs or an audio book. I have seen several people knit, draw, or create maps with magic markers as they go along. Entertaining or relaxing activities that you enjoy will keep you occupied during the long hours of the trip.

Eating While on the Bus

Depending on how long your trip will be, you may need to plan your meals in advance. If you travel a long distance across several states, the driver will announce meal breaks. Sometimes, you will be given the opportunity to run into a fast-food restaurant; other times, meal breaks take place at a bus station along the route. When the break is at a station, long-distance passengers already on board run inside the station, get something to eat, and then get back onto the bus before new passengers are allowed on. Wherever the meal stop is, be sure you understand how many minutes you have until you must be back on the bus. The driver will not wait for you. Usually, you can safely leave most of your things on the bus while you get your food, but take your wallet, electronics, or expensive items with you. If you are not sure how safe it is to leave items like your jacket, your pillow, your books, or your snacks, ask the driver.

If you can't stand the food and junk typically available at these stops, or if you are on a gluten- and/or casein-free diet, bring along your own food. You can pack some foods requiring refrigeration in a cooler, but eventually the cooler will stop working. Therefore, try to figure out what you can eat that can last the duration of your trip. Or plan a mix of a few things that can be in the cooler while it lasts and a few things that don't require refrigeration.

If you eat a very limited range of foods, this can pose a problem. Pick out one or two nutritious foods you can eat under most circumstances and pack those. Dairy products like yogurt, cream, and milk-based sauces, fish, and meat go bad very quickly. Don't eat these items if they haven't been properly refrigerated. Vegetables, fruit, hard cheese, butter, and bread or rice crackers last longer. Peanut butter and jelly also lasts a while. I do not want to advocate eating junk, but potato chips can provide you with a bit of fuel and last a long time.

During my many cross-country bus trips, I survived on orange juice, potato chips cooked in non-hydrogenated oil, and fresh green beans. For variation, I sometimes brought a small hunk of cheese or a bag of peanuts. My menu wasn't fancy but it was easy to carry and nutritious enough for a few days, plus it allowed me to avoid the greasy smells and junky quality of the fast-food outlets along the way.

Eating While on the Train

On a long train trip, you usually walk to a special dining car where you can purchase sandwiches, hot food, snacks, and drinks. Be sure to bring money to pay for what you want. On some trains like the Auto Train that runs between Virginia and Florida, you sign up for a dinner slot and go to the dining car for a sit-down dinner. It is included in the cost of the ticket. So are basic snacks, but you may still want to bring cash for extra items.

If for sensory or anxiety reasons you can't handle making a purchase in the dining car, or sitting in the dining car, ask a member of the train crew to purchase something for you or to bring your meal to your seat. My experiences with train food have been O.K. It is not as disgusting as fast food. It is not food I would voluntarily choose to eat, but I can usually find something among the offerings. To be on the safe side, call Amtrak and ask them what food choices will be available on your specific train. If you won't be able to eat any of it, follow the food suggestions for a long-distance bus trip described above.

Bathroom Advice for the Bus and the Train

Bathrooms on these trips always present challenges. On the bus, I would wait for station stops and use the bathrooms there, simply because I found it difficult to maneuver around the tiny bus bathrooms. Plus the station bathrooms are usually cleaner.

On the train, you can't use station bathrooms even if the train makes stops. The train bathrooms are even smaller than bus bathrooms and with the train rocking side to side, it's very tricky for everybody, even for those not on the spectrum. If you have motor problems or planning challenges, proceed slowly. Take a visual inventory of the environment first. How does the door lock? Where is the toilet paper?

How does the toilet flush? This will help you plan what to do. Next, find a handle to hold onto. Remember, you are in a moving vehicle that is traveling at high speeds. It is easy to get tossed around.

Sleeping on the Bus or Train

If you are taking the bus or train overnight, you are probably not going to get much sleep. The bus is worse than the train because you can hardly stretch out your legs or lean back. For the bus trip, try to bring a pillow. Soothing music on your walkman might help you sleep. If you are lucky and have a row of seats to yourself, you can stretch out, but don't count on it. Buses are usually packed. If you do fall asleep and accidentally lean on the stranger next to you, just apologize and pull yourself up into your own seat again.

Many long-distance trains have sleeper cars. If you can afford it, a sleeper room on the train is worth every penny. Sleeper sections range in size from one- or two-person booths with a seat that converts to a bed, to larger rooms for families or groups with "beds" that fold down from the walls or ceilings. These are not like beds in hotels. The beds tend to be a bit narrow. Make sure you know what kind of sleeper you are getting.

An added advantage to getting a sleeper: Your ride will be quieter. One time on the 16-hour overnight Auto Train I had a problem with Muzak suddenly piping in through speakers on the ceilings in the hall and in the private sleeper cabins. I had to talk to three train employees about autism and sensory issues before they agreed to turn off the music. But other than some unusual problem such as this, sleepers are much quieter than the coach, or regular, cars. I take the Auto Train every now and then, and besides the regular noise of the train, I almost never hear the other passengers when I am inside my sleeper.

Airplanes

Flying by airplane is my favorite method of travel. Airplanes are quick, safe, and fun. You can go almost anywhere by airplane. Some airlines are now as cheap or even cheaper than other modes of transit. The key to traveling by plane is to anticipate in advance what might happen or what might be expected of you so that you aren't overwhelmed or caught unprepared. The information outlined below can help.

The key to traveling by plane is to anticipate in advance what might happen or what might be expected of you so that you aren't overwhelmed or caught unprepared.

Buying Airplane Tickets and Choosing Seats

The easiest way to purchase an airplane ticket is online. If you go to the website of any airline, you will be able to view routes, times, destinations, and prices. Plug in where and when you want to go, and you will get a list of possible flights and corresponding ticket prices. You can then make your reservation and pay with a credit card. You can also call the airline and purchase a ticket over the telephone, again using a credit card to pay. If you buy a plane ticket online or over the phone, you will receive a confirmation number. Don't worry that you do not have an actual ticket. The day that you fly, you go to the ticket counter of your airline with your I.D. and your confirmation number, at which time you will receive a printed copy of a boarding pass.

The old-fashioned method of purchasing airplane tickets is to go to a travel agent. It may be necessary to purchase tickets from an agent for certain international destinations. To find a travel agent, look in your local telephone book or ask your family and friends for a referral. The advantage is that agents often know of special bargains you won't otherwise find. Agents usually give you a paper ticket.

If you are wealthy, some airlines allow you to purchase tickets for the first-class section, which has bigger seats, faster meal service, sometimes free drinks, and priority getting on and off the plane. Most airplane passengers purchase tickets for the coach or regular section. Usually you pick your seat, or you are automatically assigned a seat, at the time you purchase your ticket. Make sure you understand where you will be sitting. Airline cabins have different arrangements. Most have three seats, then an aisle for walking, then another three seats, but this is not always the case.

If you do not like the seat you get, call the airline. Sometimes, other seats are available but not listed publicly. Even if at first the airline tells you no other seats are available, check just as you are about to board the plane. If you explain your problem with the seat you have – for example, you get claustrophobic unless you have a window seat – airline employees may be able to reshuffle the seats at the last second.

On some airlines, if you explain that you have a disability, you can have a seat in the first row. You may have less sensory disruption up front. In addition, you can get on and off the plane much more easily. I have never had a problem whenever I have asked to be placed in the first row, so don't be shy if you would be much more comfortable with this accommodation. Just realize you will have a smaller tray table. Plus you won't be able to put things under the seat in front of you, since you won't have a seat in front of you.

Getting to the Terminal at the Airport

Airports can be confusing. Each airline is assigned a terminal, or has its own terminal. The United States does not have one standard airport system. Some airports label terminals by letter, others by number. Some associate terminals with colors. If possible, check the layout of your airport online in advance. You can also call the airline for terminal details. You will save time and anxiety if you know which terminal your plane will be leaving from, what the name of that terminal is (for example, "blue" or "C"), and how to get to that terminal.

The way to the terminal will probably be different depending on your method of transit to the airport. Public transportation vehicles usually make one stop per terminal. If you take a taxi to the airport, the taxi driver should know where to drop you off. Be forewarned: Sometimes airports have special lanes just for taxis. You may be dropped off in the taxi lane and have to walk a bit to the terminal. If this is the case, ask the taxi driver to help you carry your bags inside.

When you go to the airport by car, several options are possible. If someone drives you, he can drop you off at the curb outside the terminal, but he is only allowed to stay for a few seconds while you get your bags out of the car. Alternatively, the driver can park in short-term parking. This allows the driver to walk inside the terminal with you, help you with your bags, help you find the ticket counter, or get a soda with you before you depart.

If you drive yourself to the airport, you have to leave your car in the long-term parking lot. Make sure you understand what the rates are. Usually the long-term lots are far from the terminals, in which case you have to take a shuttle bus to your terminal. This can be a hassle if you have a lot of bags. You also need to leave ample time to get to your plane. The shuttle buses usually make a lot of stops. If you are late, you can't ask the shuttle bus driver to skip stops or hurry.

If you have rented a car and are returning it at the airport before your flight, leave plenty of time to process the return of the vehicle. The rental car lots are usually far from the terminals, also requiring a shuttle bus trip. I can't rush. I move very slowly. Therefore, whenever I have to park in a long-term lot or return a rental car, I leave an entire extra hour.

Whatever method of transportation you are taking to the airport, be sure to leave plenty of time. Call your airline and find out how early they want you to be at the airport. Most domestic flights require you to check in at least one hour before departure. You also have to leave time to get through security. If you have to park, as explained above, that adds additional time. You should also leave about an extra 1/2 hour in case of unexpected traffic or delays due to airport or road construction. This means, for example, if you have an 11:00 a.m. flight and you need to check in at least one hour in advance, by 10:00 a.m., and it takes you one hour to drive to the airport and perhaps another hour to park the car, you should probably leave your house by 7:30 a.m.

Checking In

Once you get to the correct terminal, you have to check in. Whether you have a paper ticket or a confirmation number, you either check in right at the curb or indoors at the check-in counter. Curbside check-in is quick and easy, plus you don't have to worry about your bags any more because you leave them right there. To check in inside, you have to lug your bags to the counter. But the advantage is that at the counter, you can pick your seat if you haven't already, or you can try to change your seat if you don't like the one you have. Also, at the counter, you can make sure your two permitted carry-on bags are not too big and have them tagged as luggage if they are.

If you are flying to attend a conference, a business meeting, or an event requiring specific clothing, don't check your bags as luggage. Checked luggage can be lost, especially if you are connecting to more than one plane. Lost luggage is usually traced, but this can take a day or two. While some fancy hotels may have clothing stores, what is the chance that you will find something you like, something that fits, and something appropriate for the occasion at the last minute? Don't take that chance. You should be able to fit a few suits or dresses, a casual outfit or two, toiletries, pajamas, and underwear into a suitcase that is still small enough to carry onto the plane. You are allowed two carry-on bags, so one could hold your clothes and another your computer, snacks, paperwork, or books.

Whether you check in at the curb or the counter, you will receive a boarding pass. The airline employee will also tell you from which gate of the terminal your plane will be leaving. Don't lose your boarding pass. Only passengers with boarding passes can proceed through security to the departure gates. I always pick one spot where I put my boarding pass – usually my front pocket. I know it is always there. I never move it from there. Create an Absolute Spot for your boarding pass, a concept borrowed from Chapter 2: *Maintaining a Home* (see page 38).

Airline Security

These days, airline security is heightened. Once you have your boarding pass, you will have to wait on the security line. Security officers will look at your I.D. and boarding pass. You have to place your carry-on bags on a conveyor belt so they can go through a scanner. You will be given a bin for small items like your wallet, keys, change, cell phones, cameras, laptop computers, video recorders, and sometimes your shoes and heavy or bulky coats, which are also scanned. In addition, you may be asked to turn your electronic devices on and off. Then you will have to walk through a metal detector.

If lines cause you anxiety, you may have to explain to an official that you have a disability requiring special accommodation.

If lines cause you anxiety, you may have to explain to an official that you have a disability requiring special accommodation. Officials will still have to send your carry-on bags through the scanning machines, but perhaps they can escort you to the front and then help you through the process. If you move slowly, as I do, you may want to tell the security officers in advance. I always tell them I am autistic and can't rush, so they know that I may need an extra minute to complete tasks or collect my things.

Once in a while, security officers decide they must search you more thoroughly. Do not be offended. They usually pick people randomly. You may also be picked if you bought your ticket less than seven days before flying, someone else paid for your ticket, or you bought your ticket with cash. The security officers may go through your carry-on bags by hand. They may ask you to remove your shoes, if they haven't already. If you set off the metal detector, they may also have to pat your body.

These procedures can be anxiety producing and are not part of the normal security routine. You can ask for a chair to sit on if you have to take off your shoes. If you are a woman, ask for a female officer if officials tell you it is necessary to conduct a search of your body or clothes. You can also ask for a few minutes to repack your bag somewhere out of the way when the search is over, if the officers ruffle through your possessions and mess up the order of your things. As disruptive as going through security may be, cooperate. If you refuse to cooperate, you may not be allowed on the plane.

Waiting at the Gate

After you have passed through security, you proceed to the departure gate for your plane. Usually you walk, but some large airports have flat, moving "escalators" that usher you along. Denver's airport is so big that you have to take a train to the departure gates. Departure gates have waiting areas with seats. These waiting areas are usually loud. I don't understand why airports must place televisions every few yards and then leave the volume up on all of them. Unfortunately, I have never found an airport with a quiet waiting area.

Sometimes you will have to wait a while before you board the plane. Waiting areas often have snack shops or even restaurants and stores. If you want to browse around or get something to eat, take your carry-on bags with you. Don't leave your bags on a seat even if someone nice offers to watch them for you. If carts are available, I find they are worth the few dollars it costs to rent one. Your arms will be a lot less tired.

Boarding the Plane

Eventually, you will hear an announcement over the loud speaker indicating that it is time to board the plane. If you are drowning out loud noises with a walkman (see *Sensory Issues* below), watch the departure gate. When you see people begin boarding, take off your headphones and listen for your row to be called. As mentioned earlier, just before boarding is a good time to try to rearrange your seat assignment or ask for accommodation in the first row. The airline employees won't always be able to change your seat, but it can't hurt to ask. Also, passengers who need extra time to board are allowed to get on the plane first. If you move slowly, have motor coordination issues, get anxious in crowds or lines, or need a few minutes to arrange your things, definitely board early. All you have to say is that you have a disability and you should have no problem being allowed to board early.

Sensory Issues

As mentioned, I love flying. The action of the plane flying through the air does not cause me any distress. However, some people on the spectrum have told me that the semi-weightless feeling, turbulence, and normal turns of the plane make them sick or dizzy beyond regular air sickness. This may be due to a sensitivity of the vestibular sense (see Chapter 1: *Coping With Sensory Issues*). You can take over-the-counter motion sickness tablets about one hour before departure to help prevent this feeling.

Both the airport and the plane can be loud. In the airport, TVs are usually blaring everywhere. You may also be bombarded with Muzak, regular music, loud announcements, and loud people. On the plane, you may have to endure the hum of the engines or the noises of the other passengers. Be sure to bring a Sensory Emergency Kit with ear plugs or a walkman to drown out unwanted noise. Some airlines offer music or TV while you are flying. You plug your headphones into the arm of your seat. This can be an effective way of drowning out unwanted noise and other distractions, but always have your own earplugs or walkman just in case.

Other sensory issues you might encounter include the smells of other passengers' food items or perfume, the sounds of people eating, bright lights or glare from the sun, bleeps, announcements, crying children, being touched by another passenger by accident, or being bothered by the feel of the seat or your seatbelt. Certain sensory assaults like sounds and lights are more easily addressed than others. If you wind up sitting next to someone drenched in perfume or scented products and the smell is going to make you seriously ill, the airline must switch your seat. I am terribly sensitive to perfume. Rather than explain autism and sensory issues, I find it easier and quicker to just say, "I'm allergic and need to be moved."

Tactile sensitivities are the hardest to manage on the plane. You have to stay in your seat during the flight, unless you get up to use the bathroom. Planes are narrow and crowded. I always request a window seat. Tucked in next to the window, nobody has to crawl over me to get out of the seat row. And nobody knocks into me as they pass by in the aisle. If you don't have a window seat and somebody has to step over you to get out, ask them to wait a moment. Then get out of your seat, stand in the aisle, and wait for the person to exit the row before sitting down again. When you see the person returning, get out of your seat and wait in the aisle until the person is settled back into her seat. This way, you can avoid accidental collisions. If somebody knocks into you as they pass by and you are startled, just pull away and retreat into your seat. Covering yourself with a small blanket or your coat might make you feel shielded to some degree. If your tactile sensitivities are severe, consider asking for accommodation in the first row. You'll have a little more room in front of you and perhaps less traffic.

Flying Comfortably

I find plane travel the least uncomfortable way to travel, but it is a good idea to plan for certain physical issues in addition to sensory issues. If you are prone to motion sickness, take over-the-counter tablets about one hour before departure. Besides getting plane sick, your ears may hurt when the plane takes off or lands due to changes in air pressure. Bring gum or chewy candy to ease the pressure in your ears. Also, your feet may swell. Keep your shoes on your feet. Otherwise, when you land, you won't be able to get your back shoes on.

Planes can sometimes be cool. You may want to bring a sweatshirt or light sweater, especially if you are dressed for summer weather. Lastly, if you anticipate needing a pillow or blanket, especially on an overnight or international trip, consider bringing your own because sometimes supplies run out. Just be sure to get "travel" style pillows and blankets which are much thinner and easier to pack. You can sometimes buy them right at the airport.

Eating on the Plane

For a long time, most people considered airplane food too disgusting to eat. These days, in my opinion, airlines have improved the food they offer significantly. If you are going on a long flight, an overnight flight, or an international flight, the airline will probably serve you meals. If you have special dietary needs, call at least two days before your flight and make your request. Almost all airlines can provide you with kosher, vegan, or vegetarian food. Some airlines even have an Asian food option, which is usually fish and rice. Ask what your choices are. Call again the day before your flight to make sure your request has been processed.

If you are traveling on a flight of only a few hours, you probably won't be served a meal, even if the flight intersects the usual time for breakfast, lunch, or dinner. In this case, bring your own. Almost all airlines offer free snacks and soda or juice. But if you anticipate needing more than just a snack, pack something from home or buy something at the airport. Most food stands and restaurants in the waiting areas of the airport will pack you food for the plane in an easy-to-carry box or no-spill container.

If sitting next to someone else who is eating is going to cause you great sensory discomfort, the only recourse you have is to bring a Sensory Emergency Kit with all the supplies you need to block out sounds and smells. You can't go somewhere else while your row-mates eat. I suppose you could wait in the bathroom, but that would be gross. You're basically stuck next to the other people in your row until the flight is over, so be prepared.

When You Land

After the plane lands, the pilot usually has to drive to the arrival gate. You are not supposed to undo your seatbelt until the plane crew says it is O.K. to unbuckle, but many people do. You also have to wait to get your bags from the overhead bins until the plane completely stops. Usually, everyone is so anxious to get off of the plane that when the plane does stop, they rush to gather their bags and other items. Then, after this mad rush, everyone stands in the crowded aisle with their arms loaded and waits for a long time while the plane doors are opened and exit walkways and exit stairs are secured. Eventually, at some point, the line of people begins to move, but the line is always slow and cumbersome.

If this scene is going to cause you too much anxiety, just sit in your seat and wait until everyone else is off. Why bother rushing just to have to wait anyway? It is O.K. to be the last one off the plane. You won't have to navigate through a crush of people to get your carry-on bags and you won't have to wait on a cramped line for no reason. If you need assistance with your bags, you will probably have to wait anyway. Unless you are rushing to catch another plane, it makes no sense to stress yourself out.

Also be prepared for cell phone madness. It seems that as soon as the plane lands, everyone's cell phones ring. People on the plane also make calls. Everyone chats loudly about all the details of their trip so far. If all the ringing and chatting is going to drive you crazy, be sure to have your walkman or ear plugs ready. You have to switch off your walkman as the plane is landing, but once the plane is on the ground, you can turn it on again.

Getting Your Luggage

If you checked luggage onto the plane, follow the signs to the luggage collection area. If you are lucky, your bags will be unloaded quickly. Sometimes, though, it takes a while for the bags to start appearing on the carousel. If you are going to need a cart for your luggage, get the cart first. You can usually rent luggage carts for a few dollars by inserting coins or bills into a machine that then releases the cart from a rack. Official uniformed employees of the airport, sometimes referred to as "sky caps," are authorized to help you if you need a hand. It is polite to give a sky cap a tip of a few dollars. Before you walk away from the luggage area, make sure the bags you have collected really are yours – many bags look exactly alike. Suggestion: Put something unusual or bright on your luggage, such as a ribbon or a sticker, for easier recognition.

Watch out for strangers who offer to carry your bags for you. Criminals with bad intentions may lurk around airports and steal your bags as soon as they get their hands on them. Or they will carry your bags for you, but then demand that you give them outrageous sums of money for doing so before they will release your belongings back to you. Again, if you are struggling with your luggage, get a cart or find an airport employee and ask for assistance.

Transferring to Other Transportation at the Airport

Ground transportation is usually near the luggage collection area. If someone is coming to pick you up, plan in advance whether your driver is going to park and then walk inside to meet you by the luggage carousels, or if your driver will just pull over at the curb, in

Whatever method of transportation you are going to take next, the scene can be a little hectic. Always make sure you have your bags with you. Don't leave them even for a second.

which case you should look for her outside. If you are taking public transportation, make sure you have change to pay your fare. If you are renting a car, go to the rental car counter of the company you are renting from and check in with them. They will tell you which shuttle bus you have to take to get to the rental car lots. If you are going to take a cab, make sure you understand what the fare will be (see information about taxis on page 87). Some hotels have special buses that pick up customers for free. If you will be staying at a hotel, call before your trip and find out if your hotel offers this service and if so where to find the bus.

Whatever method of transportation you are going to take next, the scene can be a little hectic. Always make sure you have your bags with you. Don't leave them even for a second. Also always make sure the transit option you are considering is official. The driver of any bus, shuttle bus, van, car service, or taxi should be licensed to transport passengers, and so should the vehicle. If somebody offers you a ride, no matter what type of vehicle, make sure the vehicle is operated by a legitimate company. Don't get into a vehicle if you are not sure.

Hotels and Motels

The classic difference between a motel and a hotel is that at motels, you drive your car right up to the door of your room, or very close to it. At a hotel, if you have a car, you park it in a garage or lot or a hotel employee parks it for you. For simplicity, I will just use the word hotel.

The first thing you have to do upon arrival is check in at the front desk. The front desk clerk will tell you which room you have, give you a key, and explain again what the hotel charges are per night. If you were told that the nightly charge would be something different, speak up and ask why the charge has changed. Hotels also charge a hotel tax, which is usually higher than the regular sales tax rate.

After you get your key, go to your room. If you do not like it, complain. For example, if it turns out your room is right next to a highway and the noise will keep you up all night, ask for a room on the other side of the building. If you can hear the elevator constantly dinging from your room, explain that you need a quiet room without noise disruptions. If the room smells like smoke or perfume, tell them the room smells funny and you would like a different one. You are paying the hotel money for a decent place to sleep. You should be comfortable. Also, if you paid for a special feature, make sure your room has it. For example, if you paid extra money for a view of the beach, but all you see outside the window is a cement wall, or if you paid extra for a room with a hot tub but it is broken, the hotel needs to switch your room or reduce your nightly rate.

Various Hotel Employees

At nicer or bigger hotels, you will notice a lot of different kinds of employees. For example, the *clerks* who work at the front desk check you in when you arrive. They also answer basic questions, such as where the hotel restaurant is located. The *hotel concierge* often has his own desk near the front desk and helps you make arrangements for entertainment or explains the local area. For example, the concierge can tell you how to get tickets to a local theater, where to go for pizza, or the open hours of a museum you want to visit. Concierges almost always have free maps and discount coupons for local tourist attractions. A *bell hop* carries your bags to your room, then collects and brings down your bags when you are ready to leave at the end of your stay. The *housekeeping department* not only cleans your room each day, but will bring you extra towels, extra coffee, or extra pillows upon request. *Room service* is usually provided by the hotel restaurant. Still others might be on staff to help you with problems with your room – for example, if you can't open the shades, the air conditioner won't turn on, or you have a problem with your hotel phone – probably someone from *engineering*.

This array of employees can be confusing. If you are not sure which department or which employee you need to speak with, call the front desk using the phone in your room and ask them to transfer you to the right person. Tipping is customary if someone does something important for you. You should give a few dollars to the person who carries your bags, for example. And when you leave the hotel, you should leave a tip for the housekeepers. But you don't have to tip every single person.

How can you tell if you should tip or not? Decide whether or not the person is solving a regular problem or an extra problem. Bringing you a few more towels is an expected and regular service. Bringing you a towel at 4:00 a.m. is unusual. Asking the concierge for a local subway map is usual. Asking the concierge to book a dozen seats for your large family on the local boat tour of the harbor for a special midnight run that is next to impossible to score tickets for is special. Ordering dinner from room service is typical and usually, although not always, includes a service fee. Asking the kitchen to cook your bag of gluten-free pasta for you and add some sauce to it is special. While hotel employees will do all these things for you to make your stay enjoyable and comfortable, tipping for these special services shows your appreciation.

Eating at the Hotel

Most hotels have restaurants. If you want to try the restaurant, be forewarned that the prices may be higher than at regular restaurants simply because of the convenience – you don't have to leave the hotel. Most hotels also offer room service. You call your order into the hotel restaurant and your food is delivered to your room. Find out what the hotel charges for room service. You can usually put the restaurant bill and your room service charges onto the hotel bill and pay for everything just once when you check out.

If you want to avoid the usually high cost of hotel food, ask for a fridge in your room. Some hotels will even bring a microwave to your room. Sometimes you have to request these items in advance when you make your reservation. In some cases, you also have to pay a fee, but it usually comes out to a lot less money than eating three meals a day in the hotel restaurant.

You can stock your fridge with simple items from home. You can also go food shopping. Just ask the front desk or the concierge where the nearest food store is. You can buy milk, cereal, and fruit for breakfast, sandwich materials and snacks for lunch, and frozen entrees for dinner. If this idea overwhelms you, but you still want to save money, you could try planning one or two meals a day instead of all three. For example, you could provide your own breakfast and lunch and just eat dinner in the restaurant. Also ask the front desk if the hotel provides free breakfast – some do.

If you have special dietary needs and the hotel cannot provide you with a fridge or microwave, talk to the hotel manager and see if the manager can arrange for you to store your food in the hotel fridge. You can also ask the manager of the hotel restaurant if he could heat up something of yours in the microwave. He may be willing to heat something up if it is a simple dish, such as gluten free pasta. But be realistic: Don't expect the hotel restaurant to help you out during the busiest times of day. Ask for the favor a little earlier or a little later than the usual lunch or dinner rush. The restaurant manager may request that you leave your food with him and let him decide when he isn't too busy. In this case, be sure to tell the manager your room number so he can call you when your food is done.

Hotel Fees

Fees at the hotel can add up. In addition to the cost of your room, you will probably have to pay every time you use the telephone to call outside the hotel. Ask the front desk what the phone charges are before you make a call. This is true for Internet service also. Sometimes high-speed access is part of the nightly room charge and all you have to do is plug your computer into the hotel's network to go online. But usually you have to pay a daily fee and have the front desk activate Internet access for you.

Sometimes you will find snacks and special drinks in your room. These are not free. Hotel staff members will check to see if the items are gone, and if they are, you will be charged. Almost always you can find the same snacks and drinks in a vending machine for a lot less money. Before you open that delicious-looking bag of potato chips or a bottle of spring water, call the front desk and ask where the nearest vending machines are located.

Your room comes with a TV. But read the signs closely. It may look like the movie channels or the video game channels are free, but they almost always cost extra. If the charges are not clear, call the front desk and ask what you will be charged before you even channel surf. Once, I stayed in a hotel where one movie each day at a set time was free, but the other movies were not. Make sure you know what the correct time slots are if you are going to make use of such a service.

General Travel Information

Communication Strategies

When taking any sort of trip, long or short, you will most likely need to communicate with two main groups of people: other passengers and employees, including officials. If you are traveling by yourself, you will most likely be sitting next to a stranger. Some strangers are friendly and want to chat the whole trip. Others mind their own business and don't want to talk to you at all. If you feel like chatting and so does the person next to you, go ahead. If you don't feel like chatting but the other person does, be polite but firmly decline. For example, you could say, "I'm really tired right now. Perhaps we can talk later, but I'm going to take a nap." If these types of interaction are too stressful for you, consider making simple Explanation Cards in advance which you can just hand out to people as necessary. (See sample Explanation Cards on page 112.)

The same goes for passengers other than the person sitting next to you who may also want to chat, who may ask you unexpected questions, or who may otherwise try to engage you in some kind of conversation. If you don't feel like talking, just say so. But you don't have to be rude about it. Try to smile and say something like, "I'm sorry, I really can't talk right now." Or, "I can't really answer your questions right now. Why not ask the bus driver?" If you don't feel like talking, but can't verbalize this, Explanation Cards can be very useful. See the sample Explanation Card below. Additional samples may be found on page 112.

Explanation Card: When you can't handle having a conversation

Hello. My name is __________. I see that you would like to have a conversation with me. I am autistic. Although I can talk, conversing is sometimes too stressful for me. I'm going to take a nap, read, or relax during the trip instead of talking. Thank you for your understanding.

Concerning staff members such as, but not limited to, bus drivers, train conductors, transit security officers, police officers, and airline employees, saying that you just can't talk or handing out an Explanation Card usually won't work. The driver of the bus may ask you where you are going. The train conductor may ask you if you have any luggage. A transit security officer may want to see your I.D. You can't just ignore these people and their questions. They need answers so transportation systems can run smoothly and safely.

If you feel extremely overwhelmed by the questions they ask, you can say something like, "I am autistic. I need more time to understand what you are asking me." Or, "I am autistic. I need more time to answer these questions." Since they probably don't know about autism, they may not realize what you need. Therefore, you may have to provide them with a little more information. In this case, an Explanation Card can help, but you will still ultimately have to respond to their questions.

One strategy I have used is to answer with as few words as possible – or no words. This seems to prevent me from going into overwhelm, yet at the same time satisfies the staff member. For example, if a staff member asks me where I am going, I show him the portion of my ticket that states the destination city. I only say something if he has further questions. This usually circumvents the start of a conversation. If an official asks if I have any luggage, I point to my bag. If someone asks me for my name, I simply pull out my wallet, open it up to my driver's license, and point. Avoiding words gives the staff person a hint that you don't want to engage verbally, but that you are willing to cooperate and provide the information alternatively.

Disruptions

For many on the spectrum, the biggest issue with travel of any type may be the disruption of your normal routine. All travel requires big changes in your schedule and your environment. If this is going to cause you extreme anxiety, plan your trip very carefully. Make sure you know what will happen during the journey, what will happen when you arrive, where you will be staying, and how you will get back home.

Also prepare yourself for disruptions while you are in transit. Delays and changes happen. You may have to switch your plans around at the last minute. Traveling requires a degree of flexibility. Bring books or other activities to distract yourself when you have to wait. Should your plans change, give yourself time to adjust. For example, if you thought you were going to take a certain flight, but the flight is cancelled due to the weather and you have to wait three hours for the next flight, sit down for a few minutes in a quiet spot and absorb this information at your own pace.

Lastly, don't feel pressured to hurry. Everyone else at the train station might be rushing around. But you don't have to. Go as slow as you need to go. I have missed a few buses, subways, and taxis because it is difficult for me to rush, but another one always comes by. You may have to rush at the airport, but you can usually avoid this if you leave a lot of extra time for unexpected delays like traffic or getting confused about where to go. If it is too hard for you to rush around or process information quickly, plan ahead and leave at least one extra hour for anything you have to do. I would rather sit and read, do a Sudoku puzzle, watch and study the hustle and bustle around me, or have a snack than rush, even if I wind up being too early sometimes.

Requesting Accommodations

Sometimes it does not feel natural requesting accommodations. This might stem, in part, from the fact that autism is a hidden disability. Most of us do not look like we are struggling. But sensory issues, motor planning, literal thinking, difficulty verbalizing under stress, and slower processing can combine to make regular traveling activities like purchasing tickets, navigating small aisles, passing through security, or eating in a large public room especially challenging.

Don't feel bad. It is the law in the United States that travel must be accessible to those with disabilities. The general public may just be finding out about autism and problems like sensory issues. You may have to do a little bit of explaining as you go along. But transportation companies should take your concerns seriously, even if they don't quite understand.

Tipping

As mentioned at various points in this chapter, you are expected to tip employees who help you while you are traveling if they provide good service. It may be hard to know when or how much to tip. Generally speaking, tip people who do difficult tasks such as lugging your bags. Tip people who go out of their way to help you. If it is not part of somebody's job, but the person does something extra for you anyway, a tip is a sign that you appreciate that this person went above and beyond the call of duty. Also tip taxi drivers, waiters, and housekeepers, who rely on tips as part of their wages. If you are ever not sure who to tip or how much, ask a supervisor or manager in private. If you can't find a manager, you can ask the employee. Most employees will provide an honest answer as to whether or not they usually receive a tip and at what rate.

General Suggestions for Tipping

- Tip people who do difficult tasks.
- Tip people who go out of their way to help.
- Tip taxi drivers, waiters, housekeepers; they rely on tips as part of their wages.

If you are not traveling with your aide, but your aide is dropping you off at the airport, you have the right to have your aide accompany you all the way onto the airplane.

Traveling With an Aide or a Service Dog

Some of us have aides to help us with the tasks of daily living. If you are traveling with your aide in your home city by public transportation, your aide has to pay the regular fare for her seat. This is also usually the case when traveling by long-distance bus, train, or plane. But I have heard of people obtaining discounts for their aide's ticket simply by calling the transportation company or airline and asking for a rate adjustment due to the special circumstances. If you are going to try to obtain such a discount, you will need proof of your disability and proof of your aide's status as an employee specifically hired to address some of the challenges you face.

If you are not traveling with your aide, but your aide is dropping you off at the airport, you have the right to have your aide accompany you all the way onto the airplane. Normally, only ticketed passengers can pass through security and walk to the departure gates. But if you explain the situation to an airline employee at the indoor ticket counter, your aide can get a special pass that will allow her to walk with you and stay with you until your plane takes off. She will have to present an official I.D. and go through security, so make sure she brings a driver's license or passport. Do not be embarrassed to request this accommodation, especially if you need help carrying your things, navigating the maze of hallways, or getting into your seat on the plane. Parents, siblings, or a friend can obtain this type of pass, too, if you anticipate needing assistance but don't have an aide.

If you have a service dog, you have the right to bring your dog anywhere you go. However, if you are traveling by long-distance bus or train or taking the plane, notify the transportation company ahead of time that your service dog will be accompanying you. This will enable officials to reseat or reschedule fellow passengers who are allergic to animals. It is wise to let hotels know as well. While the hotel can't refuse to let your dog stay, they may switch your room to take into consideration the needs of other hotel guests. Always pack a bottle of water and small water dish for the dog in case you encounter a major delay or can't get fresh water in transit. Your dog can experience ear pain on a plane, too, so bring along some chew toys, rawhide bones, or favorite snacks. If your dog is prone to travel sickness, ask your vet for tips on how to make your dog more comfortable.

Conclusion

Whether you are taking public transportation to work or going to a tropical island for vacation, it is possible to have a successful journey. The most likely sources of stress will be sensory issues and lack of structure or familiarity. Being patient with yourself is as important as planning in advance to deal with any difficulties you may encounter. Try to anticipate what accommodations you might need and then advocate for them. And never forget your Sensory Emergency Kit.

Remember, getting around independently and going new places can be fun. Accentuate whatever part of traveling you do like to offset the disadvantages. For example, if you love maps and schedules, you can study these on your way to work. If you like geography, geology, or history, you can learn and see a lot on car trips. If you like symbols and flags, look for these at the airport. You can even have fun memorizing what airlines serve which snacks. Combine your special interests into your travel plans and you'll have a better time. Your trip may require some creativity and a little extra planning, but just because you are autistic doesn't mean you can't travel.

■ ■ ■

Sample Explanation Cards

When it is too hard to answer a question from another traveler:

Hello. My name is __________. I understand you have some questions. I am autistic. Although I can talk, sometimes answering questions is too stressful for me. Perhaps you could ask the (conductor/bus driver/airline hostess/hotel manager/front desk) for more information. I'm sorry that I am unable to help right now. Thank you for your understanding.

When it is too hard to answer an official's questions:

Hello. My name is ______________. I understand you need me to answer your questions. I am autistic. Answering questions is sometimes overwhelming for me. (I need extra time to answer/I need to answer in a quiet area/I can talk, but I need to write down my answers/I need you to repeat the question a few times before I answer/I can answer your questions but I need to close my eyes while I talk so that I can concentrate.) Thank you for your understanding.

When it is too hard to eat in a cafeteria, dining car, or other large space:

Hello. My name is ____________. I understand that everybody is supposed to eat (in the dining car/in the cafeteria/in the hotel restaurant). I am autistic. Eating with large groups of people is sometimes too stressful for me because of my sensory issues with lights, sounds, and smells. I would like to eat (in my private room/in my seat) instead. Could you please accommodate me by bringing my food here? Thank you.

When you need special accommodation on the security line at the airport (or anywhere else):

Hello. My name is __________. I know I must go through the security line and cooperate with all security procedures. I am autistic. The security line is sometimes overwhelming for me. (Standing in lines causes me anxiety/I become confused when I have to move all my things around/I need extra time to put my things on the conveyor, walk through the metal detector, then gather my things on the other side. I need instructions repeated to me several times.) Could you please accommodate me (by escorting me through the line/allowing me to go to the head of the line/allowing me extra time to go through security/explaining the instructions to me slowly). Thank you very much for your understanding.

Chapter 6

Health Care

For people on the autism spectrum, a trip to the doctor, the dentist, the therapist, or other specialty appointments can pose sensory and social challenges. Concerning health matters, some of us have a very high pain tolerance and do not realize we are sick or hurt until the situation is critical. Furthermore, our concrete thinking can make it difficult to interpret and communicate subtleties about our condition. But our physical and mental health is extremely important. Taking care of ourselves is one area of life that is not optional. Certain basic survival strategies are outlined in this chapter.

When It Is Time to Visit the Doctor

How to Determine When You Must Visit the Doctor

This section of the chapter describes ways to delineate when you must visit the doctor and how to overcome some of the difficulties involved in doing so. Needless to say, these are guidelines only; everybody's situation is unique.

People go to the doctor when they feel sick or when they experience pain from an injury. But some of us on the spectrum are hyposensitive to pain and discomfort. We don't realize our foot is broken and keep walking on it. We feel a little "off" but keep going through the day, not realizing we have a high fever and the flu. Or our experience of pain is flip-flopped: A simple cut on the pinky finger might be experienced as traumatic and excruciating, but a severe burn goes completely unnoticed.

This applies to illnesses as well as injuries. We are not likely to report our internal condition to others, if we even notice it. For most of my life, even if I was aware that I was sick, it never occurred to me to tell

People go to the doctor when they feel sick or when they experience pain from an injury. But some of us on the spectrum are hyposensitive to pain and discomfort.

somebody about it. As a child I would wind up going to school, only coming to the attention of the nurse when I couldn't carry on any further or I threw up. Whether you feel very sick or you think you might just be starting to come down with something, take it seriously and assume the worst just to be on the safe side. Since it can be extremely difficult to determine how sick you are, it can't hurt to make an appointment with your doctor.

RULE: Assume injuries are bad. If you hurt yourself, go to the doctor right away. Don't wait. If you cut or burn yourself or have a very bad fall, let the doctor examine you. This is especially important if you have a high pain tolerance because you may not notice something is wrong with your body. You also may not realize the extent of your injury. Getting timely care can make a big difference in terms of how well you heal.

If you find it difficult to determine when your medical condition is serious enough to warrant a trip to the doctor, create rules to guide your decision such as those listed on the following chart. This sample chart may not include every possible situation requiring professional medical attention. Therefore, make your own chart with the help of family, friends, and your doctor. It is very important that you develop a clear understanding of when it is medically necessary to seek the help of a physician.

Other Reasons to Go to the Doctor

People also go to the doctor for a yearly checkup. It is important to go to the doctor at least once a year. At your yearly checkup, your doctor will check your entire body for any signs of problems. The physician will also check your reflexes, your lungs, and your weight, and will most likely give you a prescription to have your blood drawn either in the doctor's office or at a lab. After a complete exami-

When to See a Doctor Right Away

1. You have a fever of 102.5° or higher, or you have had a fever for more than a day or two and it is not going down.

2. You feel so ill, weak, dizzy, or nauseous that you can barely get out of bed.

3. You are unable to eat or drink, or every time you try to eat or drink you throw up.

4. You have a common complaint, but it won't go away. For example, you have a headache but aspirin doesn't help. Or you have acid indigestion even if you take antacid tablets and eat bland food.

5. You have a common complaint to start, but it takes a sudden turn for the worse. For example, you have what seems like a mild cold and you don't feel too bad. But suddenly, your ear starts hurting. You may be developing an ear infection.

6. You fall down, bang your head, or crash into something and some part of your body hurts. If you are hyposensitive to pain, get examined even if you don't hurt or the pain is mild. You may have a serious injury you can't feel.

7. You think some part of your body isn't working right, or isn't working as well as it did. For example, your heart suddenly races when you walk up a flight of stairs. Other examples include but aren't limited to difficulty breathing, going to the bathroom, moving, or sleeping.

8. You notice something unusual about your body. For example, your hair is falling out, you suddenly have a strange rash, or your eyes are puffy and red. You should have your doctor examine you to make sure you don't have the beginnings of a more serious illness.

9. You can't seem to get better. If you've tried to get better on your own and it's not working, schedule an appointment with the doctor to make sure you are correctly diagnosed.

10. You have a problem with your medication. Whether you are taking prescription medication or something over-the-counter, see the doctor if you have a bad reaction, the medicine seems to be making you worse, or you don't understand how to take the medication properly.

NOTE: Don't skip your medication because you can't afford it. If necessary, ask your doctor to help you find a way to obtain the medications you need.

nation, your doctor may order more tests with specialists. When all the information is collected, your doctor will let you know if you have any problems and, if so, what you should do about them. If you don't have a yearly checkup, problems can fester or grow worse, especially as you get older.

Women also need to see a gynecologist once a year. The gynecologist checks for special problems that women face, including cervical and breast cancer. Once you reach age 35 or 40, the gynecologist will give you a prescription to get a mammogram, a test that can detect breast cancer early. Don't skip your yearly checkup with the gynecologist. Assuming you have medical insurance and are female, the insurance company must allow you to see both a regular physician and a gynecologist for checkups once a year.

Prescription Medications

Whether you go to the doctor because you are sick, injured, or it is time for your regular checkup, the doctor may prescribe medications. You cannot buy these drugs unless the doctor orders them from a pharmacy on your behalf. Sometimes the doctor's office will call the pharmacy for you. Sometimes the doctor will write out the medication you need and at what dose on a slip of paper, which you then have to bring to the pharmacy yourself.

Remember, taking the wrong amount, not taking the whole dose, or skipping your medicine altogether can make your condition worse. If you don't understand what you are supposed to do with the medicine or if you can't read the doctor's handwriting, ask for more information or write out the instructions in your own handwriting. Also be sure to ask the doctor what to do when the bottle of medicine is empty: Do you go back to the doctor to make sure you're better or to adjust the dose? Do you go to the pharmacy for an automatic refill and keep taking the medicine? Or can you assume you are all better?

Even if you have medical insurance that covers prescription drugs, you may still have to pay a high portion of the cost. Or your insurance may refuse to pay for certain medications. Some communities have programs that help you obtain needed medications at reduced cost. You can also call the company that manufactures the medicine to see if you are eligible for any of their reduced-cost programs.

Communication Strategies

I find it very difficult to talk to the doctor because I never know what I am supposed to say. Also, I do not like talking about my body or describing physical conditions and complaints. I often can't tell if the doctor is telling a joke. Some doctors like to socialize, making it difficult for me to sort out relevant information. Several communication strategies, outlined below, can help if you have trouble communicating with your doctor.

- **Describe your complaints on paper in advance**
  I write down my physical complaints in advance. At my appointment, I simply give the doctor my sheet. The doctor then asks me questions based on what I have written down. It is much easier for me to answer "yes" or "no" in response than having to explain my problem verbally from scratch. Of course, this is only useful if I have a non-emergency appointment that I can plan for beforehand.

  It is also helpful in the days leading up to your appointment to chart your problems. For example, if you are having a terrible stomachache, write down how many times a day it hurts. Creating a chart requires anticipating what the doctor might want to know – another challenging task for some of us on the spectrum. But in general, the doctor will want to know answers to the following three questions:

  Common Questions

  1. **What does your problem feel like?**
  2. **How often do you have the problem?**
  3. **Does anything help the problem, or vice versa, make the problem worse?**

  Write down your answers ahead of time, next to your description of the problem, and let the doctor take the lead with "yes" and "no" questions that are easier to answer.

Sample Answers

1.	What does your problem feel like?	My head and neck hurt.
2.	How often do you have the problem?	Usually, late in the the day, around 5:00 p.m.
3.	Does anything help the problem or, vice versa, make the problem worse?	I have tried to take pain relievers and sometimes they help; but not always.

- **Bring a buddy**

  Sometimes the doctor wants subtle or very specific details about your condition, asking you questions that can be overwhelming. The doctor may also embody *hidden meanings* in his words – trying to inject a sense of humor into what he's saying or to convey information through body language or indirect hints. I try to bring someone with me. In addition to helping you explain what you want to say, your buddy can serve as a social and linguistic navigator, interpreting the doctor's language and implications.

  For example, when I was young, I broke my arm, and it was put into a cast at the hospital. When my arm was healed, my mother took me to the family doctor to have the cast removed. I asked the doctor, "How are you going to get the cast off of my arm?" He replied, "Oh, we'll just saw it in half!" I was terrified, imagining the kind of saw my father occasionally used in the garage. Luckily, my mother whispered to me, "He's just kidding! He uses a special kind of round medical saw that is really tiny. It might buzz a lot, but the saw won't hurt."

  Some doctors like to joke. Others are serious all the time. Your buddy can help you sort out what is important versus what is meant to be funny. A buddy can also watch for subtle cues that signal it is time to switch doctors – for example, if the doctor's jokes border on bad taste, if the doctor lacks compassion, or if the doctor responds to questions with vague answers.

Besides helping you describe your complaints to the doctor and interpreting subtleties of language and innuendo, your buddy can also "smooth over" the doctor-patient interaction. Doctors usually expect to say hello, to do personal introductions if you've never met, and to chat for a moment about something like the weather. They also expect you to make eye contact. If these social behaviors are difficult for you to do, your buddy can step in and help out in this area while you wait to answer the doctor's specific questions related to your condition.

- **Take notes during the appointment**
  Whether or not you have a buddy with you, you can take notes during the appointment. Write down what the doctor is telling you to see if you understand. If you don't, at least write down what is causing confusion. Make a list of terms you don't understand as the doctor talks to you. If the doctor asks you a question that is hard to answer, jot down the question on your pad and circle it. If you're not sure whether the doctor is trying to be funny or serious, make a note of that too.

  When it is your turn to talk, you can say to the doctor, "You asked me a moment ago if I ever felt hot on my insides. How do I determine if this is the case?" Or, "You said my stomach hurts because I'm eating too much fried food. Is that supposed to be a joke or do I really have to stop eating anything fried?" Or, "Why are you talking about my eyes? I have headaches." You might feel funny taking notes during your appointment, but I find that notes help me sort out what is being said to me. You can also go back over your notes after your appointment and call the doctor if something is still confusing you.

Sensory Issues

I hate going to the doctor because I do not like being touched by unfamiliar people. I do not like the cold feel of metal instruments against my skin. I imagine these are problems for most people, on or off the spectrum, but depending on the severity and type of sensory issues someone on the spectrum has, unexpected sensations can be particularly distressing.

I always ask the doctor to tell me before he begins to examine me or use equipment. I also ask him to verbally explain each step of what he is going to do. In general, I like doctors to tell me what I am about to experience. This way, I am less startled by sensory surprises. If your doctor does not have the time to prepare you for what is coming next, switch doctors.

The doctor's office itself can pose problems. Lots of waiting rooms are loud, with a TV or music blaring. The place might smell like medicine or aseptic cleanser. My eyes always hurt from the fluorescent lights.

If I have to sit in an uncomfortably loud waiting room for a long time, I explain my sensory issues and ask for a quiet place to wait. Sometimes, the office has a small conference room, a mail room, or an unused examining room that I can sit in instead of the public waiting room. Since this is not always the case, I bring my Sensory Emergency Kit (see Chapter 1: *Coping With Sensory Issues*), which includes a walkman to drown out noises I cannot deal with and sunglasses to deal with the lights.

Disclosing Your Diagnosis to Your Doctor

I highly recommend explaining to any doctor you see that you are on the spectrum. You do not need to launch into a long lecture about autism and how it affects your life. One or two sentences to explain how autism impacts your visit should suffice. For example, if you have a lot of sensory issues, you could say, "I am on the autism spectrum. So it would help me a lot if you would warn me first if you are going to touch me." Or, "I'm on the autism spectrum. The lights hurt my eyes. I don't have a vision condition and that's not why I'm here today. I wear my sunglasses to help with the glare." You can explain to the doctor why you have brought your buddy with you, too, by saying something simple like, "My friend came with me to help me answer questions. I'm on the autism spectrum, so sometimes it's hard for me to describe things going on with my body."

Open communication about your diagnosis of autism will enable your doctor to understand you better and to offer you better treatment. It is also important for your doctor to know if you need instructions explained with visual aids or if you need directions explained directly and sequentially. For example, you may want the doctor to show you how to take a certain medication or how to rearrange your bandages as opposed to just telling you how.

When You Probably Don't Need to See the Doctor

A lot of times, we feel sick or have a minor injury, but this does not mean we have to go to the doctor. If it is difficult for you to determine the extent or severity of your physical condition, go to the doctor for an examination. Also go if you are ever unsure of what condition you have. But if you have a common complaint, the tips below can help you determine what to do at home.

Visual Aids for Determining Common Complaints

Visual clues can help you determine what to do when you contract a variety of less serious common conditions. Make a small poster depicting people with various complaints such as a headache, a stomachache, a cut, or a bruise. You can clip pictures of people suffering from these ailments out of magazine advertisements for over-the-counter medications. You can add written descriptions to your pictures, too, that further explain how someone might feel or what might be happening physically.

Next to the picture or description, you can list, draw, or add pictures of what to do. For instance, next to a picture of someone with the flu, you might put the following on your list: Get back in bed, drink a lot of water, take your temperature, take medicine if you have a fever, or call a relative or friend to check on you. These visual prompts will help you determine what ailment you have if you don't feel well and what steps you need to take to get better.

REMEMBER: If you are not feeling well and you are not sure how sick you are, check with a doctor. Even if you have a fairly common complaint such as a headache, you need to check with a doctor if you are getting symptoms very often or if common remedies do nothing to help you. Common complaints can be the beginning of a more serious condition.

Learn How to Self-Report

Teach yourself the valuable skill of self-reporting. As mentioned already, it often doesn't occur to those of us on the spectrum to report our inner conditions or problems to others, including doctors. There are several reasons for this. We may not notice subtle fluctuations in our inner state, we may not intrinsically realize that people help each other, or we may not understand or have the skills for the level and type of social interaction involved in such an exchange.

Make it a rule that when you feel something unusual in your body, you tell somebody else immediately. Your family members, your spouse, or a close trusted friend can help you determine what condition you have and what to do about the symptoms. They can also let you know if they think your condition requires professional medical attention. If you don't tell, you could get worse without anyone realizing it.

Self-reporting does *not* mean you go up to anybody anywhere and graphically describe things that are happening to your body. Don't go up to your family and friends and tell them things to gross them out or to get a reaction. When you discuss a physical problem with someone to solicit advice, talk in private. If you are extremely embarrassed to discuss your personal issues even with someone you trust, or if you lose your voice under stressful situations like being sick, use your visual aids (see page 121) to communicate. You can show someone a picture of what you think might be happening to you to indicate you need help or more information.

As well, if someone asks you how you are doing, you can mention that you have been sick. But don't give them every detail of your illness. You can say, "I haven't been feeling well lately." They will almost always follow up with, "Oh really? What's wrong?" To this question, give a basic answer like, "I've had a cold." They will then usually conclude with a sympathetic statement like, "I'm sorry to hear that. I hope you feel better." The appropriate response is a simple, "Thank you."

Emergency Rooms and Hospitals

Going to an emergency room or any part of the hospital for any reason can pose many of the same challenges as going to the doctor, but with the added stressors of crisis and severity. Again, it may not be obvious to you that you need to go to the emergency room immediately.

A list of a few of the conditions that require an immediate and unquestionable trip to the emergency room is included below. Make your own list and post it somewhere accessible. A few minutes can sometimes make a crucial difference in the outcome of your condition.

When to Go to the Emergency Room Right Away

1. You are bleeding profusely from any part of your body.
2. You have been in an automobile accident – no matter how minor. Sometimes you are so stunned from the accident you can't tell you are hurt, or the accident seems so minor that you don't realize you are injured.
3. You have been bitten by a person or an animal. This may seem silly, but if the bite has broken the skin and bacteria enters your system, you can develop a serious and sometimes fatal infection.
4. You experience so much pain in some part of your body that you can't move that area. ***Note:*** If it is your back or neck that hurts, don't move. Stay put and only let emergency workers move you once they arrive. They are trained to move people with back and neck injuries using special techniques. If you have broken your back or neck and you move or are moved in the wrong way, nerves can be severed, causing paralysis.
5. You have a fever of 103.5° or higher, or your temperature is going up and down erratically. A high fever can cause brain damage quickly and requires prompt medical attention.

6. You are disoriented, especially after a fall or bonking your head. Being disoriented means you're not sure where you are or who you are, the world looks fuzzy (even with your glasses if you wear them), or you can't answer basic questions like how many days are in a week.

7. You feel tightness or vague discomfort in your chest area. This could mean you are having a heart attack. Don't delay.

8. You can't stop throwing up. When you throw up constantly, you can become dehydrated very quickly, causing serious damage to your kidneys and other organs.

9. You have ingested poison, eaten rotten food, or swallowed something toxic like paint, medications that are not yours, or an overdose of illicit drugs.

10. You stop breathing or are having great difficulty catching your breath. This includes choking. If you've choked on something but got it up, still go and get checked. You may not have gotten all of the particles out of your airway.

11. You have any serious and unusual physical symptoms that you can't identify or that you never had before. For example, if you can't stop coughing and hacking, if you suddenly pass out or faint, or if you have a seizure. People with chronic medical conditions like asthma, diabetes, and epilepsy sometimes learn how to manage their symptoms and problems over time. But since you haven't ever been diagnosed with anything and don't know how to respond appropriately, you need to get professional treatment right away.

12. You have a severe allergic reaction. For example, if you eat something and your lips swell or your throat starts to close, or if you are stung by a bee and your arm develops an enormous red bump at the spot. You may think you have no allergies at all, but you can still have what's called an anaphylactic reaction to any substance at any time. Swollen lips, a tight throat, red welts, itchy hives, or a rash that is spreading rapidly are indications that you are going into anaphylactic shock. If you don't get to a hospital for treatment within a few minutes, you can stop breathing and die.

13. You have been the victim of a crime. No matter how mild your injuries may seem and no matter the nature of the crime, you will want an official examination and documentation of what has happened to you. This is of extreme and particular importance for women who have been sexually victimized. Don't be embarrassed. What happened to you is not your fault.

14. You are having severe mental, emotional, or behavioral problems. Emergency rooms are not for physical problems only. If you do not have a regular mental health worker whom you can call for help, go to the emergency room.

Always have a Sensory Emergency Kit ready to go in case you have an emergency. It is crucial to have one for trips to the hospital. The kit should include ear plugs and/or a walkman with fresh batteries to drown out the bleeps of heart machines, the noises of other patients, sirens, alarms, and the drone of hospital equipment. Hospitals are notorious for uncomfortable room temperatures, so always have a thick sweater and a T-shirt in your kit in case you are too hot or too cold. Your kit should also include a pair of sunglasses if you are sensitive to lights.

And don't forget an Emergency Card that states your name, your address, your diagnosis, and any special behaviors or sensitivities that you have. This information is important for workers in the hospital because not everyone is familiar with autism. For example, if you are in a lot of pain, you may not be able to explain why you need to keep your sunglasses on. The nurses may try to take off your sunglasses thinking they are helping you. Or if rocking back and forth soothes you, this is also important information for emergency workers to know so they do not misinterpret your behavior and falsely assume you are on drugs, for instance. The following is a sample Emergency Card. Remember – everybody's card will be different.

Emergency Card Sample

My name is John Smith. My address is 123 Main Street, Boonesville, NY 10003. I am autistic. Sometimes when I am under stress, I rock back and forth to soothe myself. I also wear sunglasses indoors because bright lights hurt my eyes. Please allow me to continue wearing my sunglasses. Also, when I am stressed out, I sometimes lose the ability to communicate verbally. If I'm not able to answer questions or if I cover my ears with my hands as if I am frustrated, provide me with a quiet room and alternate means to communicate such as a pen and paper or pictures I can point to.

Thank you for your cooperation.

Familiarity with the hospital is helpful in reducing stress. Before you wind up in your local emergency room, or before a scheduled visit to the hospital, go there and see what it is like. Where is the front door? Who works there? Do you need a pass for the main part of the hospital? What does the emergency room look and sound like? Where is the bathroom? If you know you are going to be staying in the hospital, what does your room look like? Will you probably have a roommate? Does the cafeteria have food you will eat?

Asking for Help

While in the hospital, it will be necessary for you to ask for help. For example, you will need to describe your experiences and explain your symptoms and problems. If it is hard for you to express emotions or make facial expressions, even if you are frightened or hurt, hospital staff may have difficulty realizing you are scared or in pain. Or they may ask you questions that you find overwhelming. Their job is to help you get healthy, but they rely on you to communicate what you need, as challenging as this may be for you.

Why is asking for help so difficult? I have trouble articulating changes in my condition, asking for comfort measures like extra pillows, or demanding immediate attention when warranted. Sometimes I don't even notice changes in my condition, or I notice a change but this does not translate into a corresponding action. I find it difficult to solicit help or I don't realize it is normal and expected for me to do so. The following suggestions, based on personal experience, can help you navigate the social act of asking for and receiving help in the hospital.

Usually, your hospital bed will have a button you can press to summon help if you feel worse, if you need more medication, if you need assistance going to the bathroom, or if you are uncomfortable. Don't be afraid to press it. You might be sick but that doesn't mean you have to lie there and be miserable. After pressing the button, you have to wait a few minutes for somebody to arrive. The staff member will ask you to describe your problem. Then, you may have to wait a second time if the staff member has to go get medicine, additional staff members, or supplies. The nurses and doctors are helping many people. Everyone has to wait for a turn. But if you don't press the button, no one will know you are having a problem.

Top 10 Reasons Why You Might Press Your Help Button

1. You don't feel well or your condition is getting worse.
2. You are in pain.
3. You need medication.
4. You need to use the bathroom and require assistance.
5. Your IV or other medical devices and gadgets are not working correctly or are causing you discomfort.
6. You are too hot or too cold.
7. You are hungry or thirsty.
8. Your bed is uncomfortable.
9. You can't get your TV or telephone to work.
10. You feel disoriented.

Whether you call for staff with your help button, or nurses come by for a routine check, certain rules of behavior apply. Don't yell at hospital workers. It can take a few attempts to explain to them what your problem is. Be patient if the doctors and nurses have to help someone else worse off than you first. Don't yank out or rearrange your medical equipment. Tell someone you need an adjustment if you are uncomfortable. If you are supposed to remain in bed, don't try to get up and walk around.

Vice versa, you deserve to be treated with respect by everyone who works at the hospital. If you do not like the way you are being treated, if your nurse refuses to believe you are in pain, if no one will help you eat or go to the bathroom, or if you do not understand why you have to undergo certain tests or take certain medications and you can't seem to get a satisfactory explanation from anyone on your medical team, you need to complain. Sometimes you can complain to the head nurse on duty. Sometimes she is too busy; sometimes she is the one causing you a problem. In this case, hospitals always have a designated person with whom you are allowed to talk. This person is usually called a patient representative. She listens to your complaints and attempts to resolve your problems as quickly as possible. If it is late at night or a weekend, you may have to wait to talk to her. Be patient but be persistent. You shouldn't have to suffer or lie in your bed confused and upset.

NOTE: Try to be as cooperative as possible even if change, surprises, and random events cause you anxiety.

If for some reason you are unable to reach the patient representative or another person who handles complaints, or you feel very upset about your physical condition, you can ask to talk to a clergy member of your religion. Again, you will probably have to wait your turn. But all hospitals have priests, rabbis, and ministers on staff who visit hospital patients. In addition to praying with you and talking to you about your problems, clergy members can sometimes help you resolve grievances or at least get in contact with someone who can.

Lastly, hospitals also have social workers on staff. If you are not sure that you are getting the care you need, if you are not sure you have the right diagnosis, or if you are worried about how you will take care of yourself when you leave the hospital, ask to speak to the hospital social worker. Social workers can help you sort out your issues. They can also refer you to agencies and community resources that provide the assistance you may need after you go home.

Dealing With Hospital Routine

One of the hardest parts of staying in the hospital is dealing with the hospital's schedule – or rather, lack thereof. I have never been able to rest in the hospital. Hospital workers flow in and out of the room all day, starting early in the morning. It is next to impossible to get a schedule of what will be happening when. Someone pops in at the crack of dawn to draw your blood. Just as you fall asleep again, someone else arrives to mop the floor. Before you know it, breakfast is delivered. After you've eaten and laid down for a nap, the doctor bounces in the room to discuss your case with you. When he leaves, you anticipate some peace and quiet. But a half-hour later, a technician comes in and says you are being wheeled downstairs for an X-ray. This goes on all day. You are exhausted by evening time, but then your brother shows up to visit!

You can try to ask what happens when for certain activities like meals, cleaning, and sometimes doctor visits if your doctor keeps a fairly regular routine. Otherwise, you will just have to adjust to the rhythm of disruptions and interruptions. You can ask your doctor to try to give you as much notice as possible before a test or diagnostic procedure. You can ask technicians and nurses for a few minutes to get used to the idea that you have to give blood, go for an X-ray, or have your IV changed. But remember they are taking care of many people. You may not like being surprised, but they do have to do the tests and move on to the next patient.

Dealing With Hospital Meals

Mealtimes can also be stressful. Many hospitals have been trying to improve the quality of the food they serve. Some hospitals allow you to choose what food you want to eat, at least to some degree. Even so, you may get some of the wrong items on your tray. If you don't like your food or you are served the wrong food, ask for something else. It will probably take a while for the new food to arrive. Often the entire floor or wing has to be served first before a food delivery staff member can go back to the kitchen for you.

Also, meals are typically served only at specific times, even if you are not hungry or you are accustomed to eating at different times. If you are hungry between meals, the nurses can usually find you a snack but don't expect them to fetch you juice or crackers instantly. Save some food such as a roll and butter or dessert from your meal tray just in case.

Practicing and Preparing

If you know you have to go to the hospital, practicing scenarios in advance can help you prepare. For example, practice explaining a problem to the doctors. Practice asking the nurse to help you make your bed more comfortable. Role-play getting someone's attention when you can't find a nurse. You can also make a list of acceptable and unacceptable hospital behaviors and what you should ask for help with. You can then refer to the list as necessary during your stay.

Everyone feels anxious when going to the hospital. You are hurt or sick. Maybe you can't get there on your own and have to go in an ambulance. Maybe it is the middle of the night. I hope you are not alone. Even planned visits to the hospital can be nerve-racking and full of anticipation.

For autistic people, it can make all the difference in the world to know what the hospital is like, what happens when you arrive, what kind of people work there, and what you can expect in terms of the care you are likely to receive. Do whatever it takes when you are not sick to get ready in the hopefully rare event you do need hospital treatment.

The Dentist

It's not optional: All of us have to go to the dentist once or twice a year. What makes the dentist such a nightmare for autistic people is, I believe, the awful sounds of dental equipment. The scraping, screeching, and drilling are horrible for anyone, but all the more so when you are on the spectrum and have auditory sensitivities. The easiest way to deal with excruciating auditory stimulation is to drown out the dental noise with a walkman. Unfortunately, even the loudest walkman just can't drown it all out.

One approach might be to ask the dentist to do work on you in smaller increments, even if that means that you have to go a few extra times. On the first visit, maybe he will do all the scraping and it will only take about five minutes. On the second visit, he can do the scrubbing, which also might only take five minutes. But at least you don't have to sit through 10 full minutes of auditory torment in one day.

Concerning extreme olfactory discomfort in the dentist's office, you can wear a filter over your nose while you wait (see page 359). Unfortunately, you will have to remove the filter when the dentist is ready to look inside your mouth. But at least it cuts down on the total number of minutes of exposure. If it isn't the whole office that smells, but mainly the gels and pastes the dentist uses during the checkup, ask for unscented and unflavored alternatives.

As with doctors, having the dentist explain exactly what he is going to do before he does it can reduce anxiety. Ask him to break down procedures into comprehensible steps with an indication of how long they will last. A digital timer can help you estimate how many more seconds or minutes you must endure a certain procedure. Have the dentist show you the tools he is using and ask for a mirror so you can see what he is doing. Sometimes knowing what is going on, understanding how long the task will take, and watching as the task progresses can help enormously in reducing discomfort and eliminating panic.

Always interview or try several dentists before you decide which one you want to see regularly. Some dentists are more sensitive to their patients' needs than others. Is the dentist's office quiet and comfortable, or is there an alternative quiet room you can sit in while you wait? Does the dentist explain what is happening in a gentle manner or is he in a rush? Does he think you are crazy because you need time to get used to the noise of a machine he is about to use? Find a dentist who is willing to give you a chance to get comfortable, who doesn't make you feel bad about your issues, and who is willing to work with your special needs.

I recommend explaining your diagnosis to the dentist precisely so he can understand why you need accommodations. If the dentist isn't interested or doesn't care, he may not be the best dentist for you. If, on the other hand, he listens carefully to your concerns and agrees to make accommodations, chances are he'll be willing to work with you over the years. Some dentists may ask you to come for appointments at odd times like early in the morning so they can spend more time with you explaining procedures and making the accommodations you request. Ask your dentist what is the least busy time in his office and schedule your visits then.

It is also important for the dentist to know how autism might impact your visit in less obvious ways. Once, the dentist had to give me a shot of Novocain. After the injection, he left for a few moments while the medicine started to work. When he reappeared, he asked me if my mouth was numb. Well, it was numb comparatively speaking. So he began working on my cavity. I almost jumped out of the chair because the pain was so bad.

He said, "But you told me your mouth was numb!"

"It is."

"So it shouldn't hurt."

"Well, it does."

It was in that moment that I realized the crux of the miscommunication: He hadn't asked me *how* numb my mouth was. It was numb, but only slightly. The medication needed more time to take effect. I had interpreted his question literally: yes/no. I also did not pick up on his expectation that I would automatically describe the level of numbness in response to his question. I explained briefly that because I am on the autism spectrum, he needs to ask me questions that request all of the information he is seeking. He cannot rely on me to pick up implications. So now he asks me point blank, "Are you a lot numb, or just a little numb?"

Like visiting the doctor's office, it is helpful to have a buddy go with you to the dentist's office. In a situation such as the one in the above example, a buddy could have poked me and said, "What the dentist is really trying to ascertain is if your mouth is numb enough to start working." Then my answer would have been a resounding "No!"

Lastly, good oral care at home can help prevent the kinds of dental problems that cause the most sensory distress. By brushing, flossing, and rinsing every morning and night, you can potentially reduce the chance of cavities, heavy cleanings, and root canals. It is also important to learn how to recognize when your teeth hurt and to go to the dentist when the pain first starts. Delaying is only going to make the dental problem worse. Ultimately, if it is impossible for you to go to the dentist for sensory, tactile, or other reasons, consider finding a dentist who provides treatment to patients while they are put to sleep artificially with anesthesia. The health of your teeth is so important to your overall health that skipping the dentist is not an option.

The Therapist

Many people, not just those on the autism spectrum, seek out therapy for a variety of issues that can come up in life. For example, you may need counseling if you are going through a lot of changes, you just discovered your diagnosis, you can't seem to find happiness, or you are experiencing great difficulty in getting along with the people in your life.

Don't be embarrassed if you feel like you need to talk to a professional therapist. The therapist can help you sort out your feelings and will help you discover steps you can take to feel better. If you are having a severe emotional crisis, you feel suicidal or like you can't go on in life, your mind feels like it is out of control, or you can't control your behavior or feelings, you may need emergency mental health care. If you don't have a mental health worker whom you see on a regular basis, or you can't find a therapist to see right away, go to your local hospital emergency room. The emergency room has counselors, therapists, and doctors on staff who can help you with both talking therapy and medication, depending on the situation.

When to See a Mental Health Specialist Right Away

1. You feel so bad about your life that you want to kill yourself or all you do is think about different ways to die.
2. You have been very sad for no apparent reason or for a very long time without any relief.
3. You never experience happiness any more, not even from your special interests and personal projects.
4. You are so anxious or depressed that you can't get to work or school, or can't even leave your bedroom or house at all. This can include anxious thoughts running through your mind over and over again to the point that you're too distracted to concentrate on work, school, or taking care of yourself.
5. You hurt yourself physically or you can't stop thinking about doing so.
6. You lash out physically or emotionally at other people with no provocation, even at people you love, or can't stop thinking about doing so.
7. You can't handle your anger or anxiety.
8. You are unable to do anything to take care of yourself, including eating or bathing.
9. Your habits change drastically – for example, you start doing drugs or drinking alcohol, you begin hanging out with new friends who get into trouble a lot, you purposefully seek sexual relationships with strangers just to be provocative or to escape your life, or you suddenly quit a job you love for no apparent reason, placing yourself in financial jeopardy.
10. You become addicted. People can become addicted not just to drugs or alcohol but to unhealthy sexual relationships, overeating, gambling, driving dangerously, or stealing. If you have an addiction that is destroying your life and putting you in danger, get help.

Different Types of Therapists

It may be overwhelming to decide which type of therapist you need. At a minimum, all therapists should be certified and have a license to practice. A *psychiatrist* is a therapist who is also a doctor and who can therefore dispense medications. If a therapist is not a medical doctor, but has received extensive training and education in the therapy field, he or she is called a *psychologist* or a *psychotherapist*. Psychologists have different methods of therapy or different philosophies about how people can improve their lives. If you are considering going to a certain psychologist, find out what kind of therapy she practices to be sure you agree with the methods and values of the system she will use with you.

Psychiatrists or psychologists will look at the root causes of your problem. They may explore with you how your childhood is affecting your adult life. They assist you in discovering what hidden influences and motivations are causing your behaviors. Usually, psychiatrists and psychologists base their work on verbal exchange: You will talk about yourself. Then they will ask questions to guide you or to clarify information. Some therapists use a cognitive-behavioral approach and give you concrete exercises to reduce anxiety in certain situations, to confront your fears, or to manage your behavior differently. A psychiatrist may prescribe medications for conditions like depression, anxiety, and obsessive-compulsive disorder.

Some people prefer to go to *social workers* and *certified counselors*. Social workers must have a college degree in social work. Certified counselors usually take courses that prepare them to do work in certain areas of therapy, such as drug addiction or family issues. Social workers and counselors tend to take a more practical or day-to-day approach than traditional psychologists or psychiatrists. For example, a social worker may help you outline a job plan if your main problems are vocational in nature. A counselor at a family center may help you come up with new strategies for managing a problem with a family member. Social workers and counselors often, but not always, provide shorter-term therapy than psychiatrists or psychologists. But again, social workers and counselors rely heavily on a verbal exchange of information.

Different Kinds of Therapy

If you feel as though you can discuss your inner emotional states with another person and that doing so would help you see yourself in new ways, learn new ways of expressing yourself, or otherwise improve your sense of getting along in the world, therapy can be very useful for you. However, some people on the spectrum find the talking and self-reporting that traditional therapy relies on to be too overwhelming or too abstract. They sit in the therapist's office wondering what to say or do. They don't know why the therapist is asking them to interpret problems through the lens of subtle feelings. The social dynamic of therapy can be too taxing, negating any therapeutic value. The reflection of the inner self through the therapist's eyes may be too indirect for someone on the spectrum to benefit much from.

If talking therapy doesn't work for you, consider alternative forms of therapy that can be just as useful in sorting out your problems. Short-term therapy of a few weeks' or months' duration that focuses on one specific problem might be easier. For example, you could find a counselor who would be willing to spend eight weeks working with you on improving your way of dealing with anger. Others on the spectrum have tried art or drama therapy. Therapy that provides concrete behavioral exercises, emphasizes concrete plans of action, or otherwise assists you in discovering information about yourself without you automatically having to know what to talk about may be more useful than traditional therapy models.

How to Find a Therapist

It often takes a while to find a therapist who meets your needs. If you have health insurance, call the company and ask what your policy covers. All health insurance companies have rules about whom you can see and how many times you can go. You may also have to pre-certify your

***REMEMBER:** If you don't have a mental health care worker whom you see regularly, but you are having a crisis or a problem such as one of those listed on page 133 and you can't find a therapist to go to, go to the emergency room of your local hospital.*

visit – that is, receive approval before your first appointment. Assuming your plan covers mental health visits, the insurance company can give you referrals to therapists.

If you do not have health insurance, you can find therapists at mental health clinics and at large mental health agencies who will reduce their fees or base the fee on your income. Look in your phone book under "mental health services" or "social services." If you can't find any options, try calling your local hospital or the local board of health. You will have to do a bit of research, but low- or no-cost mental health services are available.

Local autism groups often list mental health workers who have helped others on the spectrum. The advantage to getting a referral from an autism group is that the therapist already has some experience working with autistic people. Also, it is fair to assume that you wouldn't be given a referral to a therapist that nobody likes. That being said, you still may not like the first therapist you go to. Keep asking around for more referrals until you do find someone you like.

Lastly, you can contact national associations for referrals. Try the American Psychiatric Association for psychiatrists, the American Psychological Association or the American Psychotherapy Association for therapists, or the National Association of Social Workers for social workers (check association websites or your phone book for numbers and referral procedures).

WARNING: Even though the referral is coming from a national association of therapists, the practitioner may not be great or may not be a good match for you. Get the names of a few so if one doesn't work out, you can try another.

What to Expect From Your Therapist

Always make sure that the therapist you are going to work with is certified. Give yourself a few sessions to decide if you like the therapist and the kind of therapy she offers. It is O.K. if you decide you do not like the therapist or the type of therapy. The therapist is there to help you grow as a person and learn more about yourself. If your therapy sessions aren't helpful, it's time to switch therapists.

Also remember that your therapist is a professional person who is paid to listen to your concerns. If a therapist tells you that your problems aren't real, or if a therapist belittles your concerns, don't keep going to her. Your therapist should care about you as a person. She should be alert, ready to listen to you, and willing to help you. If her phone keeps ringing, if she falls asleep, or if she looks away from you like she isn't paying attention, you aren't getting the help you deserve. Quit going to that therapist and look for a new one.

Unfortunately, some therapists take advantage of their clients. When I was first seeking a diagnosis after learning about Asperger Syndrome, I went to a psychiatrist who said he would be able to determine if I had the condition. He was very expensive and accepted only cash payments. During the first session, he asked me a lot of questions. At the end, he said he couldn't tell yet and that I needed to come back. He did this three or four times – emptying me of my savings before I caught on. He never intended to diagnose me or help me. He just kept asking me questions and saying he needed to see me one more time, presumably to make more money off of me. If you suspect that your therapist is taking advantage of you in some way, you need to quit that therapist and find another one.

Clarify What You Can Expect From the Therapy

When you start therapy with a new therapist, discuss your therapy goals and understand your therapist's expectations. If you are getting a diagnosis, how many sessions are required? What tests, if any, will you be given? Will you be interviewed as well as tested? You should be, since tests alone can't tell the whole story. In order to be diagnosed properly, the therapist should interview you extensively in addition to administering tests in order to gain a sense of who you are.

Certain tests like the Millon™ Clinical Multiaxial Inventory-III may be next to impossible anyway for someone on the spectrum to complete

If you are beginning psychoanalysis with a psychotherapist, a very long-term process that can take years, find out how you will be billed for the sessions.

accurately due to the cognitive and linguistic challenges associated with autism. The Millon test is a sheet of vague statements such as, "Sometimes I feel so blue I can't get out of bed," to which you must answer "Yes" or "No." After filling in the answer circles, a computer generates a report that is supposed to give an accurate psychological profile.

Using the above example, I suppose everyone has felt that blue once or twice in life. Most people would understand the implication buried inside the question and answer, "No," as in they do not feel suicidal. An autistic person is likely to miss the implication and answer literally "Yes," as in all people do *sometimes* feel that blue, creating a false psychological picture. If you are going to be administered abstract, vague, or confusing tests such as this one, or you find yourself struggling with such a test, ask for an accommodation to have the questions clarified as necessary and insist on a diagnostic interview to corroborate or correct any computer-generated reports.

If you are beginning psychoanalysis with a psychotherapist, a very long-term process that can take years, find out how you will be billed for the sessions. Can you pay once a month? Will your health insurance pay for one session a week? If you are seeing a psychiatrist who may prescribe medications for you, will your health insurance pay for these medications? If not, will your psychiatrist help you find a program that can assist you in obtaining reduced-cost or free mental health medications?

If you are seeing a social worker for help with a specific problem, ask her how she has helped other clients. Does she have demonstrable experience helping people in this area? Will she do role-playing with you? Is that something you want to do? How long does she estimate it will take for you to learn the set of skills you are hoping to gain or to come up with concrete resolutions?

Trust Yourself

Lastly, keep in mind that while you are relying on your therapist to help you understand yourself and improve your life, ultimately you know yourself the best. One therapist told me I couldn't possibly have Asperger Syndrome because I had a girlfriend. Another therapist told me that if I just stopped feeling sorry for myself, I would fit in with my peers better and my problems would go away. He added that women often think they have problems when really they just have premenstrual syndrome. That didn't sound correct. I knew in my heart that I wasn't feeling sorry for myself. Actually, I was really enjoying my life at that time. But I knew I had a problem or some issue that made certain aspects of life a challenge. My literal thinking and super-focused mind also posed challenges at work. I needed real answers and respect.

You won't always agree with the therapist, and that is O.K. A healthy disagreement can help the therapeutic process. The whole point of therapy is to learn new ways of looking at things and new ways of getting along in the world that you haven't thought of on your own. This can be uncomfortable at first. You may have to face your fears, which can also be uncomfortable. Give yourself time to get used to therapy. But, on the other hand, if what the therapist is telling you doesn't seem right, ask someone you trust for a second opinion. If you think your therapist doesn't believe you or isn't taking your problems seriously, follow your instincts and find a new therapist.

Other Types of Appointments

Many times we have to go see specialists – the eye doctor, a podiatrist, a physical therapist, or a message therapist, for example. The same advice given for visiting doctors, dentists, and therapists holds true. Bring a Sensory Emergency Kit. Bring a buddy if you can. And again, if something doesn't seem right, ask somebody to help you sort out the issue.

One time I went to have my eyes checked. The eye doctor said that my vision was "not in the prescription range" but that I could still benefit from a pair of glasses. Why should I get glasses if my vision is fine? I think the eye doctor just wanted me to buy a pair of the fancy glasses for sale in the office lobby.

It is . . . crucial to develop ways to communicate our health problems, to get the proper treatment, and to maintain our health with preventative care.

Autistic people are particularly vulnerable to suggestion and pressure because we tend to automatically trust what people tell us. When a professional suggests something that does not seem logical, such as ordering glasses even though your vision is O.K., purchasing expensive vitamins that you can buy at a local drug store for a lot less money, or suggesting diagnostic tests for problems you do not have, you are probably right that something is amiss. Check with someone you trust first before proceeding.

I always find it difficult to summon help or express discomfort. For example, my acupuncturist would leave me on the table for 15 minutes, instructing me to call her in from the other room if I had any unusual pain. But I was never able to yell out to her. If yelling out for somebody is too hard for you to do, ask for a bell to ring or a buzzer to press instead. If you aren't sure if something is hurting, remember that you can always say, "I don't know if it hurts or not – it's hard for me to tell." You'll have a chance to think about it before proceeding. And if something does hurt, definitely point this out one way or another.

Conclusion

Obtaining physical and mental health care services can be challenging for those on the spectrum because we may have sensory issues, we may have trouble communicating our inner experiences, we may not know the social rules, and we may not know how or when to ask for help. It is therefore crucial to develop ways to communicate our health problems, to get the proper treatment, and to maintain our health with preventative care. As difficult as going to the doctor, the dentist, or a therapist may be, your health and safety should be your top priority in life. Don't skip getting the care you need just because it can be a challenge. Using the techniques outlined in this chapter, you will have an easier time reporting and recognizing your health complaints, navigating the social complexities of exchanges with health care providers, and ensuring that your best interests are served.

■ ■ ■

Chapter 7

Vocational Challenges

One big problem in the adult autism community seems to be chronic unemployment and under-employment. Many of us have great potential and much to offer society but a breakdown happens somewhere. I am not immune to vocational challenges. I cannot speak from the perspective of one who has surmounted the difficulties in obtaining and maintaining a steady, viable job. But I do have a wide berth of employment experiences. Based on these experiences, I can highlight where the troubles often surface and what can be done to address vocational challenges.

To recap my experiences briefly, I journeyed across the United States for five years in the early 1990s, during which time, and for several years before and after, I worked at every type of job imaginable: Dishwashing, farming, setting up conventions, unloading trucks, cat sitting and dog walking, counting cars and recording license plates for a traffic research agency, packing and shipping, driving a cab, conducting opinion surveys, delivering telephone books, telemarketing for a carpet cleaning service, cashiering, merchandising, and cleaning are just some of the jobs I did. I also worked as a secretary and an editor in corporate and non-profit offices, was Santa Claus at a vet clinic (because dogs can't join the family at the mall), apprenticed myself to an electrician, and worked in several kinds of factories.

After traveling, I came back to New York City, my hometown, and finished my undergraduate education. I excelled at the academic research I had to conduct as part of my joint major in ancient history and women's studies. But I had no idea how the university system works, how to net-

This combination of mostly solitary work in informal environments, self-employment, and project variation is going well for me so far.

work with others, how to get published, or how to obtain a teaching position while I continued my research at the graduate level. Since I am good at writing and editing, I earned a master's degree in technical journalism. I was able to obtain internships and jobs in the field. For example, I wrote and edited docent training manuals and popular articles for the American Museum of Natural History and edited blurbs for an online financial newspaper. But I could never sustain employment over the long term. Now, I am working as a heavy equipment operator, running my own Internet business on the side, and writing in my spare time. This combination of mostly solitary work in informal environments, self-employment, and project variation is going well for me so far.

A summary follows, describing what areas – based on my personal experiences – autistic people do well in, what types of jobs we are not likely to succeed at, and why. The chapter is divided into three main sections – how to determine what might be an appropriate job, where to find a job, and how to manage once you get a job. I also include information on self-employment. Though not many people have a chance to work for themselves, self-employment can be a great option in some cases.

Determining What Job Might Be Right for You

Some jobs I've held were great. Others weren't. Over the years, I discovered that, when looking for a job, it is important to consider two things:

1. Your personal work style
2. The characteristics of autistic workers in general

Knowing about your individual personality as well as broadly defined autistic traits will help you match yourself to a job where you can more easily reach your potential.

Discovering Your Personal Traits

Knowing yourself thoroughly is key to finding the right job. If you can't sit still, don't look for jobs that require you to stay at a desk all day. If you can't stand being outdoors in all weather, don't work at a park or a zoo. Perhaps you enjoy contact with people and chatting about your favorite topic – trains. In this case, a job at a toy train shop or as a docent at a train museum could be perfect for you. But if talking to people all day long is stressful or impossible, maybe you could clean, repair, or organize the trains instead. If you are a highly skilled computer programmer, but not good at team computer projects, perhaps a job as a freelance programmer or programming consultant, going from project to project and from company to company, is better suited to your situation.

Before you even begin looking for a job, take out a sheet of paper and answer the following questions. Your answers can help you figure out your preferred work style and work conditions. I came up with some of these questions for myself to gain a sense of what vocational direction I should go in and added a few others for this book. I am sure books written about finding work have better questions, methods, or advice. This is simply what I did on my own. It may work for you.

Discovering Your Personal Work Style

Likes and Dislikes

1. What are you good at doing?
2. What do you like to do?
3. Do you have any hobbies or special interests that could translate into a job?
4. What do you absolutely hate doing (or refuse to do)?

Sensory Issues

1. What environmental or other conditions are intolerable?
2. What conditions do you prefer?
3. Do you have any sensory issues you know you need to prepare for in advance?

Communication Style

1. Do you enjoy talking to other people?
2. Is conversing, formally and informally, easy or difficult for you?
3. Are questions easy to answer?

Social Style

1. To what degree do you enjoy socializing?
2. Does socializing make you anxious?
3. Do you have trouble understanding other people?

Project Style

1. Do you work better on your own, with a leader, or with a group?
2. Do you like concrete tasks or open-ended projects?
3. If you usually work alone but then must collaborate with others on a special project, would the switch in style be a big problem?
4. Do you mind repetitive work?
5. Are you easily distracted?

Action Level

1. Do you move slowly or quickly?
2. Do you need a lot of action and motion or do you prefer to be still?

Personal Issues

1. Do you have any anxiety issues to consider?
2. Are you organized and neat, or messy?
3. Do you like to dress up?

There are no right or wrong answers to these questions; they simply help you define yourself and your needs. You should have a good idea of what work would be suitable for your personality after taking a good look at and being honest about your abilities. If you can't handle chatting with people, that's O.K. You can find jobs that do not require chatting, or where workers who do not enjoy chatting are still tolerated and respected. But it is important to know this about yourself before you look for a job. If you do not know what you can and cannot tolerate, you risk winding up in a less than ideal situation.

Considering the General Traits of Autistic Workers

Some people are very uncomfortable discussing the traits of an entire category of people. We are, after all, individuals. Just because I have Asperger Syndrome and you do too does not mean you and I are automatically similar. Respecting the fact that individual personalities are unique, it is still possible to describe tendencies that autistic workers share. If these generalizations are not true in your case, skip to the next section. However, it may be very useful to understand typical autistic behaviors and thought patterns as they relate to vocational issues when trying to determine what type of job would be best for you.

For example, those of us on the spectrum tend to have the ability to concentrate deeply and focus intensely on some aspect of our work that we value highly or find interesting. But we may also be easily distracted from assigned tasks because of sensory issues. We often have difficulty managing disruptions. Interruptions are hard because we have to change our focus from one thing to another rapidly. This takes a lot of mental energy. An environment that allows you to work on your assignments with minimal or no disruptions is probably best.

Those of us on the spectrum also may function better on the job when work tasks are measurable and quantifiable. If you must fill 52 wholesale orders of peanut butter, pack and then ship the boxes, it is very clear at the end of the day whether you completed all of the orders or not. If you must write a report on the sales rate of your corporation's newest product, you have a defined topic and also probably a set date that the report is due. Jobs that have such easy ways of measuring progress and success may be better for us because we can see concretely whether we are too fast or too slow, on schedule, getting all our work done to the boss's satisfaction, or having some sort of problem that can then be addressed.

But more open-ended tasks, such as managing a group, deciding what to write about for a newsletter, or coming up with a new way to market ceiling cleanser, are much more dependent on a subjective analysis of how the task is progressing, or of how well you have succeeded. How do you measure ability to lead, or your creativity? Because it is much harder to grade your performance on these open-ended tasks, you may not be able to accurately gauge how you are doing. Your boss may not be able to tell how you are doing either, especially if you have a hard time articulating your experiences and your perspective.

Most jobs require some open-ended tasks, but seriously consider whether or not you can handle a job comprised essentially of tasks that are difficult to quantify both while performing and upon completion. This is related to another area that can be a challenge for us: prioritization.

We may have many things to do as part of our job, and each one can seem vitally important. We may not be sure which tasks can wait, which have to be attended to immediately, or in what order the tasks should be accomplished. Some jobs require juggling so many different activities practically at the same time that it is tricky to complete any of them. We are more likely to succeed if we have one defined project to work on at a time. If you are considering a job that has many different components, decide how you would structure each piece into your day and be sure to determine how much help with prioritizing your supervisor or boss will be offering.

Literal thinking also plays a role in our success or failure on the job. I would fail as a waitress because I take what people say very literally. Can you imagine what would happen if a customer asked me for an egg "over easy" and for coffee "with milk"? I would stand there wondering what on earth an egg over easy could be – over what? And I would likely wind up serving two drinks – a mug of coffee, and a glass of milk. I once heard a waitress at the diner yell out to the cook after I placed my order, "Cheddar easy all sides and a V." Apparently, this conveyed to the cook that I wanted a grilled cheese with cheddar, toasted instead of fried, French fries, a pickle, and a vanilla milkshake. All jobs and professions have special words or "lingo" that you can figure out easily enough. But consider what could happen if the job you are applying for requires you to understand a whole lot of jargon at an extremely fast pace.

Those of us on the spectrum also tend to be visual thinkers. On the one hand, this can pose a challenge if you must filter information and instructions visually. For example, you may need visual aids to understand the day's events, visual clues to organize your work materials, or a list of steps to complete a task. You will probably have to make these visual guides yourself (see the section *Survival Tips for Life on the Job* for more information).

On the other hand, visual thinking skills can be an enormous asset. Many of us are able to "see" in our minds how something should work or look, as if we are watching a video. When I was in charge of scheduling events for all departments at my synagogue's office, I could "see" all the different locations, classrooms, and meeting halls in my mind at once, visually juggle every event that had to have an assigned space on a certain day or within a certain week, and then transcribe this "video" onto the Intranet calendar, completely eliminating the problem of double-bookings and maximizing the efficiency of space assignments.

If you are a strong visual thinker, consider finding a job where you can put your visual thinking skills to good use. Examples include jobs designing objects, machines, or procedures if you can see how things work; organizing physical spaces and production systems if you can see where things should go or where things should be done to maximize efficiency; scheduling, assigning numbers, cataloging, or formatting if you can see the order in which things should go or how they should be arranged; and, of course, illustrating if you can depict ideas, concepts, plans, or schematics with your drawings.

Many of us have difficulty socializing on the job partially because social interaction requires extra energy and partially because we may not

Many of us have difficulty socializing on the job partially because social interaction requires extra energy and partially because we may not know how to interact appropriately for all the different situations that arise.

know how to interact appropriately for all the different situations that arise. Interacting with the public, for example, often requires a worker to modulate his voice, his social approach, and his topics of conversation according to the type of customer he is talking to. Jobs sometimes require socializing with the public, other co-workers, authority figures at the company, and anyone associated with the company's business, such as bankers or suppliers, all in the course of one day. Each of these interactions involves a different set of social rules.

Some jobs don't just require you to interact with the public, say, to complete a sale. Most jobs also require a special kind of socializing that enables others in the work environment to include you in the work community, a vital part of receiving additional work assignments or various types of recognition.

I loved my science writing internship at the American Museum of Natural History. I had dreamed of working there since childhood. I went above and beyond my assigned project and wrote articles for Museum publications, one of which was even selected for the Museum website. But I didn't know that being a good, motivated writer wasn't the only qualification when it came time to be selected for a full-time position. The social and political steps involved in gaining entry into Museum life were elusive to me and I was passed over. I never figured out how to become part of the Museum culture. I was lost in the shuffle and my dream disintegrated.

While the social aspects of work can be daunting, we can be very loyal and devoted to our places of employment. We tend to do better in environments where people come to know us and value us for our skills instead our ability to socialize. We are more likely to succeed at jobs where we are recognized for our contributions based on performance and where we have opportunities to be promoted based on commitment to the company. In other words, when thinking about what kind of job you might want, it is important to determine how much socializing will be expected of you not just to get through the day and perform your assignments, but also to be recognized for what you can do and to be rewarded for your efforts.

Lastly, we may have trouble attending to self-care on top of working. Personal hygiene, meals, home responsibilities, and dressing may require so much conscious effort that it is as if you are working two jobs, leading to extreme fatigue. If dressing in corporate clothing is next to impossible for you, find a job with a more informal atmosphere. If you need a lot of time in the morning to wake up, shower, eat, get dressed, and gather your things, a job with a long commute is not a good idea. If taking public transportation to work will push you over your sensory limits before you even arrive on the job, you may have to look for work within walking distance.

Don't neglect this issue. Your chances for success at work increase when you are eating well, sleeping enough, taking care of your body, and living in a sanitary and peaceful home. Look for a job that won't decrease your ability to complete personal care activities.

Characteristics of Autistic Workers

- Usually able to concentrate intensely
- Often frustrated by disruptions/interruptions
- May be distracted due to sensory issues
- Better able to handle and assess concrete tasks
- May have trouble prioritizing responsibilities
- May be confused by literal thinking
- Possibly possess strong visual thinking skills
- Sometimes lack social skills to complete job tasks or to be recognized for contributions
- Tend to be loyal
- May have trouble balancing personal and work life

Jobs That Are Usually Good for Autistic Workers

Throughout my work history, I have found that the following types of jobs mesh well with the characteristics of autistic workers.

- **Apprenticing to an expert in an area of interest**
  Until the apprentice is ready, he can rely on the master to set priorities and make major decisions. But the apprentice is not stripped of all responsibility and has a sense of being included and important. When I was an electrician's apprentice, I found it additionally enjoyable to work with a journeyman who taught me about electricity and electronics as we engaged in projects.
- **Researching and fact-finding**
  Some of us may have the ability to focus so intensely on an area of interest that we can follow the trail of obscure details and information without getting lost, bored, or side-tracked. When conducting research, you can usually also go at your own pace, set your own schedule, and apply the special abilities of your mind to something productive. Libraries have the added sensory bonus of being quiet.
- **Merchandizing/inventory/loading and unloading**
  Many of us love organizing, stocking, shelving, and counting. Categorizing items is exciting for me. The atmosphere in warehouses is informal. Workers wear jeans and T-shirts or uniforms. Social life on the job can be more flexible or less pressured. And usually, workers do not have to jockey for position and recognition. The social rules and the methods for determining a worker's worth in this type of environment are very clear.

- **Some types of factory work**
  Factories usually produce products in an orderly progression of tasks, which can be soothing. When I worked in a peanut butter factory, I liked being able to focus on one station at a time. On my own initiative, I even learned about the machines and joined extra shifts to clean and repair them, increasing my value as a worker and gaining important skills.
- **Solitary jobs**
  Solo jobs, where a worker is basically by himself all day, often require very little socializing. Doormen, security guards, cab drivers, machine operators, truck drivers, delivery personnel, and messengers may have to come in contact with others periodically as part of the job, but most hours are spent alone. When I drove a cab, I had to ask passengers questions and then interact with them to collect payment, but otherwise I could chat with interesting riders or remain silent at my discretion. I have a friend who is a night doorman for a fancy residential building in New York City. He doesn't mind chatting when necessary if someone needs help with the elevator or a Chinese food delivery, but these interactions are informal and brief. Most of the time, he is all by himself, just as he prefers.
- **Jobs with animals**
  If you enjoy animals, cleaning, walking, feeding, and caring for all types of animals may be a viable option for you. I loved walking dogs and cat sitting and still do on occasion. It is comfortable and fun to interact with animals. I have never failed at a social interaction with a dog or cat, and interactions with their humans are usually casual and quick.
- **Self-employment**
  When I took some time off work to develop an online design-it-yourself jewelry business, Intelligirl Jewelry Maker, I was able to set the tone, the pace, and the style of my work environment. I picked what projects to do and how tasks would be completed. I also relied only on myself. This was also true when I took on freelance editorial assignments during college. Self-employment is risky but affords the maximum degree of control over work conditions.

Most people respond to job advertisements. These job ads are located in a number of places. Local newspapers always have sections for job ads. The Internet is another place to look.

Where to Find a Job

Once you have an idea of what job you want to do, how do you go about getting one? Most people respond to job advertisements. These job ads are located in a number of places. Local newspapers always have sections for job ads. The Internet is another place to look. Do a search for "jobs" and you will get several websites specifically devoted to listing available employment opportunities. You can also find job ads posted at job locations. For example, the supermarket and other local businesses often hang signs in the front window or on a special bulletin board when jobs are open.

Usually, when you apply for a job, you submit a resume, which is like a summary of your vocational and educational experiences. Often a cover letter accompanies the resume, which is a letter you compose introducing yourself and briefly stating why you are so interested in the position. Hundreds if not thousands of books have been published about writing resumes and cover letters. I include a list of a few that have helped me in the Resources section on page 361. Also consult your local library for additional materials on how to format resumes and cover letters, what to include, and how to make yours standard for your field of work if necessary.

If you have responded to several ads and no employer has called you back offering a personal interview, realize that newspapers and websites reach thousands of people. A company often receives dozens or hundreds of applications for one spot. You may have to change your job search tactics and try a few of the alternatives listed below.

Whatever method of finding a job you choose to pursue, remember you are trying to show what a good worker you will be. Don't paste ribbons to your resume or type your resume in red ink. This will not get you positive attention. Don't stand outside a company all day and then follow the boss when he leaves in an attempt to talk to him. This is not behavior a boss wants to see. And don't call the company you want to work for over and over again to ask about positions or the status of your application. The secretary is busy. If you have followed the regular application procedure, the company will call you if they are interested in offering you an interview or a position.

- **Networking**

  Networking is a type of socializing. People network for a purpose, usually to see if the other person knows about any open jobs. You can network virtually anywhere at any time, as long as you are polite. Keep your eyes open for networking opportunities. If you are at a friend's party and you meet somebody who has the kind of job you want, ask the person if his company is hiring. Ask him how he obtained his job and if he has any tips for you. If the conversation is going well, you can ask him if he would introduce you to his boss. Personal introductions give you a boost above all the unknown people responding to ads.

  The key to networking, as I mentioned, is to be polite. Remember, you are trying to show what an enthusiastic and responsible worker you could be. Depending on the kind of job you are hoping to obtain, consider ordering some inexpensive business cards to hand out while networking. You can even inexpensively print out these cards at home. The card only needs your name, your phone number, your email address, and perhaps a title indicating your field of interest such as "John Smith, Dog Groomer." Your card enables someone to contact you easily *and* to continue the networking cycle by handing out the card to others on your behalf. You can also leave your cards at an appropriate location where potential customers will see it. Remember to ask the owner for permission first.

- **Volunteering**

  Volunteer positions are plentiful. While working somewhere as a volunteer, the manager or boss has a chance to see how well you work. Should the organization suddenly need someone for a paid position, everyone there will already be familiar with you. Or perhaps while volunteering in one position, you will hear of a different but paid position opening up before job ads are even placed.

This gives you a chance to approach the manager or hiring officer before word gets out to the public. Since you already volunteer at the place, and since you are the first to hear about the paid slot, you will be given more consideration than strangers answering ads. This is how I obtained my job at my synagogue. I volunteered in the office for about two months, filing, doing data entry, and editing. The executive director had a chance to see both my strong editing and computer skills and offered me a full-time position tailored to my abilities.

In the event that your volunteer position does not ever turn into a paid position, at least you have current experience to add to your resume. Job applicants who have lots of experience – paid or unpaid – are always more appealing to a company. You can list your fellow volunteers or the head of the organization as recent references. This is also appealing and makes you stand out from other applicants.

- **Employment agencies for disabled persons**

  I have had very little success with programs that endeavor to place disabled people into employment situations. For example, when I contacted VESID, the state agency in New York that handles employment training and placement for disabled people, I was instructed to attend a workshop first. Although the workshop made it obvious that VESID mostly places candidates in positions that would underutilize my intelligence and skills, I continued the process with an open mind and sat down with my assigned case manager afterward. She told me she could help me obtain two types of jobs: mopping floors or washing bathrooms. I was deeply disappointed. I have also tried private agencies that help the disabled. One such place, Just One Break, had a poster from the 1950s on the wall of a pretty woman in a wheelchair answering the phones behind a desk. I realized that Just One Break had been working with disabled people long before society was as accepting as it is now, so I was optimistic that they would have viable opportunities. I waited a long time in an enormous plastic chair. I had to fill out numerous forms. I was told to staple my resume to one of them. Then, the counselor called my name.

She asked me to list jobs I would be good at. I was prepared: editing textbooks, fact-checking for a law firm or not-for-profit organization, preparing lists of information such as the ingredients for a product, writing blurbs for a zoo or a museum. She listened politely and nodded a few times. When I was done with my cheerful and honest suggestions, she said plainly, "We don't get in jobs like that really."

"Well, what kind of jobs do you get?"

"More like, can you answer a phone?"

"Sure I could do reception work. But I do best in quiet work environments with few interruptions, some structure, and an informal social atmosphere."

"I see. What is this – Asperger – Asperger Syndrome?"

"A type of autism."

"Oh I see. You should try VESID."

I also tried the National Jewish Council on Disabilities, NJCD. Two women interviewed me. They said they had just attended a workshop on Asperger Syndrome and knew all about the condition, so again my hopes went up. The older woman said verbatim after reviewing my work history, "You are a real gem of a worker. We just have to find you the right placement." Both of them were absolutely confident they could help me. They asked for writing samples, which I had brought with me. My preparedness impressed them. Again, I outlined what I would be good at with confidence and explained my weaknesses honestly with concrete suggestions as to how to manage them so that I could get and maintain a decent job. I had a master's degree after all, and I knew my capabilities.

The two women said they would call me over the next week to let me know about potential placements and to help me prepare my resume and papers for pending employment. They never called me back. When I tried to reach them, neither of them was ever available. I left a couple of messages that were never returned. I was carefully polite and didn't want to seem pushy or desperate, but I did ask them to call me with an update because I was excited and ready to work.

Eventually I got a call from the younger one. She apologized and said the office was extremely busy. She said she was working on my case and gave me no indication to lose faith. But the weeks went by, so I called again. When I still received no response, I wrote a letter. Nobody answered my letter. I was despondent at first, but then I decided to use the volunteering tactic just described, and that worked much better for me.

If you want to try using a public or private employment placement agency, I have two main suggestions based on my personal experiences: One, make sure the agency has some familiarity with autism; and two, be very clear about what the agency will and will not do to help you. What kind of jobs does the agency place people in? Do these jobs match your skills and potential? How long does the process take? When will they call you back? Do you call them? Can you have a written timeline of what will happen and when? Do they offer other services, such as editing your resume or teaching you how to pass a personal interview?

Don't be shy. You are availing yourself of a service. The agency should be able to answer all of your questions and should be able to give you honest answers about what services they provide.

- **Temp agencies**

  If you need to work right away, but are having trouble finding a full-time position, try working for a temp agency. Temp agencies place workers in temporary positions for brief periods of time. For example, you might replace a regular worker who is on vacation for a few weeks. Temp agencies can send almost anyone out on a job right away because they know about a whole range of projects and positions that are not advertised publicly. These agencies should never charge you anything to find you jobs (with one exception, see below).

  You are allowed to keep looking for regular jobs while you work at temp jobs and most temp workers do. This situation is ideal if you must earn money right away, plus your temporary employers can provide references. If you know your goal is to find a full-time position, ask the temp agency for "temp-to-perm" opportunities. These are temporary assignments that have the potential to become permanent. You may not get a temp-to-perm assignment at first. But while you work at other temp jobs, the temp agency will see what a good worker you are and will be more likely to refer you when a temp-to-perm slot does become available. Another advantage of a temp-to-perm position is that usually you have a few weeks to decide if you want to stay. You and your new boss can see how you do and make sure you are a good fit before committing.

  If you discover that you really enjoy a certain temp position, and the boss at the company likes you as a worker, he may offer you the job or a similar job at his company. But usually, unless the position was specifically designated as a temp-to-perm arrangement with the agency in advance, you or the boss will have to pay a fee. This is because the temp agency was paid by the employer to place you only temporarily. The agency will lose money if they can't keep sending you out anymore. The best policy is honesty. If you want to stay, and the boss wants you to stay, find out what fees the agency requires or if the agency requires you to wait a period of time before accepting the position.

  Temp agencies often have specializations – office work, industrial work, professional work – so make sure you sign up with an agency that offers assignments you want. A nice feature of working for a temp agency is that you do not have to accept an assignment if

The interview allows you to learn even more about the position and allows the interviewer to learn more about you. Even if you have not yet been called for an interview, begin practicing. Interviews can make anybody nervous, on or off the spectrum.

you don't want it. But if you constantly turn down assignments, the agency is not going to look favorably upon you. They will call other workers and give them first choice. They may also describe your work habits negatively if, when applying for a regular job, a potential employer calls them for a reference. In other words, if you sign up with a temp agency, be prepared to work.

- **College career offices**
  If you are a student, take advantage of whatever career placement opportunities your college offers. Even if you are not a student any more, call your old college and ask if alumni can keep using these services. It doesn't matter when you graduated, even if it was a long time ago. Some companies specifically advertise on college campuses only. Career placement offices usually have information on volunteer or internship placements that could turn into paid positions. If you can afford to take three to six months to do an internship in your field, you can segue from there into a paid position. Also, colleges occasionally offer networking dinners, workshops, lectures, or social activities to both current and former students (see more about networking on page 155). The career placement office will know of any upcoming events. You'll be able to meet others who have the same college degree, or similar work interests, and they might know of opportunities at their companies.

Disclosure: If You Are Called for an Interview

If a company calls you after reading your resume, cover letter, and/or application, this means they may want to hire you, but they are not sure yet. You will almost always have to appear in person to interview with members of the company. An interview is not a promise of employment. The interview allows you to learn even more about the position and allows the interviewer to learn more about you. Even if you have not yet been called for an interview, begin practicing. Interviews can make anybody nervous, on or off the spectrum. Again, hundreds of books have been written about passing job interviews. Read the suggestions in the Resources section on page 361 or check your library for books and videos that can guide you on how to talk, what to say, and how to answer tough interview questions.

Since so much information on interviewing is available, I will discuss two points that probably are not in many books. The first issue is *whether or not to disclose the fact that you are autistic*. Some argue that you should never tell a boss or supervisor that you are on the spectrum, least of all while interviewing for the first time. Because of stereotypes and a general lack of information about autism, it is true that you run the risk of being pre-judged to one degree or another. You don't want a potential employer to assume your abilities are limited or that anything you do is simply because you are autistic.

On the other hand, disclosing upfront that you have a disability can be to your advantage, which leads to the second point I want to discuss. *If you have specific social challenges, you may not have a choice*. For example, it is expected during a job interview that you will look in the interviewer's eyes at appropriate moments to show you are an enthusiastic person and that you are paying attention. If you can appear to have certain social skills or can fake social signals like eye contact, perhaps you can wait for a different moment to disclose your diagnosis, if you want to tell at all. But if you absolutely cannot tolerate eye contact, especially in high-pressure situations like an interview, you need to explain your behavior before the interviewer makes an incorrect and negative assumption about you. This means you will have to delicately weave a discussion about autism into the conversation.

I believe in disclosure when it comes to work, and I believe in disclosing the diagnosis during the interview when possible and if necessary. Be ready to explain autism in general and autism as it applies to your life, in positive ways. The person interviewing you – usually the boss or a manager who will supervise you if you get the job – is going to wonder why you are bothering to discuss your diagnosis, so you need to explain your strengths and weaknesses in terms of the specific job. The boss doesn't need to know you had a hard time making friends in college or that you find shopping difficult. But she does probably need to know if sometimes you forget common social graces like saying hello in the morning, if she might see you rocking back and forth, or if you won't be able to attend formal monthly business luncheons because of sensory or social issues.

The point of such a discussion is to show the boss that you can overcome your challenges with basic accommodations or that you can still be a member of the team even with your behavioral differences. Therefore, when explaining difficulty with social skills, for example, phrase your issues as positively as possible. Statements such as, "I often forget to say hello in the morning because I am so eager to get to my desk and start my projects," or "I often walk in and go straight to work because I'm concentrating so hard on what I have to do to have a successful business day," are better statements than, "I don't like to chat with people," or "Socializing makes me very uncomfortable so I'd rather not do it."

Disclosure does pose certain risks. The boss or manager could incorrectly assume it would be too hard on the company to hire and train an employee who has disabilities. Discriminating just because you are autistic (or otherwise disabled) is illegal, but everyone knows it happens. This is why some people on the spectrum prefer not to disclose at work. If you are not going to disclose your diagnosis, have a plan in place for how you will address any challenges that come up, should you get the job and then run into difficulty later on (for more on this issue, see the section, *Survival Tips for Life on the Job*).

One advantage to disclosing your diagnosis is that you no longer have to work hard at appearing non-autistic. But ultimately, only you can make the decision to disclose or not. Remember that if you change your mind and want to disclose your diagnosis weeks or months after being hired because it turns out you do need special accommodations due to your disability, the conversation will probably be uncomfortable for both you and your boss. Your boss may wonder why you weren't honest during the hiring process, so make the decision to keep your diagnosis hidden carefully.

This is why I advocate disclosure: People cannot possibly make the leap to accept me if I don't first afford them an opportunity to understand me. Honest dialogue poses risks, but by sharing your strengths and weaknesses openly, others can take the first steps toward including you and giving you a chance.

Survival Tips for Life on the Job

If you are lucky and you have been hired for a job, what happens next? You may discover that getting a job is less of a problem than keeping one. I almost always sail through interviews, but dealing with the day-to-day rigors of the job causes me great difficulty. The hardest part of a job for many of us on the spectrum is managing all the social interactions that arise in the course of a typical day. Upon happily arriving for the first day on the job, we suddenly feel dumped into a social jungle gym without a rule book. I made a list of social skills that any worker typically uses to demonstrate just how complicated a job can be for someone autistic. I could list hundreds more skills, and all of them could come into use before lunch.

Sample List of Social Skills Used in the Work Place

- Shake hands at the right moments and with the right pressure and speed
- Remember rules of polite interaction
- Remember pleasantries like, "Good morning"
- Determine when to exchange pleasantries
- Determine whom to exchange pleasantries with versus when to leave someone alone
- Determine tone of voice and content of pleasantries, depending on audience (boss vs. UPS man)
- Decode idiomatic expressions
- Decode humor
- Respond appropriately to humor
- Offer humor appropriately
- Keep up with social expectations (for example, lunch requests)
- Determine with whom to chat
- Determine when and how to chat casually
- Determine the content of a small chat
- Modulate voice during the chat
- Listen carefully for conversational clues that indicate interest, boredom, confusion, etc.
- Determine one's turn to talk/respond
- Respond appropriately to what the other person contributes to the chat
- Handle interruptions smoothly even when frustrated
- Notice the feelings and comfort level of others
- Respond to co-workers who may be dissatisfied, upset, hurt, or confused by you
- Respond to co-workers who may be happy, satisfied, concerned about, or jealous of your work
- Receive and give constructive criticism
- Handle requests and complaints from customers, clients, suppliers, boss, etc.
- Organize desk and projects, taking into consideration others working in the same environment
- Share and ask for supplies
- Communicate regarding sensory issues
- Figure out social norms

- Compensate for sensory issues without overstepping social norms (for example, no sunglasses at executive meeting)
- Cope with the irritating behavior of others (for example, slurping coffee or snapping gum)
- Defend oneself against unjust accusations politely, while at the same time taking responsibility for weaknesses constructively
- Know when to ask for help
- Formulate appropriate requests for help
- Balance the need for help with the ability to learn/work independently (for example, balance seeming too dependent versus seeming too independent)
- Pick up slack left by lazy co-workers without being used
- Decode social politics (for example, why person X complains about person Y, then treats Y to lunch)
- Determine personal boundaries (for example, if someone is taking advantage of you by asking you to do her filing)
- Ask for clarification of tasks, requests, jokes, conversational meanings, and innuendos
- Explain problems and relay relevant details
- Balance priorities, responsibilities, and loyalties to different people
- Know when to do a favor versus when to report an ethical or behavioral irregularity (for example, to tell the boss person X is late again for the 50th time, or not)

While social skills training can be useful, rote memorization of broad social rules doesn't always help on the spot in the middle of an average Tuesday when you can't understand why someone said you must be having a bad hair day, why the secretary who told on you to the boss is inviting you out for a soda, and why your co-worker in the cubicle across from you has asked you to do her filing again.

What follows in this section is a list of 10 tips and suggestions to help you survive once you are on the job. Many of us on the autism spectrum also have trouble balancing personal and work responsibilities. Getting dressed and fed and to work each morning – then home and fed and to bed again – can require as much energy as the full-time job. As a result, you may find yourself totally exhausted, mentally and physically, at the end of the day. A few suggestions for coping with work-life balance follow the suggestions for surviving the myriad social aspects of holding down a job.

Ten Suggestions for Getting Through Daily Life on the Job

1. ***Plan for problems in advance***
   Whether or not you have decided to disclose your diagnosis to anyone at your place of work, create a plan in advance for how you will deal with any problems that arise. Have some ideas of what you can say in different scenarios. For example, if you have a sensory issue with lights near your desk, you could ask the boss for permission to wear dark glasses or to use a full-spectrum bulb. All you have to say is, "The fluorescent lights at my desk are hurting my eyes. Would it be possible for me to ____________ (fill in the blank)?" Or if you have an issue prioritizing your work, you could turn to your supervisor and say something like, "I am really good at collating all the records and updating the database, but I can't tell which to do first!"

2. ***Plan for emergencies***
   Whether or not you have disclosed your diagnosis, have emergency plans in place. Even if you carefully prepare your environment, you may still have a sensory emergency or an unexpected social problem. What will you say if you have to run out of the room? Do you have a quiet spot to retreat to if you become extremely overwhelmed and need a few minutes to regain your composure?

3. ***Keep disclosure discussions simple***
   If you tell your co-workers about your diagnosis, keep it simple and related to work, unless they ask you further questions. Be prepared for questions that seem ridiculous or even offensive. For example, they may want to know if you memorize phone books in your spare time. Don't feel bad. They probably know very little, if anything, about autism.

4. ***Select a "Work Buddy"***
   Consider using a Work Buddy to serve as a social translator, helping you navigate social aspects of workplace life that may be obvious to everyone else, but not to you. A Buddy can also help you respond appropriately to social challenges and expectations. If you disclose to your boss and/or supervisors, you can ask for a Work Buddy as one of the accommodations you need. If not, you can still approach someone at the office who seems friendly, open-minded, and socially adept. Ask to speak to this person in private and then describe your situation. For example, you could say, "I may need to ask you who to talk to about a certain work-related problem," or "I may need tips on how to make friends with the other technicians in the department." If the person agrees to be your Work Buddy, set up a regular time to meet every week or even every day if necessary. Again, you don't need to mention autism if you are not comfortable doing so or your diagnosis is hidden. You could say something like, "Sometimes it's hard for me to catch on socially. Do you think you could be like my social navigator around here if I have questions or don't understand what's going on?"

5. ***Designate a personal work area***
   Make sure you have one spot to work at and that this spot is yours permanently. If you move around a lot at work because of the nature of the job, still carve out an area where you can put your things down or store items for future use. Having one spot for all of the things you need at work will reduce problems that result from disorganization, plus if you aren't running around looking for a paperclip or your notebook you'll have more energy for your actual assignments. Label things like tools and supplies with your initials so others won't move or take them (if labeling is allowed).

6. ***Use visual aids to understand the day***
   Color code or chart a schedule of how your days go. For example, if you come to work, drink a cup of coffee at your desk, focus on small projects for a couple of hours, take a break to go to the bathroom, then do filing before lunch and longer projects after lunch, a nice map of the day can help you stay on track. Disruptions may also be easier to handle. You can go back to your schedule once the chaos is over and you will know exactly where to resume.

   Today's Events

   7:30 arrive at work
   7:40 get a cup of coffee and make schedule for the day
   8:00 work on small projects
   10:00 take a 10-minute break
   10:10-12:00 do filing
   12:00-1:00 lunch
   1:00-3:30 longer project
   3:30-3:45 15-minute break
   3:45-4:45 continue longer projects
   4:45 check email
   5:00 go home

7. ***Take notes on social language***
   Keep a log book of common expressions and conversational patterns. For example, if you keep hearing people say, "She's having a bad hair day!" or "He's ill!" write these phrases down. Privately ask your Work Buddy or someone you trust what they mean or look in an idiomatic dictionary and write the definitions nearby. In this case, "bad hair day" means someone is frustrated, and "ill" means someone is cool.

   Also notice and record how your co-workers talk to each other and what they say. When they see each other in the morning, do they say, "Hey Bill! How's it going?" or do they say, "Good morning, Mr. Smith. How are you today?" If a holiday is approaching, do they ask each other what they plan to do to celebrate? On Mondays, do they ask each other what they did over the weekend? What are the "correct" or most common responses? Do they ever ask each other about their families, or do they stay away from that topic? Like a keen social scientist, keep all of this information in your log as a guide to proper social conduct that you can refer to periodically or if you are confused.

8. ***Ask for help***

When you are having trouble, always ask for help and don't delay. It doesn't matter if the trouble is because you are autistic or not. Everyone needs help once in a while. You can ask your co-workers or supervisor for help if you are having trouble completing your work. They often can give you suggestions. And by asking them for help, they will feel as though you respect them and value their opinions.

If, however, if you are having a problem with a person at work, do not talk to your co-workers. They will consider this gossiping. Besides, your co-workers cannot help you with "people problems." Ask your boss (or your supervisor if it is not customary to discuss day-to-day office life with your boss) to help you if you are having a problem with another person and request that the information remain confidential. Your respect for the other person's privacy, even though you are having trouble with him or her, will show the boss you are not gossiping but truly asking for help in resolving the problem.

9. ***Be willing to compromise with creative suggestions***

If you anticipate serious trouble with some event, suggest alternatives. For example, if you cannot sit through formal meetings, ask the boss if you can listen from the next room, where you promise to take notes and consult with her privately later. If you cannot tolerate the thought of attending the company picnic, volunteer to be the one who stays behind to answer the telephone.

10. ***Communicate***

Lastly, be yourself – just be sure to explain yourself. The social pressure will be a lot less intense when your officemates understand why you do the things you do. For example, if you must eat lunch alone, but you notice everyone eats in a group or individuals invite each other out to eat, you can explain to them that you need a bit of quiet at mealtimes, a chance to wind down and refocus for the rest of the day. Don't worry too much about what they think. You've given them an explanation for your behavior. They should respect who you are, as long as you respect their feelings and don't leave them wondering why you don't like them, which they are likely to assume if you don't join the lunch crowd or follow the usual lunch routine.

Another example: If you aren't good with social pleasantries like saying good morning or goodbye, just tell your officemates plainly that sometimes you are concentrating so hard you forget to interact on your way in or out. Again, this will help them understand you. Most adults can accept somebody who acts differently when they are reassured that the behaviors they see – eating lunch alone, forgetting to say hello – have reasonable explanations and are not due to unfriendliness.

Work-Life Balance

If you are having extreme difficulty taking care of yourself on top of working, it is time to reassess your job situation.

- **Try to pinpoint why you are having trouble**
  Sensory issues may be to blame. Don't let sensory issues bother you indefinitely. Excess noise, noxious smells, and burning lights can rocket your nervous system into such high gear that you just want to crawl into bed when you come home at night.
- **Check your commute**
  Does it take you a long time to get to work and back home again? Some people actually like commuting. They use the time to read the paper, catch up on work from the day before, or sleep. But long commutes can take a toll on your life, especially if you need non-stressful time in the morning and evening to take care of yourself. If you find that you just can't shower, dress, eat, and do your chores on top of your commute, you may need to find work closer to home. As much as you love your job or worry that you won't be able to find a new one, you need to take care of yourself.
- **Look at how you prioritize**
  Using the Weekly Easy Chart method described in Chapter 2: *Maintaining a Home* (see page 43), create a chart for self-care tasks, including the recreational activities you enjoy. You can fill in your mornings with showering, dressing, and eating breakfast and your evenings with picking out your clothes and packing a lunch for the next day. Get as specific as necessary. You may need to include smaller tasks like shaving, washing your hair, brushing your teeth, applying deodorant, ironing your shirts, or dropping your suits or your uniform off at the dry cleaner. And don't forget to include the activities you do to unwind or relax. For example, you can include reading or walking in the evenings, your weekly swim class, or your autism support group meeting.
- **If time management is an issue for you, assign amounts of time to each task**
  For example, perhaps you wake up at 7:00 a.m. Do you want to give yourself 10 minutes to wake up, 15 minutes to shower and shave, 15 minutes to get dressed, 30 minutes to eat breakfast, and then 15 minutes to do some chores? In this example, that would mean you

Once you figure out a time schedule that is right for you, hang it up on your wall where it is easy to see or put it right onto your Weekly Easy Chart. You can refer to it as you go along.

would be ready to leave your house at 8:25 a.m. Does that give you enough time to get to work?

Also make a time schedule for the evenings. Once you figure out a time schedule that is right for you, hang it up on your wall where it is easy to see or put it right onto your Weekly Easy Chart. You can refer to it as you go along.

- **If you are having such difficulty working and taking care of yourself that both aspects of your life are suffering, consult a professional therapist who can help you sort out your competing responsibilities**
  The more trouble you have taking care of yourself, the harder it will be to function at work. Conversely, the more trouble you are having at work, the worse you will feel when you get home at night. This cycle tends to escalate until things are out of control. Because life and work are intertwined, you will need to find a way to manage both.

Weekly Easy Chart for Self-Care Tasks

	Monday	Tuesday	Wednesday	Thursday	Friday	Saturday	Sunday
AM	Shower Put on deodorant Shave Take medications Go over backpack checklist – gather anything missing	Shower Put on deodorant Shave Take medications Backpack checklist Charge cell phone	Shower Put on deodorant Shave Take medications Backpack checklist Drop dirty uniforms at dry cleaner	Shower Put on deodorant Shave Take medications Backpack checklist Charge cell phone	Shower Put on deodorant Shave Take medications Backpack checklist Leave 1/2 hour early for walk through park	Shower Put on deodorant Shave Take medications Synagogue 9:00 a.m.	Shower Put on deodorant Shave Take medications Organize lunches & snacks for upcoming week, pack tomorrow's lunch
PM	Clean lunch box, pack lunch Trim cat's claws Pick out clothes for tomorrow Brush teeth Set alarm	Clean lunch box, pack lunch Swim 6:00 p.m. Pick out clothes for tomorrow Brush teeth Set alarm	Clean lunch box, pack lunch Therapy 5:30 p.m. Pick out clothes for tomorrow Brush teeth Set alarm	Clean lunch box, pack lunch Pick up uniforms Watch "Survivor" Pick out clothes for tomorrow Brush teeth Set alarm	Clean lunch box *Free night* Brush teeth Set alarm	Swim lesson 2:00 p.m. Polish workboots Brush teeth	Pick out clothes for tomorrow Charge cell phone Watch "60 Minutes" Brush teeth Set alarm

Note: This person uses her Weekly Easy Chart for self-care activities to schedule important daily tasks she must remember, such as taking her medication and setting her alarm at night. On Saturday she goes to synagogue and has a swim lesson. On Sunday, she makes sure she has all the lunch and snack items she needs for the following week. She even assigned a set time to review her backpack checklist and make sure all the items she needs when she is away from home are in the bag. A chart such as this can help you manage all the non-optional and optional tasks you must complete each day in order to take care of yourself properly.

The pressure of self-employment is enormous, but working for yourself can also be very joyful. Success or failure is completely up to you.

If You Want to Work for Yourself

As mentioned, I started my own Internet company, Intelligirl Jewelry Maker, an interactive website that allows users to design their own jewelry online and then order it. I took some time off at first to develop and launch the website. After about one year of development, the business was launched in the spring of 2005. Now, I am working at a job again while the business grows. I hope my newest venture succeeds. As of press-time, it is unknown what direction the business will take.

Based on my experiences developing Intelligirl and doing freelance editorial jobs in college, I can describe some of the pros and cons of being your own boss. The pressure of self-employment is enormous, but working for yourself can also be very joyful. Success or failure is completely up to you. You usually wind up working most of the time and rarely doing anything else! But if you love doing the work necessary to make your business succeed, working for yourself can be a good choice.

When you work for yourself, you do not have to deal with the ordinary social pressures of most workplaces. You can work hard without interruptions, and sometimes you can go at your own pace. However, you have to set priorities and goals and then achieve them without a boss or supervisor urging you to complete your tasks. For this reason, you need to be motivated and self-disciplined enough to get your work done without any external enforcement.

And even though the social pressure on a daily basis is low, self-employment involves a greater or lesser degree of networking and socializing, depending on the field. But you can conquer this challenge in unique ways. For example, if you have to meet with other business leaders or clients, you can bring someone you trust to the meeting. I often bring my wife or my mother, both of whom have roles in Intelligirl any way. I do the straight reporting – facts, figures, the PowerPoint slides, the technical jargon. My mother or my wife handles the social nuances that are not my strong point – introductions, exchanging business cards, chatting, ensuring a relaxed but professional mood. We use secret hand signs that guide me through the social aspects of the meeting. I make sure we never hold meetings over dinner due to sensory issues, and I only conduct meetings in quiet conference rooms with natural sunlight so I can avoid wearing my sunglasses.

If you must approach potential customers or clients, bring someone who enjoys socializing. For example, if you are starting a dog walking service, go to the nearest dog walk or dog park with your friend when it is very busy. Have your friend interact with the dog owners and then introduce you at the right moment. Upon being introduced, describe the details of your service. Your friend can nudge you when it is time to present your business card or say goodbye. If you don't have any friends, ask a sibling or a parent to help you.

I have learned that my autistic strengths are useful for self-employment. I am excellent at developing efficient systems, keeping records, filing data and information, and quickly learning new computer skills to keep up with the ever-changing state of technology. I can concentrate for very long periods of time. I also have great stamina when it comes to doing something I enjoy.

Most self-employment ventures do not succeed overnight, so if you need steady income, you will need to work at an external job while your business grows. Some ventures fail altogether, and then you have to start on a new idea. Should your attempt at self-employment fail, or take a while to come to fruition, it is not just because you are autistic. Starting a business, running it, and making it succeed requires many skills and talents and excellent planning. Be sure to check your library for books on how to start and run businesses, take classes to learn business skills you don't have, and ask relatives and friends who run their own businesses to mentor you.

Self-employment can be an avenue to success if you have the right mix of personality traits and good ideas. I think the opportunities to work for oneself are wider than they may appear at first. If you want to work

Those of us on the spectrum can work, and we can be some of the best workers in the world.

for yourself, figure out what you do well and then start doing that for friends and your local community. Keep building on your skills. It takes time, creativity, and ingenuity, but if you think working for yourself would be the best option, don't give up hope of succeeding.

Conclusion

All disabled people, including those of us on the autism spectrum, can work. Having a job is an excellent way to engage with the world. On the job, people feel as though they are contributing to the world and receiving from the world in return. Work allows an individual to express his interests and his inner self. Without a job, life can seem aimless or unkind.

Those of us on the spectrum can work, and we can be some of the best workers in the world. We have intense focus and intense passions. We are driven when we feel a connection to a task. I hope the suggestions in this chapter help you find a job that you find interesting and that meets your needs as an autistic worker.

■ ■ ■

PART 2:
LOVE

The chapters in this part of the book depart from the tasks of daily living to focus on concrete suggestions for issues primarily concerning our relationships to other people – and to ourselves. Instead of zooming in on one topic only, such as dating, I wanted to include a broad spectrum of suggestions for all types of relationships and ultimately weave them together with the core concept of self-esteem. When we see value in the way we think, feel, and love, self-acceptance opens doors of opportunity not just in terms of relationships, but in all of life, tying this part of the book with the first.

■ ■ ■

Chapter 8

Dating on the Spectrum

People are often surprised to hear that someone on the autism spectrum would even be interested in an intimate relationship. While many do chose to remain single for a wide range of reasons, just as many yearn for the companionship and personal growth that intimacy can provide. Yet dating and relationships pose special problems for autistic adults: How do you go on a dinner date if restaurants trigger your sensory issues? Do you have to meet someone at a loud, noisy bar? How can you tell if someone is flirting with you if you already have trouble decoding nonverbal signals? How far away do you stand from someone you are romantically interested in? What body language do you use to communicate your feelings? How do you create intimacy if eye contact and tactile stimulation are challenging for you? And this list is just the beginning.

The assumption is that all human beings acquire the knowledge to pursue intimacy automatically or by osmosis, but that is not the case for autistic people. This chapter covers dating choices, deciphering the feelings of others, communicating your own feelings, disclosing your diagnosis and when, personal safety and health issues, using the Internet responsibly, managing frustration and loneliness during the dating process, and handling big decisions. Dealing with the stressors common to all relationships and navigating the phases of a relationship as it changes over time are also discussed. One chapter cannot possibly cover everything you need to know when venturing out into the world of dating, but it's a start.

Some of us on the spectrum find it very uncomfortable and awkward to initiate a friendship. If you have this problem, you can always ask for help from the people you trust.

Before You Start Dating

Before you jump into the dating world, it is a good idea to assess what you are looking for or why you think you should be dating. Many people who feel lonely assume that only dating somebody will cure the blues. Examine your life before you start dating by determining what makes you feel lonely. If you are lonely because you lack friends or don't have enough to do, or if you decide you are not ready to date, you can ease your feelings of loneliness in many ways.

One of the best ways to make friends is to take up a hobby. If you like astronomy, join a club at a local science museum. If you like cooking, join a cooking workshop at the local Y. Even if you are not enrolled in a degree program, you can usually take classes at local colleges. So if you love math, sign up for an advanced math class just to keep your brain working. Classes, clubs, teams, and hobby groups enable you to meet others who like to do the same things you like to do. If you can't figure out what to talk about, you can always talk about the activity you are sharing.

You can also volunteer. Volunteering is a great way to get out of the house and meet others. If you like animals, volunteer at the zoo, a nature center, or an animal shelter. If you like art, volunteer at an art museum or a gallery. Religious institutions often need volunteers and usually offer a supportive environment. If you are unable to work, you may still be able to volunteer at a parent's or friend's office – even once or twice a week – where you can meet and befriend co-workers.

Some of us on the spectrum find it very uncomfortable and awkward to initiate a friendship. If you have this problem, you can always ask for help from the people you trust. For example, maybe your science teacher knows somebody else at your college who is as interested in electronics as you are and would arrange a meeting or create a project for the two of you to work on. Don't be afraid to ask your parents, your siblings, your priest – anyone you trust – to help you find a friend.

If you're not up for much socializing, you can still feel better and less lonely when you are taking good care of yourself. Go on a walk instead of flipping on the TV. Get off your computer for a while and do something totally unusual like planting flowers on your terrace or putting together a science kit. Get creative: If you like cargo ships, go watch them in the harbor. Even a little trip to your favorite library can lift your spirits. When you are enjoying your life, the loneliness won't be as bad.

If after spending some time thinking about your life you decide you do want to start dating, a clear idea of what relationships are all about will help you figure out how to proceed.

Some people think that being in a relationship and falling in love solves everything: You'll never be lonely again, you'll always have someone to talk to, and you'll always have someone who cares about you. It is true that dating someone can be fun, exciting, and comforting. Relationships are often a source of strength. The person you date may teach you new things, introduce you to new activities, or share a new way of solving a problem. Usually, two people who are dating like to do some of the same things together. When you are dating someone you love, the two of you have a wonderful chance to enjoy life in a special new way. After dating for a while, your feelings may grow into a more serious commitment that can lead to marriage and maybe a family of your own.

But being in a relationship can be difficult, too. A relationship is hard work. Being with somebody every day does not play out the way it does in the movies. It takes a long time to build up trust with the person you are dating. You'll have to communicate constantly. Part of being in a relationship means figuring out the other person's feelings, sharing your own feelings, and compromising when the two of you cannot agree. You always have to consider your partner in everything that you do. You might find yourself missing your "old life" when you could do whatever you pleased or go anywhere at any time without having to see how your partner feels about what's hap-

Dating and relationships are very broad concepts. You can think of dating as a spectrum from the most casual to the most serious.

pening or having to let your partner know where you are going.

Communicating with someone else day in and day out takes a lot of energy. The rewards can be great as the two of you get to know each other more deeply. But being in a relationship requires an adjustment – just like every change in life. If you are not ready for the responsibilities of dating, or if you aren't sure you are up for all of the socializing, exchanging of feelings, and constant communication involved in an intimate relationship, try some of the other ways of dealing with loneliness mentioned earlier.

Dating Versus a Relationship: What's the Difference?

It is impossible to say, "You will know you are ready to start dating when________ ." You can't go by a set age or by a specific event such as graduating from high school. Sometimes you may not know you are ready to date until you suddenly like somebody romantically. Or you may think you are ready, start dating somebody, and then discover you can't handle it. Other times, you just know inside of yourself that you would be able to handle dating if you met somebody you liked. Ultimately, only you know what you are ready to experience and what you want to experience. Because in our culture people who are dating can promise each other many different levels of commitment, understanding your options will help you determine the situation that is right for you.

Dating and relationships are very broad concepts. You can think of dating as a spectrum from the most casual to the most serious. Would you like a casual date a few times a month for dinner, conversation, roller skating, or a walk? Or are you looking to get married? Or something in between? It is hard to predict in advance what might happen, but knowing what sort of relationship you are looking for can help you make the right decisions as you begin meeting potential partners.

Dating is usually a little bit different than having a relationship. Dating is less formal and usually centers on having fun. Most people date when they are young, but people of any age can and do go on dates. You usually ask somebody to go on a date with you. Then the two of you decide on a specific activity to do on the date. If things go well, you may ask the person on a date several times in a row, picking new activities to share and getting to know each other even better. But unless the two of you have a discussion and agree on a more formal commitment, you can date other people at this stage. People who are dating casually sometimes hold hands, kiss goodnight, or get more involved physically. If you go on one or two dates and discover you are not having fun or do not like each other romantically after all, you tell each other nicely that you would rather not date, in which case you can either remain friends or go your separate ways. Because you were only dating informally, this situation is not considered a major breakup.

Sometimes, after a few dates that go really well, or as the level of physical intimacy increases, two people choose to date each other exclusively. That is, they agree not to go on dates with anyone else so they can build up trust and focus just on one another. This is considered "getting serious" and is a commitment you should enter into only if you can be true to your word. Otherwise, you will hurt the other person's feelings. If you and your date are getting serious, dating exclusively, or having sexual relations, usually dating changes into a relationship.

Having a *relationship* is harder to define. People have very different kinds of relationships. They may live together; they may not. Some get married; others never do. Some have children; some don't want children. Some see each other every single day; some decide to see each other on specific days or the weekends. Relationships can take many different forms, but what they almost always have in common is a commitment: The two people commit to each other. Whereas dating is more casual and centered on activities, a relationship is more like sharing your life with someone. You no longer want to just date. You begin to want to care about your partner in a deeper way, desiring to help your partner with all that goes on in life and getting more involved in your partner's daily living. For example, even if you don't live together, you may share dinner or help each other get ready for work in the morning.

This area of life does not have specific rules. You may date someone for years and be perfectly content with this arrangement, never moving to a more serious relationship. Or, you may have a very serious relationship with somebody you only get to see once a week. Some couples date for only a few months and know they want to get married. Others date seriously for a year and then stop. Many date a variety of people very casually before finding the one person with whom they want to have a more involved relationship. This can be very confusing. The important difference between "just dating" and "having a relationship" is how you feel about the other person and the promises you make each other.

Relationships change too. You might be in a serious relationship with someone and then decide to go back to just dating or being friends. The most important thing is to always talk to your partner. It is perfectly O.K. to ask, "Are we just friends, dating, or getting serious?" Ask your partner how s/he feels. Do you both feel the same way, or does one of you feel differently? Obviously, you can't marry somebody who does not want to marry you. Your partner's feelings will be part of any equation. But by knowing what *you* want – a friend, a date, a serious partner, a husband or wife – you can make better decisions in life as you start going out with people and looking for your ideal situation.

Dating Autistic Style

When it comes to dating and romance, one problem for autistic adults can be society's expectations. It seems like everybody knows how to follow some secret "script" – except those of us on the spectrum. Yet, while it may appear as if other people know exactly what to do when it comes to dating, everyone is just as confused, scared, and excited as you are.

The important point to remember is that, despite what you could easily conclude from all the messages we get from the media, anyone can go on a date and have fun, no matter your style or activity preferences. In other words, you just have to be yourself. After all, the other person is dating you, not the activity. What follows are suggestions that may help you with the different aspects and stages of casual dating, taking into consideration the special issues that often come up for autistic adults.

Meeting Someone

The first step in dating is to look for someone you want to date. Where on Earth can you meet someone? One stereotype in our culture is that people meet in bars. Some people do meet dates at bars and clubs, but many people don't. Often, people meet dates while doing an enjoyable activity. When you are doing a hobby, taking a class, volunteering, or playing sports, for example, you have the chance to meet people who share some of your interests.

People also meet potential dates while just doing life; for example, at the gym or at college. In fact, you could run into someone you are interested in dating almost anywhere – even while grocery shopping! Although in the old days parents introduced their children to potential dates, this is not common any more in our culture because it can be very awkward to have your parents involved in your love life. But friends and siblings might be able to introduce you to somebody. They are about the same age as you and probably know you well enough to determine if the other person is a good match.

NOTE: Meeting someone happens easiest when you aren't trying too hard. The important thing is to be involved in activities you enjoy. If you're enjoying yourself and you like your life, other people will sense and respond to your positive energy. Remember, too, that sometimes you'll make friends with somebody first, developing a romance over time after you get to know each other. Life is full of possibilities.

Asking Somebody on a Date

So assume you have met somebody somewhere and you want to ask this person on a date. What is the next step? How can you tell if someone is interested in you? How can you indicate that you are interested?

The clues most people use to indicate interest may not be obvious to you. For example, people often send signals of interest with their eyes. They might gesture with their hands or smile in a certain way. If possible, have a friend or a sister or brother demonstrate common interest signals for you. Practice making the signals yourself, and practice recognizing someone else's signals. Don't be embarrassed. Practice helps you figure out your style and gives you experience in determining if another person is romantically interested in you.

TIP: Practice helps. Ask a friend, a sibling, or somebody you trust to role-play with you. Practice how to start a conversation with somebody who seems interesting to you. Try different kinds of conversations, different types of questions, and different responses. Create different scenarios – at school, at the mall, in a crowd, at the gym. What could you say to somebody you would like to talk to? How do you think they would feel if you went up to them with different possible approaches?

Even if you have a good understanding and perception of social signals, it can still be hard to tell if the other person is attracted to you. In such a case, you will just have to take a risk, especially if you meet somebody you like in a random place like a store. This happens to people not on the spectrum, too. It is usually considered O.K. to ask someone on a date even if you are not 100% sure the other person is interested in you romantically, as long as you are polite and your behavior is appropriate. Don't use lewd language, ask nicely, and don't touch people you just met. Also, if the person says no, don't keep pestering. Leave him or her alone and go on with whatever you were doing.

Whether you have a clear signal of interest or not, don't ask someone on a date in the middle of a crowd of friends. Try to ask in a quiet spot if possible and preferably when the other person isn't tired, sick, or in a hurry. Although sometimes people pass a note or send a friend over to ask, it is best to ask someone on a date in person, face-to-face. Your potential date, whether the answer is yes or no, will appreciate your effort.

Before you ask, choose your style. Do you want to be bold and go right up to the person you are interested in and ask, "Would you like to go on a date with me?" Or do you want to use a more gentle approach such as, "I noticed that you really like ice skating. Would you like to go ice skating with me this weekend?" Different styles elicit different reactions. If you don't know someone at all, asking for a date in a bold manner may turn the person away. On the flip side, if you use a subtle approach, the person may not realize you have romantic intentions. However, a subtle approach is usually your best option: The person will appreciate your polite manners, and if it turns out that you don't like each other romantically or the attraction is not mutual, you can still be friends.

If you are going to approach somebody you have never met before, use extra caution and common sense. In the movies, the gorgeous star goes up to a cute stranger and just smiles. Suddenly, they like each other. Then the star asks for a phone number. He calls her. They fall in love. This is not how it works in real life. If you go up to a stranger and ask for her phone number, she will probably think you are weird, she may be scared, or she may quip, "But I don't even know you!" You run the risk of startling her – after all, you are a complete and total stranger.

This doesn't mean that strangers never talk to each other. Otherwise, how would we meet new people? But you do have to practice a few techniques so you can avoid freaking people out. Introduce yourself and talk for a few minutes before you bring up dating. What is the

You can exchange phone numbers or email addresses, but make a plan to meet in public for your first few dates. This will give you time to get to know the person before you meet in private.

person doing? Does she have bags from a certain store, or a milkshake from a certain restaurant? You can use these facts to start a conversation. You could say, "Hi there. I see you like Joe's Widgit Shop, too. I love that store. I like to shop in there all the time. Did you check out the new Ultra Widgits?"

Give the person a chance to respond. If she walks away or doesn't answer, she clearly does not want to talk to you. If the two of you do strike up a conversation and are having a fun time chatting, you can then try asking for a date. Ask to do something simple together. You could say, "My name is Bob, by the way. I'm having a great time talking to you. Would you like to get a soda?"

If the answer is yes, you are on your way to your first date together. If she seems very interested in you but the answer is no, it is possible that she is just too busy right now. In this case, you can ask once, "Well, would you like to hang out some other time?" If the answer is yes, go ahead and arrange another time to meet, just remember to be safe. This person is still a stranger. Never agree to go to someone's private home, and don't give out your address. You can exchange phone numbers or email addresses, but make a plan to meet in public for your first few dates. This will give you time to get to know the person before you meet in private. (For more about dating safety, see the section *Your Health and Safety When It Comes to Dating*.)

If the answer is clearly and absolutely no, chances are the person is probably already involved with someone else or isn't interested in dating right now. That's life. Politely say goodbye and move along. Don't pester her or keep asking. And don't follow her around. These behaviors are annoying and could be incorrectly or correctly considered sexual harassment, a serious crime. Your feelings may be hurt, but you will meet other people. (For more information about proper dating etiquette, see the section *Inappropriate Versus Appropriate Behaviors* below).

In the United States, "age of consent" or "age of majority" laws protect children from sexual activity. The exact age of majority, or year at which it is considered legal for someone to consent to sexual activity, is slightly different from state to state, but is usually 16, 17, or 18 (ask your parents, another adult you trust, or a school counselor). At school or in your neighborhood, you will see teenagers dating, but they are roughly the same age. Age of majority problems occur when one person is an adult (over 18) and the other person has not reached the age of majority in your state. To be on the safe side, if you are over 18, do not go up to somebody younger than you in the supermarket, a movie theater, or other public location and ask for a date. And never approach somebody romantically if you cannot be sure they are old enough to be dating. You can be (and probably will be) arrested.

Alternative Dating Possibilities

So you met somebody you like romantically, and you made your approach. Having practiced various techniques and conversation styles, you asked if she would like to go on a date, and she said yes. Now what? Don't think you have to go to a fancy restaurant for your first date just because in the movies and on TV, romantic couples often go out for dinner. A dinner date is not your only option.

Alternative ideas include quiet activities like going on a walk or to a museum. Unusual ideas include asking someone to go on a trip to the library or to watch planes at the airport. Be creative. You may feel silly asking someone to do something other than go to a restaurant or a movie, but you'll have more fun if you respect yourself and pick an activity you will enjoy sharing with the other person.

If the other person would really like to do an activity you don't want to do or aren't sure about, you may have to compromise. For example, if your date wants to share a meal with you, but you cannot tolerate restaurants, ask if she would like to go on a picnic or get takeout instead. If your date wants to go to an amusement park but you have never been or you don't know if you would like it, be honest. Perhaps you could agree to go only for a couple of hours at a very slow time, like early in the morning on a Tuesday, when it would be much less crowded and noisy.

Alternative Dating Ideas

- Go to the library to look something up or to share your favorite books.
- Watch cargo ships in the harbor.
- Have a picnic in the park.
- Have a picnic at the garbage dump, so you can watch the trucks smash up the trash.
- Watch planes take off at the airport and score points for different airlines.
- Visit a museum, an aquarium, a science center – they often offer free admission days.
- Take a trip to the zoo.
- Go hiking at a nature center.
- Take a walk in a neighborhood you've never been to.
- Go to a concert, a play, or the opera – many colleges have cheaper but very good events.
- Take a public bus line you've never been on and see where it winds up.
- Count the number of stores (or movie theaters, restaurants, beauty salons, etc.) in your city.

All of the dates on the list above spark easy and fun conversations while you are doing the activities. Brainstorm and make your own list of activities that do not cause you anxiety and do not trigger any sensory issues. Avoid activities that put you in harm's way. For example, if you look at the list above, taking a public bus line to see where you wind up is not a good idea if the bus line goes through dangerous neighborhoods, but could be fine if the bus just wanders a little through some quaint neighborhoods and shopping areas. If you have a list of safe, fun date activities prepared in advance, you will have lots of ideas in mind when it comes time to plan a date. Someone who likes you will not make fun of you and will respect your needs and interests.

Dealing With Sensory Issues on a Date

Even if you anticipate that your date plans will not overwhelm you, sensory issues can come up in the middle of a date. For example, you could be having a quiet picnic lunch in the park when an outdoor band starts playing loud music nearby. If you have auditory sensory issues, what can you do? It is probably not a good idea to launch into an explanation of your diagnosis in the middle of the date. But it is O.K. to say, "This music is too loud! Let's go somewhere else." Or, "This bowling alley is much louder than I expected. Can we go on a walk instead?" You can always explain that the current activity is not working out for you and that you would like to do something different.

Dressing for your date can also pose sensory challenges. If you have sensitivities to lights and you need to wear sunglasses, again a simple and brief explanation at this stage is enough. Just say to your date, "I need to wear sunglasses because bright lights hurt my eyes." Or, "I wear sunglasses all the time because my eyes are really sensitive." If you have sensitivities to smells, ask your date in advance not to wear perfume or cologne. Again, a simple explanation will suffice. You could say something like, "I have a sensitivity to perfume/ cologne, so if you could avoid wearing it that would be great."

Tactile issues can also surface. If you don't like unexpected touch but your date keeps trying to hold your hand or touch you somehow, you could say, "I'm not ready for all of this touching yet." This is a polite way to get the person to back off a little without giving the idea that you are not attracted at all. You could also counter-initiate a kind of touch that you enjoy. For example, you could say, "Please don't touch my back – that startles me. But I'd like to hold your hand." Remember, you always have the right to stop any kind of uncomfortable or unwelcome touching. Just tell the person to stop. If your date won't stop touching you and you don't like what's happening, get away or get help (see the section *Your Health and Safety When It Comes to Dating* below).

Again, practice helps. Make a list in advance of any sensory issues you are likely to have in different scenarios. Then role-play with a friend or sibling and try to explain your sensory issues politely using simple language that other people can understand. Also, practice and role-play what to do if you have a sensory emergency while on a date. If you are prepared, sensory issues don't have to ruin a good time.

TIP: If possible, go to the site of your pending date a day or two beforehand to make sure the environment is O.K. for you. Plan out an escape route should you have a sensory emergency. Make sure you know where the bathroom or some other quiet or private spot is so you can excuse yourself politely and go there for a break. If you have sensory issues with smells, make sure the place isn't clouded with incense, perfume, or scented candles. If you have light sensitivities, see if the place has spots that are less

Remember, it is important to talk with your date if something makes you uncomfortable, if you are not ready for physical contact, or if after going on the date you would prefer to remain friends.

bright. Some restaurants or cafes hang bright lights right over the table – that obviously won't work for you.

How to Be Yourself

When you are on a date, do you have to pretend to like everything? Do you have to smile every single minute? Do you have to love every single thing about the other person? Do you have to know what to do in every situation? Do you have to say clever things?

The answer is no. The important thing is to always be yourself. If you are trying to impress someone by acting a certain way, that won't last because it isn't the real you. Your best chance for success on a date is when you are honest about who you are.

Awkward situations will come up – this is only human. Just make a brief statement appropriate to the situation and then move on. For example, if you are out to dinner and you drop food all over yourself, you could say, "I'm so embarrassed. Sometimes I'm a little clumsy. I'll just go clean up." Burping, farting, and picking your nose should be done only in private. If you burp or fart by accident, your date will probably find this offensive. Apologize or excuse yourself, but then get right back to the conversation or activity.

You may feel awkward if your date makes a facial expression you do not understand. It is O.K. for you to say, "What does your facial expression mean?" This is a clear and non-offensive way to ask for more information. It is also O.K. to say plainly, "I'd like to kiss you. Do you want to kiss me?" if you can't figure out your date's signals or you don't know what signals to use to initiate contact or send a nonverbal message. When in doubt, ask. Your date will appreciate your respectful behavior.

Remember, it is important to talk with your date if something makes you uncomfortable, if you are not ready for physical contact, or if after going on the date you would prefer to remain friends. Always be polite and honest. Your date deserves the truth and so do you.

If someone is not honest with you, or if someone rejects you just because you expressed yourself, that person is not worth dating. Move on.

Learn to Compromise

The key to a successful dating experience is compromise. You can't have everything go your way all the time. Part of loving somebody else is considering the other person's feelings and needs. Accusing somebody else of not caring about you because she doesn't want to do something you love to do won't get you far. For example, you may have no idea how on Earth your partner could not want to watch your old *Star Trek* videos. Maybe your partner will agree to try one *Star Trek* video if you agree to try one of her favorite videos. Maybe your partner won't ever watch a *Star Trek* video, but she would be willing to watch *Dr. Who* with you.

For another example, perhaps you enjoy playing a game on the computer that takes six hours, but this would drive your partner crazy. Save your serious gaming for times when you're alone and play shorter video games or shut off the computer when you're together. Negotiating and compromising are important skills in a relationship.

If you can't find anything that the two of you enjoy doing together, and if it feels impossible to reach a compromise, perhaps you're not compatible and you need to take a look at whether dating this person is right for you. On the other hand, it can take time to learn a style of compromising that works. So don't give up too easily. If you're having trouble sharing activities, try something completely new for both of you. You'll discover new interests and new hobbies and, best of all, you'll get to discover them together.

Dealing With Rejection

If you ask someone on a date and the answer is no, take heart. This has probably happened to every single person on the planet. You aren't a bad person, you aren't ugly, and you aren't undeserving of love just because somebody said no. Sometimes the other person is not ready to date, or already has a girlfriend or boyfriend. Other times, the person is just not interested in dating you specifically. It is natural to feel sad and dejected. Time will ease the painful feelings. You will find someone new that you are interested in, and maybe next time the answer will be yes. The important thing is to keep enjoying your life and feeling good about yourself.

You may go on a date with someone, really like her, and hope for a second date – only to be turned down when you ask. This is what people mean when they say their feelings are not mutual – you both don't feel the same way. This is disappointing, especially if you are very attracted to the person. You could try taking some time off from dating and then ask again in a few weeks. Sometimes the other person just wants to get to know you slowly. But, ultimately, if somebody just doesn't like you the way you like her, you will have to face the rejection with bravery.

Trying to make the other person jealous of you as a punishment never works. For example, say you ask someone out on a date. You think the two of you had a great time, but at the end of the night she doesn't want to kiss you goodnight and she says she'd rather just be friends. Your feelings are hurt. You are very sad. So the following week, you go out with a cute woman you can't stand, just to piss off the woman who hurt your feelings last week. This is not fair to the woman you don't really want to date. And the woman you do like who just doesn't like you is probably not going to care one way or another. She is probably moving on to new people or is busy with her friends. By behaving this way, you are wasting your time and maybe hurting someone innocent. (For more information about dating and relationship behaviors, see the section below, *Inappropriate Versus Appropriate Behaviors*).

It is never easy to move on after being rejected. You may need some time to feel better. You may not be interested in anyone new for a while, as you struggle to get back on your feet and get over the person who rejected you. But if you find that you just can't stop thinking about the person who clearly does not want to date you, if you are too depressed to resume your regular activities or hang out with your friends, if you just can't concentrate at work or school, if you start to feel very bad about yourself as though you are unlovable, or if you feel like giving up altogether, it's time to get some help. Talk to somebody you trust or a professional counselor who can help you sort out and manage these confusing emotions.

Internet Dating

Many people are meeting dates online these days. Going online to meet someone can be fun. You have a chance to describe yourself without having to worry about facial expressions, voice tone, voice volume, nonverbal clues, modulating your voice, managing eye contact, or dealing with sensory issues – a great relief for those on the autism spectrum. You can also screen out people who don't share your values and interests.

But be extremely careful. People online can and do lie about themselves easily. Before discussing the actual mechanics of Internet dating, safety rules are explained for both using dating websites and for going on dates should you choose to meet someone in person. Make sure that you understand these safety rules and that you are capable of adhering to them before you actually try Internet dating.

Safety Rules for Using Internet Dating Sites

1. ***You have to be 18 years of age to use online dating sites.***
If an online dating site does not have an age requirement, don't use that service. You can wind up in jail if you email somebody under the age of 18 for romance, even if you do so by accident. You can't tell the authorities that you didn't realize the other person was too young. And you can't blame it on the other person even if the other person is the one who lied about his or her age. It's your job to make sure that you use an online dating website with age restrictions in place and that you confirm the age of anyone you are going to contact.

2. ***Make sure the online dating service has a customer service department.***
Some dating sites charge a fee. Find out exactly what the fees are and the phone number or email address of the customer service department so you can contact them in case you have a problem. It is best to use large, well-known online dating websites. One of the most popular services is www.match.com. Some sites cater to specific religions or lifestyles. For example, if you are Jewish, you can try www.jdate.com. If you are gay, you can try www.planetout.com.

3. ***Never put your full name, address, phone number, social security number, or driver's license number on public display or in the section where you describe yourself.***
Don't give out this information to anyone for any reason. If you find someone you like and you begin writing to this person by email, you can tell the person your name. Avoid giving out your phone number until you've really gotten to know the person by email. Even then, remember that people online can lie about their age, their gender, and their intentions. Serious crimes have been committed as a result of people divulging personal information online.

If you have met someone online and both of you now want to meet in person, proceed with extreme caution. Even though you have written each other several email letters, or perhaps had a few telephone conversations, the other person is still a stranger. Follow the safety rules below.

Safety Rules for Meeting in Person After Meeting Online

1. ***Always agree to meet in a crowded, public place.***
   Meet at a busy museum, a coffee shop, or some other public location. Make sure other people are around. Do not meet at a movie the first time – a movie theater is dark. And do not go to a quiet park where no one will hear you if you need help. Never agree to go to somebody's private home or apartment.

2. ***Tell a friend, a parent, or a sibling where you are going and when you expect to be home.***
   Bring a cell phone so you can call this person for help if the date does not go well or if you feel uncomfortable. If you do not have a cell phone, borrow one from your friend, parent, or sibling. You could always bring change for a public telephone, but what if you can't find a pay phone?

3. ***After the date, say goodnight and leave.***
   Arrange to have a friend or a sibling pick you up when the date is done. Do not agree to walk home together – you do not want the other person to see where you live. And do not offer the person a ride home or accept a ride in the other person's car. If you had fun, you can arrange more public dates to get to know each other better before meeting in private locations. Your date should respect these safety precautions. If your date pressures you to go home with him, or he insists on walking or driving you to your house, say no and call for help immediately on your cell phone.

4. ***Don't show the person where your home is under any circumstances.***
   Meet in public and say goodbye in public. As mentioned in safety rule #3, it is best if someone you know comes to pick you up at the end. Your safety is the most important thing in the world. Don't take chances, even if you think your date is a terrific person who would never hurt you. It can be very difficult to interpret the social behavior of someone you just met for the first time. Your date should respect you and should agree that these safety precautions are important.

The Mechanics of Internet Dating

Now that you know what rules to follow if you are going to try Internet dating and perhaps even meet an Internet contact in person, you may be wondering, how does Internet dating work anyway?

The first step usually involves registering with the dating website. Assuming the dating website is legitimate, with age policies, a customer service department, and a privacy policy in place, it is O.K. to give the company your name and the other information requested during the sign-up process. If the website charges a fee, you have to pay before proceeding.

Once you are signed up and have paid any fees, the dating website will give you an online form where you describe yourself. Some areas of the form allow you to simply check off answers to basic questions. Other areas of the form ask you to write a paragraph about your interests, your hobbies, what you like to do in your spare time, or what you are looking for in a partner.

Try to make a favorable impression. If you do nothing in life but sit in front of the television, at least talk about your favorite shows. It is O.K. to acknowledge your faults and weaknesses, but do so in a positive light. For example, instead of saying you don't do much, say you prefer to hang out at home. Then talk about what you like to do at home – read, play with your dog, cook. Instead of saying, "I hate sports and I'm totally not athletic at all," try, "I am more interested in reading, taking quiet walks, or playing computer games. I'm a whiz at Tetris." Remain honest but positive when describing your personality traits. For example, instead of saying, "I have no tolerance for people interrupting me when I'm doing something," try, "I have a very intense focus and enjoy long periods of time to concentrate on my projects."

It is not a great idea to bring up your diagnosis at this point, unless you are using a dating website for disabled people. Let others get to know who you are and what you like to do first. If somebody is interested in you for all the things that are special about you, learning about your diagnosis later on will only help them learn more about you. (For more information about disclosure, see the section, *When to Disclose Your Diagnosis*).

Practice writing a basic description of yourself that is positive. Even if the description is never used in an online dating context, the exercise will help you learn how to describe yourself in a positive way, sharing what is unique and exciting about who you are.

Some dating websites allow you to add a photograph of yourself. You don't have to post your photograph, but fewer people will email you if you choose not to. An alternative idea is to say in your text description that you'll share a photograph once you begin an email dialogue. If you decide to post a photograph, choose one that is flattering and recent. Don't put up a picture of yourself from five years ago, or a picture of you frowning. And don't put up a picture of yourself with your ex-girlfriend or ex-boyfriend cut out of it. Doing so is considered cheesy.

Look at other people's website descriptions as samples or for ideas of what people commonly include; just don't copy other people's paragraphs. Practice writing a basic description of yourself that is positive. Even if the description is never used in an online dating context, the exercise will help you learn how to describe yourself in a positive way, sharing what is unique and exciting about who you are. Show your description to a friend or a sibling and see what they think. They may have suggestions and ideas to improve your profile. They can also let you know if your description is exciting and clear.

Your Health and Safety When It Comes to Dating

Preventing Diseases and Unwanted Pregnancy

Although it may be embarrassing for you to talk about subjects like dating, sex, and relationships, it is vital to understand how to protect your health and safety. If you are going to have sexual contact with someone, you must take steps to avoid sexually transmitted diseases and unwanted pregnancy. You have to take precautions even if you are just "fooling around" (having any physically intimate contact other than sexual intercourse). Always use birth control to prevent pregnancy and condoms to prevent sexually transmitted diseases, including AIDS. Ask your doctor or gynecologist to recommend and explain the different birth control options that are available for both women and men. If birth control and condoms are against your religion, you need to wait until you are married to have sexual contact with somebody.

This book does not focus on sexual education. For more information about birth control and preventing sexually transmitted diseases, talk to an adult you trust or your doctor. You can obtain information from your school nurse if you are still in high school or college. You can also find more information at a Planned Parenthood clinic or the Planned Parenthood website at www.plannedparenthood.org. Planned Parenthood provides counseling and medical care and will scale the cost of birth control and sexual health medical services if money is an issue for you.

Protecting Yourself From Unwanted Sexual Contact

Just because you decide to go on a date with someone does not mean you must touch the other person or have sex. You always have the right to say no. If someone tries to touch you in an unwanted way, tell the person to stop immediately. If the person won't stop, get away, scream for help, or call the police. Be cautious – even someone you trust or have known for a while and think is still cool could try to touch you in ways you don't like or want, also requiring you to get away or call for help.

If your date tries to pressure you to have physical contact or sex, this is wrong and you have the right to say no. For example, if your date says, "But I paid for our dinner. We had fun. Now you have to kiss me," he is pushing you in an unacceptable way. Another example of unacceptable pressuring: "You would have sex with me if you loved me." No matter what somebody tells you, don't give in to the pressure. You can say politely, "I'm sorry you feel that way. I'm just not ready." Or, "If you loved me, you would respect my feelings."

Vice versa, it is absolutely wrong to force somebody to kiss you, touch you, or have sex with you. Even if you take somebody out on a date and the date goes well, the other person may not want to be physical

When you start going out on dates, chances are you will experience new feelings that you have never felt before. Some of these feelings are great, others aren't.

with you, yet or ever. If this hurts your feelings, it is O.K. to express your disappointment. You can say, "I thought we had a great time. I'd like to give you a kiss goodnight. I'm sad because I think you aren't attracted to me." But if your date says no, that's the last word. Say goodnight and leave. You can wind up in serious trouble if you do not respect your date's right to say no. (For more information on inappropriate dating behavior, see the section, *Inappropriate Versus Appropriate Behaviors.*)

Emotional Changes

When you start going out on dates, chances are you will experience new feelings that you have never felt before. Some of these feelings are great, others aren't. Your feelings in a relationship will be much more complicated than usual. Two important tips will help you cope.

1. **You can always take some time off to sort out your feelings.** It is totally fine to say to your date, "I don't know how I feel about this issue yet. Let me think about it." You can also say, "I'm really angry and upset right now, but I don't know why. I think I need a break to sort it out."
2. **You can have more than one feeling at once.** For example, you might feel like spending more and more time with your new boyfriend and yet miss your old friends at the same time. One feeling does not have to cancel the other. You can say to your boyfriend, "I really love spending time with you, and in fact I want to spend more time with you. But I need time to see my friends, too. I'd like to go the movies with my friend Bob next weekend, but would you like to meet me for dinner beforehand?"

   You can experience conflicting emotions, too. For example, say you and your girlfriend make a plan to go to the zoo. When you get there, she declares that it is too hot to walk around. Right away, you feel disappointed, wondering if the whole day is ruined. The best way to deal with conflicting, confusing emotions is to talk about them and to ask for clarifying information. Maybe it's too hot for your girlfriend to see the outdoor animals, but maybe she would be willing to see the indoor animal exhibits where it's air conditioned. Before you jump to the conclusion that the date is ruined, talk to your date about all the different possibilities.

Anyone, not just autistic people, can have trouble figuring out what another person is thinking or feeling. But if you have difficulty picking up social clues, dating behavior can at times be completely baffling. Don't be afraid to ask what's going on. Someone who loves you will be happy to explain. If your date says something and you can't tell if it's a joke or if it's a serious comment, ask. If your date uses an idiomatic expression that doesn't make sense, ask what the phrase means. If people are laughing and you have no idea why, ask what's funny. It's better to ask and get the information you need than to remain confused and feeling left out. It's also easy to feel hurt by someone who is just teasing or kidding around if you don't realize that's what the person's doing.

If you make a blunder, be polite and apologize, but don't be ashamed. For example, what if your date is teary-eyed, but you don't pick up on the emotional signal? She may get mad at you and say, "Can't you see I'm upset? Couldn't you tell I've been crying?" You can be honest and say, "Actually, I didn't realize you were upset. I'm sorry. What can I do to make you feel better? Do you want to talk about something?" Then make a mental note so that next time, if she is teary-eyed, you recognize this as a clue that she might be feeling sad. Be patient with yourself. As you get to know someone, it will be easier to decipher the other person's signals.

Inappropriate Versus Appropriate Behaviors

Certain kinds of behavior are considered not acceptable by society whether you're just going on one date or you are planning to get married. The chart on page 203 visually organizes four categories of dating and relationship behaviors. Refer to the chart and become familiar with the different categories. Talk to your parents, a trusted adult, or your religious leader to see if anything needs to be added for your specific community situation.

Category 1: Behaviors That Are Absolutely Unacceptable

The first category deals with behaviors that can land you in jail. Laws exist to protect people from different kinds of violent assaults and criminal activities. You will go to jail if you rape somebody or force somebody to touch you. You can also wind up in jail for sexual harassment, stalking, or having sex with somebody under the age of 18 if you are over 18. Society is very clear that these behaviors are unacceptable under any circumstance. You need to know what these behaviors entail so you can protect yourself from danger and so you can avoid doing the behaviors yourself.

Our society does not tolerate physical, emotional, or sexual abuse. This is also called "domestic violence" if it happens when you are married or in a committed relationship. It is considered abuse if your partner hits you, pushes you, throws things at you, or forces you to have sex. If your partner says cruel things to you and you've told your partner to stop but she or he just won't, that is considered abuse, too. Get help immediately. Talk to someone you trust or a professional counselor. This is a confusing part of life, but unfortunately even people who love each other are capable of abusing one another. Never stay in an abusive relationship, no matter how much you might also love the person.

It works the opposite way as well. Although sometimes partners fight and hurt each other's feelings, it is absolutely not O.K. to call your partner stupid or to curse at your partner. It is not O.K. to call your partner names or to deride your partner. Even if you have never been so frustrated or angry in your life, try not to scream. Take a break before it gets to that point. If the fighting is out of control, get professional help to solve your problems or to determine if the relationship is really right for both of you.

Another totally unacceptable behavior is called stalking. If somebody follows you around all the time, calls you on the phone every minute, or waits for you around every corner in a way that makes you uncomfortable, you are being stalked. If someone is stalking you, have a friend walk with you wherever you go. If the stalking gets to a point where you cannot leave your house, walk to work safely, or do your normal activities and routines like shopping or attending college classes, tell the police so they can protect you.

Similarly, you do not have the right to follow the other person around, spy, constantly call on the phone, or track the person down at school or work and force him or her to talk to you or pay attention to you. Stalking is a crime, whether the stalker is someone you know or not. If the person you are interested in romantically is not interested in you, eventually you will have to face the situation and leave the other person alone.

Lastly, except in the state of Nevada, society does not accept prostitution. If someone offers you money for sex, or you try to get money from somebody for performing sexual favors, you are engaging in prostitution. You can be arrested and put in prison. Prostitution is not a healthy way to deal with your loneliness.

Category 2: Behaviors That Are Considered Very Bad

The next category of behaviors is also unacceptable. If you and your partner have made a commitment to each other, but one of you goes on a date with someone else, this is considered cheating. In some cultures and most religions, cheating is a crime. In the United States, cheating is also called adultery if you cheat while married and is grounds for immediate divorce.

Nobody approves of cheating and adultery. Just because you see people on TV, in the movies, and in public life having affairs and cheating on their partners does not give you permission to cheat, too. In real life, cheating is rotten and mean. If your partner cheats on you, you will probably feel like your trust was violated and you'll want to break up

Certain kinds of behavior are considered not acceptable by society whether you're just going on one date or you are planning to get married.

right away. If you do the cheating, your partner's feelings will be very hurt and almost always your partner will not give you a second chance.

If you find yourself attracted to someone new, don't cheat. Be honest and tell your partner that you're feeling like you need to break up and meet new people. Wait until after you have finished breaking up to ask out the new person. Your partner might be very hurt to hear you want to break up, but it will hurt a lot less than if you cheat. Your partner deserves respect.

Other behaviors that society disapproves of severely include lying, blabbing about your sex life or your partner's secrets, betrayal or breaking your promises and commitments, and controlling your partner's life. If you want people to respect you, don't do these behaviors. People also strongly disapprove of "leading someone on." This means telling somebody you love him or her, when you really don't. Sometimes the truth hurts, but conducting a "fake" relationship is worse.

Category 3: Gross Behaviors

The next category of behaviors is not considered criminal or truly horrible, but people who do these behaviors are considered gross or rude. This list would include but is not limited to farting and burping on purpose to disturb others, scratching or grabbing your private parts in public, urinating in public (in some cities like New York, this is actually a crime and would go in the first category), spitting, not minding your manners, and not attending to your personal hygiene. No one wants to stand next to you if you smell bad or never wash your clothes. Your date will not want to kiss you if you never brush your teeth. And nobody finds it funny much after elementary school to watch you do something disgusting with your body to get people to laugh, such as chewing up your food and then opening your mouth to show everyone.

Inappropriate vs. Appropriate Behaviors

Category 1: Absolutely Not Allowed – You Will Go to Jail	*Category 2: Very Bad – Society Does Not Like People Who Do These Things*	*Category 3: Disgusting – Others Will Think You Are Gross*	*Category 4: Very Good – People Will Appreciate Your Behavior*
Rape/Date Rape – forcing someone to have sex when they told you NO or STOP ***Forcing Touch*** – making someone kiss you, making someone hold your hand ***Abuse*** – hitting someone, calling someone bad names, throwing things at someone ***Stalking*** – following somebody all the time, spying, constantly calling or emailing when the other person told you to stop ***Sexual Harassment*** – saying things about someone's body, making somebody kiss you or touch you for a favor ***Prostitution*** – paying somebody to have sex with you, or accepting money from someone in turn for sex (exception: Nevada) ***Under-Age Sex*** – dating someone under 18 if you are over 18, emailing someone under 18 for romance	***Cheating*** – dating more than one person at a time without letting your partners know the true situation ***Lying*** – faking your age, faking your situation in life ***Discussing Your Private Life*** – telling others what you do in bed, telling your partner's secrets ***Telling Someone You Love Them When You Don't*** – also called, "leading somebody on" ***Betrayal/Violation of Trust*** – breaking your commitments and promises ***Controlling*** – refusing to let your partner see friends and family, dictating what your partner is allowed to do in life	***Farting, Burping, or Picking Your Nose*** – especially on purpose to annoy others ***No Attention to Personal Hygiene*** – smelling bad, wearing dirty clothes, never brushing your teeth ***Scratching or Grabbing Your Private Parts in Public*** ***Spitting or Salivating*** ***Pissing in Public*** – not only gross, in some cities also illegal ***Bad Manners*** – chewing like a cow, eating with your fingers, pulling gum out of your mouth, eating with your mouth open	***Being honest*** – tell the truth nicely, even when it is hard ***Asking First*** – before touching, kissing, having sex ***Being Responsible*** – don't drive drunk, don't use drugs, protect your body from sexually transmitted diseases/unwanted pregnancy ***Taking Care Of Your Body*** – use birth control, use condoms to prevent disease, take a shower, wear clean clothes ***Following Communication Rules*** – don't interrupt, take turns in conversation, talk at appropriate volume, use nice language ***Being Polite*** – say "excuse me," explain your sensory issues nicely, apologize when you make a mistake ***Being Kind*** – be kind even if you don't like someone any more, even if you have to break up

Category 4: Very Good Behaviors

The behaviors in the last category on the list are ones you should strive for. Be honest, even when the truth is difficult to hear. Be kind, even if you have to tell someone you want to stop dating or you are unhappy in the relationship and want to move on. Remember the rules of conversation – take turns, don't interrupt, ask for more information if you are confused, and monitor the volume of your voice. Ask your partner first before initiating physical contact, particularly in the beginning when you are just getting to know each other and it is harder to tell if your partner is ready for sexual intimacy. Take care of your body and mind your manners. Be responsible – don't drive a car if you are drunk, take steps to avoid pregnancy and sexually transmitted diseases, and talk openly to your partner about what you ready for emotionally and physically.

NOTE: Nobody is perfect. You will make mistakes. Everyone is capable of hurting another's feelings. And even non-autistic people misunderstand social cues and conversational signals. But if you follow the basics of good dating and relationship behavior, you'll be able to learn from your mistakes, apologize when you've done something wrong, and continue to grow as a person.

When to Disclose Your Diagnosis

It is difficult to determine the exact moment at which you should disclose your diagnosis to a romantic partner. The timing is different for every couple. Usually after a few dates, the other person has had an opportunity to see you for who you truly are. When someone has had fun with you and has seen the special things about you that make you unique, it is less likely that this person will reject you simply because you are autistic.

At the same time, remember that chances are your date knows very little about autism. She may ask a ton of questions that to you seem stupid. Be patient. If you are going to talk about your diagnosis, pick a quiet time to do so and be prepared to give honest answers about what challenges you face, if any, and how autism impacts your life. If your partner really cares about you, she wants to understand you and wants to be helpful.

This section will discuss the two main reasons why you disclose your diagnosis to a romantic partner – to handle miscommunication and to enhance understanding – and how to make disclosure go smoothly.

Disclosure and Handling Miscommunication

Sometimes autism can play a role in miscommunication because those of us on the spectrum have difficulty decoding emotional and social signals. For example, if you couldn't tell that your date was just joking around with you and you got angry about a comment that was meant to be funny – which in turn hurt your date's feelings – it might be time to sit down and have a talk about autism and how autistic people sometimes have trouble decoding nonverbal social language. Keep it brief and mention that autism impacts your ability to read social cues. Explain that it can be very difficult for you to tell when someone is joking because it is hard for you to pick up social signals like changes in tone of voice or accompanying smiles that indicate humor. Apologize for getting angry, but point out that it would be helpful if from now on your date could let you know when something is meant as just a joke.

Disclosure and Sharing More of Yourself

Perhaps you haven't had any specific incidents like the example above, but as you get to know someone, you usually want to share more about your life. Tell your partner that you are bringing up the subject of autism precisely because you want to share more of yourself. Don't pull out 16 books on the subject and deliver a two-hour lecture the first time you discuss autism. Answer questions as best as you can. If your date isn't that interested in autism, it could be that she just accepts you as you are and isn't concerned that you have a disability. Let it go, and bring it up again only if autism is affecting your ability to communicate effectively, to socialize comfortably, or to otherwise enjoy your relationship. If your date does happen to be very interested in autism, then you can go into greater detail or suggest books and websites that you can look at together.

The important thing to remember is that people's feelings change. If your date is surprised to hear that you are autistic and backs away from you, she may just need some time to adjust to the news, to learn more about autism, or to get comfortable with this new information about you. That doesn't mean she is going to give up on you. Unfortunately, it is a fact of life that ignorant people sometimes reject someone solely on the basis of disability. If someone rejects you just because you are autistic, you don't want to be dating someone so callous anyway. Such a person is not worthy of your love and attention. Recognizing this is the best way to cope should it happen to you. Move on and find someone new.

Moving Beyond Dating: Time for a Serious Relationship

Perhaps you have been dating someone for a while. You want to know where this is going. Will you be together forever and get married, or is your love going to fade out? You might start growing apart or realizing that you're not so compatible after all. But the reverse is true, too. Your love for someone can increase over time, especially as you share more of your life with each other. Feelings change over time. It is important to stay in touch with yourself by periodically asking yourself and your partner how you feel about your relationship. It is also important to recognize that relationships, not just people, change.

The Evolution of Relationships

When you start dating someone, you usually feel excited and happy. It seems like you always have fun when you are together. But, as time goes on, regular life creeps back in. Maybe you have an argument. Maybe you need to discuss serious and complicated feelings. The relationship is taking up a lot of energy. Maybe your feelings got hurt. This doesn't have to mean it's all over. It's just a fact that, as you and your partner become more serious about each other, the issues and challenges magnify.

When two people are in love with each other, they truly enjoy each other's company. They like spending time together and miss each other when they're apart. They want to take care of each other. They are concerned about each other's feelings. They feel a special connection that they don't share with others. Two people who are in love usually commit to each other exclusively. They agree not to go out with other people because their feelings for each other are very serious and they're just not interested in dating anyone else.

But this doesn't mean they have to like everything about each other. People who are in love still have disagreements. They still treat each other with respect. They feel like they can go to each other with their problems. They have a discussion until they work something out, even if the truth hurts or it is extremely difficult to come to a compromise.

Some people say the initial excitement of dating wears off a little when you settle into a long-term, serious, committed relationship. But you will find new sources of excitement and fun as you get to know each other better, as you learn to communicate on a deeper level, and as you learn how to solve your problems together more effectively. You'll discover how much work it takes to maintain a relationship, but at the same time you'll feel the rewards of all the work as your bond deepens and your trust grows.

Rules to Guide Social Behavior

Social behavior can be very complex. Even couples who are not on the autism spectrum often rely on rules agreed upon in advance to help smooth out interactions and to prevent miscommunication. It is O.K. for you and your partner to decide on some basic rules to govern your relationship. The rules will help you know what to do. For example, you might have a rule to wait until you get home to discuss serious feelings and problems so as not to get into an argument in public.

If the flow of conversations is difficult for you to decipher, you might have a rule that each person indicates when she or he is done talking to prevent accidental interruptions that can hurt feelings. If it is too hard to explain very complicated feelings verbally, you might have a rule that it is O.K. to take a break and write down your feelings first before you talk, giving you a chance to sort them out rather than getting into a fight due to confusion.

Everyone's rules are different. You don't need a rule for every single minute of your life. But if you and your partner experience the same problems or difficulties over and over again, come up with some rules to help you figure out how to handle your specific situations better. (For more information on techniques for enhancing communication and cooperation in a relationship, see Chapter 9: *Spectrum/Non-Spectrum Relationships – A New Perspective on Making It Work.*)

Sample Rules for Social Behavior

1. Only discuss problems in private.
2. Signal when you are done talking.
3. It's okay to take a break to try to sort out your feelings.

Being Autistic in a Relationship

Don't assume that all the problems in your relationship are because you are autistic. All people in relationships have to work hard to get along and find ways to solve their problems, autistic or not. That being said, you may encounter special challenges and issues because you are autistic. Don't be afraid to solve relationship problems with creative or unusual ideas. Anything that helps you and your partner strengthen your relationship can be useful. Remember also that you do not have to do all the changing in a relationship. You will encounter and have to deal with the downsides of neurotypical behavior. Both you and your partner are responsible for compromising, for helping each other, and for finding a way to meet each other's needs. (For more information on solving relationship problems, see Chapter 9.)

Time Management in Long-Term Relationships

In the beginning of your relationship, you may want to spend all your time with your partner. But you need your friends, your family, and your own activities, too. Being with someone is about sharing yourself, so don't give up on the other relationships and activities that you enjoy. You may feel jealous or sad if your partner is ready to "go back" to old friends and activities before you are, but rest assured this is not a sign that your relationship is failing. Your partner just wants to stay in touch with the people and things he has always loved.

When you allow each other the space and time to have your own friends, visit your family, and do your own activities once in a while, you'll actually have more "self" to share and more things to talk about. If your partner will not let you see your family members, spend time alone, or hang out with friends, that is a big problem. Someone who truly loves you will encourage you to explore your interests and maintain your friendships and family ties precisely because he wants to see you grow and be happy.

Making Big Decisions: Living Together, Marriage, and Children

Deciding to live together or get married is an enormous decision. Don't make this decision quickly. Spend plenty of time getting to know someone before you move in with each other or get engaged. If you are going to be together for your whole life, a year or two to make sure you are truly compatible won't change your love.

Living with someone you are in love with can be a lot of fun, but it can also be difficult. Living together changes everything and brings up a whole new set of challenges. For example, when you live together, you usually share money, which can be very complicated. Always talk to your friends and family while you are making these kinds of big decisions. Ask them what they think. If you are young, ask them to help you determine if you are ready for such serious responsibilities.

Deciding to have children together should never be done in a hurry either. It might seem like children are so cute and it would be so much fun to have a baby. But having a child is the most enormous responsibility you can take on. Once you have a child, that responsibility is irrevocable. You will be a parent forever, every single day and night of your life. Your child will depend on you for many years.

Take steps to prevent pregnancy until you are stable enough to provide a child with everything he or she needs to grow up healthy and happy. Make sure you know what methods of contraception (birth control) are available to you and make sure both partners are involved in preventing an unwanted pregnancy.

Breaking up or Divorcing

Sometimes it is obvious that you have to break up with your partner. For example, if your partner is abusive or if your partner cheats, stalks, or harasses you, it is time to leave. Under these circumstances, it is clear that the relationship should end. Get professional help if you're having trouble separating from an abusive partner.

Most of the time, though, it is not so obvious if and when to end a relationship. If you aren't happy in the relationship, maybe you just need more time alone or more time with your friends. If you think the two of you still love each other but things have gone stale, take a break. A little time apart can make you feel excited to see each other again and can refresh your relationship.

Or maybe you just need to figure out better ways of communicating. Sometimes two people really love each other, but need help learning how to share their feelings and resolve problems. If this is the case, but you can't come up with ideas on your own, couple's therapy or joining a group for couples at a community center can help. Going to see a therapist or marriage counselor doesn't mean your relationship is doomed. In fact, getting help often makes your relationship stronger.

Even if you are happy with your partner and don't have difficulties communicating, you can grow apart, especially if you are young. The two of you may go off to different colleges, where you will want freedom to meet new people. Or maybe after being together romantically for a period of time, you discover that you're just two very different people who would be better off as friends. Try to leave each other on amicable terms. You shared some fun times together, so what is the point in being mean?

Scenarios where both of you decide at the same time that it would be best to part ways for whatever reason can still be sad and difficult, but are easier than unexpected and unplanned breakups. If you still love your partner, but he comes home one day and announces that he is leaving, you may be shocked as well as hurt. You can try to find out why he has so abruptly changed his mind about the relationship, but chances are he won't have a reason that satisfies you. When someone leaves you suddenly, without warning and without an obvious reason, you can feel absolutely devastated. You can also feel angry or like you'll never be able to trust somebody else in the future. Your feelings may range from severe abandonment to intense rage.

You will need to monitor yourself carefully in the days and weeks, even months, after a devastating breakup. People going through serious breakups sometimes find it hard to eat, sleep, concentrate, or take care of basic responsibilities. Remind yourself that time does heal a broken heart and try to get through each day one at a time. Turn to your friends and family for comfort and assistance. Keep reassuring yourself that when you are feeling better, you will have a chance to meet someone new and will be able to trust in love's possibilities again. If after a breakup you feel so depressed that you can't go to school or work or do all the things you normally do, or if you find that you absolutely cannot take care of yourself, seek out professional help.

On the flip side, try not to break up with someone abruptly yourself. If you feel the need to end the relationship, but your partner is happy and doesn't want to break up, don't just announce one day that you've had it and you are leaving. Think about the devastation she would feel (see

If the two of you are married or have children, breaking up can be very tricky. When either or both of you want to dissolve a legal marriage, you will have to go to court or at least file court papers.

the previous two paragraphs). You will have to be honest about the fact that you are no longer in love, but give your partner a chance to absorb this information. Explain that you feel the need to move on in your life, or that you are not able to get what you need from the relationship, but at the same time give your partner a chance to adjust to the fact that you want to leave. She may have questions. She may try to talk you out of your decision. She may cry a lot or be angry, but still want you to comfort her. If you are sure you need to leave, be firm. Don't give mixed messages or hints that you might stay if you really don't mean it. But be as kind, polite, and gentle as possible during the separation period.

If the two of you are married or have children, breaking up can be very tricky. When either or both of you want to dissolve a legal marriage, you will have to go to court or at least file court papers. If you have children, you will almost always have custody issues that will also have to be resolved in court. This is why it is essential that when you decide to marry someone and start a family, you are mature enough to handle any unanticipated problems, including a difficult separation. In other words, even if you and your spouse are extremely angry at each other, you must be mature enough to split any assets you own jointly as equitably and as peacefully as possible. And no matter what you and your spouse think about each other, which can become extremely negative quickly, especially when courts and money are involved, you will have to be mature enough to remain amicable for the sake of any children in the family.

What happens in the weeks and months after a serious breakup is official? If you miss your ex, you can make a phone call or send an email. You can chat for a few minutes if you run into each other naturally. Some ex-partners remain friends, or become friends later on after they've had a chance to heal. But no matter how sad or angry you are after breaking up, you have to leave the other person alone and move on with your life. If your ex-partner states clearly that she does not want to talk to you or see you, stop trying to make contact. For some people, it is just too hard to see or talk to an ex-partner. Don't call on the phone, don't email, don't go by her new house, and definitely do not show up at her place of work. Remember, pursuing your ex-partner after she has specifically ended contact with you can be considered stalking, a serious crime.

If You Are Gay, Lesbian, Bisexual, Transgender, or Transsexual

Coming to Terms With Your Identity

As you go out into the world and begin dating, you may discover that you are not attracted to the opposite sex, or that you actually are the opposite sex, or that you fall somewhere in the middle of a wide scale of possible sexualities and gender identities. This discovery can be extremely distressing if alternative sexualities and genders are against your religion or the norms of your community. If you choose to recognize and follow an alternative path, your family and old friends may reject you. But doctors and mental health workers now agree that repressing or trying to hide an alternative sexuality or an alternative gender is not healthy and can cause psychological problems. You may need help coming to terms with your new identity, especially if your community is not favorable toward these issues.

Even if you have no problem with the intellectual concept of alternative sexualities and alternative genders, you may still have difficulty accepting yourself, figuring out a healthy way to express your identity, or deciding how to live in the world with your new identity. Seek help and advice from community centers and support groups, which you can find in most big cities and many larger towns. Check your local yellow pages under "Social Services" or do an Internet search. The center might be called the Gay and Lesbian Community Center, but you can still usually find help and support there if you are bisexual, transgender, transsexual, questioning, or undefined.

You are not abnormal. You are not a freak. Don't be afraid to reach out. Other people in the world are going through the same things you are, and they can help you and support you.

Actual dating and relationships are similar for heterosexual people and people with alternative identities. But alternative couples may have added stressors to deal with, especially if they are rejected by family and friends.

Special Safety Precautions

No matter whether your discovery of and transition toward a new sexuality or gender identity is rocky or smooth, you must learn special precautions and measures to keep yourself safe. Some people are homophobic, or biased against people who express these types of alternative identities. Without having to hide who you are or feeling like an unworthy misfit, you need to acknowledge that violent people may try to hurt you just because of who you are. Therefore, don't hold hands with or kiss a member of the same sex in public unless you are sure you are on a safe, well-lit street in a supportive neighborhood. Walk home in groups after dates, especially if it is dark or you are cross-dressed. Don't ever go home with anyone you don't know: Some homophobic people will trick you into thinking they like you, only to attack you when you leave the community center or the bar or the dance club. Carry a flashlight and a whistle with you at all times so you can signal for help in a crisis.

Dealing With Dating and Relationships

Actual dating and relationships are similar for heterosexual people and people with alternative identities. All human beings deal with the same issues of getting to know each other, taking care of their bodies and behaving responsibly, dealing with rejection, learning to communicate feelings, making big decisions, and sometimes breaking up. But alternative couples may have added stressors to deal with, especially if they are rejected by family and friends. They may face violence on the street, may have to keep their true identities hidden for safety reasons, or may have to fight expensive legal battles to take care of each other, to share and inherit each other's assets, or to establish joint custody of their children. These pressures can take a toll on even the strongest, happiest, and most loving relationship.

If you are feeling isolated or stressed out, get help. As mentioned, community centers can provide you with support, referrals, and important information. Also find activities, groups, and other people who are supportive, sympathetic, and tolerant. Churches and synagogues specifically catering to people with alternative identities can be helpful and exist to provide supportive communities. Almost all big cities have one or two such religious organizations. Gay bookstores, gay cafes, and even some gay bars can provide you with lists of community support resources. These businesses also sometimes offer healthy recreational activities that will give you and your partner a chance to meet other couples who are dealing with similar issues. Don't try to get through your life alone!

Conclusion

Dating and relationships, like all social activities, can be both fun and difficult. You have a chance to experience lots of wonderful feelings. It can take some time to practice all the social skills that go into asking somebody on a date, approaching someone you like, planning a fun activity to share, sorting out your feelings, discussing your diagnosis and challenges, making serious commitments, and sharing your life with your partner. Don't be embarrassed if you make a few mistakes along the way – all people do. Never be ashamed to ask for help.

Be sure to protect your physical and mental health. Ask your family and friends for guidance. You don't have to be like everybody else to be lovable, but you do need to follow the basic codes of acceptable social behavior, and you need skills to navigate the social world successfully. You'll have a lot more fun and success in the dating world when you are honest with yourself about what you can handle, what you want, and how you feel. It may seem impossible to meet somebody to date, and you may go through periods of great loneliness. But don't despair. It is possible even as an autistic person to find a partner, go on dates, fall in love, or get married and have a family, if this is your goal.

■ ■ ■

Chapter 9

Spectrum/ Non-Spectrum Relationships – A New Perspective on Making It Work

Many couples where one is on the spectrum and the other is not have described a gulf or chasm that can develop and even destroy bonds of intimacy simply because each one's way of being is foreign to the other. Early in my marriage to my partner, Gena, we sought new ways of bridging our differences in communicating, thinking, and feeling that did not focus only on the relationship problems caused by the autistic partner. In fact, Gena has always acknowledged the strengths, skills, and fresh perspectives an autistic spouse can bring to a relationship.

This chapter takes a new approach to resolving relationship challenges and does not include tactics for "putting up with" autistic behavior, as if autistic characteristics are separate from a person's essence or are less desirable than the traits of non-autistic partners. Non-spectrum behavior can cause relationship problems for the autistic partner! It is important to move beyond blame and find healthy ways to meet each person's needs. Equitable compromises can be made that enhance closeness and cooperation, but both partners must adapt to each other.

The chapter starts with mini-stories about two hypothetical partners, Sue and Bill, to illustrate main areas of conflict in spectrum/non-spectrum relationships. Then, methods, tools, and techniques that can address

Although the focus of the chapter is on suggestions for two partners in an intimate relationship, where one is on the spectrum and the other is not, the suggestions work for all types of relationships.

these sources of tension and conflict are explained and described. How these tools enhance emotional communication is demonstrated throughout. Managing sensory issues and accentuating autistic strengths are discussed at the end.

Although the focus of the chapter is on suggestions for two partners in an intimate relationship, where one is on the spectrum and the other is not, the suggestions work for all types of relationships. Parents, children, siblings, friends, caregivers, teachers, and co-workers can all benefit from the material, not just spouses. For an easier read only, I refer to a male-female partnership throughout the chapter.

NOTE: For the sake of grammatical simplicity, it is assumed that your partner is not on the spectrum, but that you are. Therefore, references to your non-spectrum partner or spouse may be shortened to just partner or spouse. Also only for grammatical simplicity, I continue to refer to you as male and your non-autistic partner as female.

Main Areas of Conflict From the Perspective of the Non-Spectrum Partner

- **The spectrum partner is not able to decode body language and other nonverbal signals.**
  Sue enters the apartment, arms filled with packages. She gives Bill a look that asks nonverbally, "Can you help me?" Bill has no idea what Sue is doing with her eyes and continues fixing his computer.
- **The spectrum partner has problems modulating voice volume.**
  Sue and Bill are lying in bed late at night talking. Sue is talking quietly, almost in a whisper. Bill is talking to Sue as if she is somewhere on the other side of the house. This hurts Sue's ears, so she asks

Bill if he could talk more quietly. Bill feels dejected, thinking Sue isn't interested in the conversation.

- **When emotions are flying and the argument is heated, the spectrum partner "shuts down" or tunes out.**
  After arguing for a while about many different and complicated issues, Bill is drained and totally overwhelmed. He has no idea how he feels anymore, and he decides he is no longer going to discuss anything. Sue is confused and hurt by Bill's silence and withdrawal, wondering why Bill doesn't want to resolve their conflict.

- **The spectrum partner is not able to describe his/her feelings, especially if the emotions are subtle or "mixed."**
  Sue goes to Bill's office one day to help Bill with a special project. Sue finishes her part and decides to go home early. Bill seems disappointed. So Sue asks Bill, "Do you want me to stay longer?" Bill has no idea how to answer that question.

- **The spectrum partner views interactions in terms of rules as opposed to responding out of instinctive desire or spontaneous emotion.**
  Bill has to go to a holiday dinner at work. He announces happily, "I assume you'll come with me. That's the rule – families always go together, right?" Sue asks Bill if he would like her to attend, to which Bill replies, "Yes, that's the rule. Families always go to the holiday dinner together." Sue is surprised at his response. She asks Bill again, "But would you enjoy having me there? Do you want me to come, like deep down inside?" Bill just keeps repeating the rule. Sue is a little hurt.

- **The spectrum partner does not know an appropriate way to respond to his/her partner's feelings.**
  Sue calls Bill on her cell phone. She's really upset and launches into an explanation of what just happened. Bill is totally silent.

- **The spectrum partner expresses emotions very strongly and seemingly out of proportion to the situation – or may not have a keen sense of when and where to express emotions.**
  Sue and Bill go to the store for ice cream. The store is out of Bill's favorite flavor. He is crushed. The whole night is ruined. Nothing is fun any more. Sue tries to get Bill to order something else, but he does not want a different flavor. They were going to go to the movies, too. But now Bill just wants to go home and sulk and play video games.

Main Areas of Conflict From the Perspective of the Autistic Partner

- **The non-spectrum partner always seems to need an answer right away.**
  Sue calls in from the other room, "Bill, what do you want for dinner?" Bill thinks about this question for a few moments. Wondering why Bill hasn't answered after four long minutes, Sue assumes he is rudely ignoring her. "Did you hear me?" she shouts. Now Bill is frustrated – he thinks he was taking a reasonable amount of time to gather his answer. His train of thought has been derailed and he has to consider the question all over. Additionally, he can't understand why Sue is asking him if he heard her, since she knows he is not deaf.
- **Conversations always have to be structured according to non-spectrum conversational rules.**
  Sue asks Bill how he feels about visiting her mother next month. Bill does not appear to be answering her question. Sue is frustrated and asks the same question slightly differently. Now Bill is getting annoyed – he has a second question to answer, when he hasn't even answered the first! He needs to answer in his own time and in his own way.
- **The non-spectrum partner must discuss something even though the spectrum partner is in the middle of an important and serious personal project.**
  Sue comes into Bill's computer room and wants to know how he would feel about adopting another cat. Bill can't believe she wants him to discuss this right now! He is in the middle of tracking ship traffic between China and Panama.

- **The non-spectrum partner makes a joke or teases the spectrum partner, expecting the humor will be understood.**
  Sue laughs and says jokingly, "No, dummy! That's not how you beat eggs!" Bill puts down the fork and steps back, looking upset. Sue taps his shoulders and adds, "Oh come on! I was just kidding!" Bill is wondering how on Earth he was supposed to know Sue was just teasing. He doesn't feel like helping make the cake any more.
- **The non-spectrum partner wants to be physically affectionate after a fight.**
  Sue and Bill have just resolved an argument. Bill needs some space after all that intensity and would like time to play video games or go on a walk by himself. Sue is shocked and hurt! She wanted to cuddle up with Bill and be close again.
- **The non-spectrum partner doesn't understand why the spectrum partner wants time off from social interaction.**
  It's the weekend. Sue envisions quiet romantic time with Bill – watching movies, taking walks, cooking dinner together, or decorating the house. Bill needs a break from a week full of social interaction and envisions uninterrupted time to read his new book on international shipping, or perhaps some time alone to watch cargo ships in the harbor.
- **The non-spectrum partner disrupts the household systems or does not follow the rules.**
  The rule in the house is that the recycling bins always stay in the front closet. Sue moves the recycling bins into the backyard a few hours before the big July 4th barbeque. She figures it will be easier to collect all the empty soda cans and beer bottles if the bins are right near the party tables. Bill comes home and discovers that the recycling bins are missing from the front closet and is very agitated. Sue tries to explain, "But we're having an outdoor party tonight. It's just for one night. Besides, this way people don't have to track through the living room to throw something out." Bill is very upset and says adamantly, "The recycling bins always go in the front closet! That's the rule!" He proceeds to put the bins back into their right place.

Techniques for Bridging the Relationship Gap

Based on the examples describing typical areas of conflict and additional examples you may think of from your own life, the gap between a partner on the spectrum and a partner who is not may seem impossibly wide. The autistic partner is frustrated by endless demands for social exchange and emotional interaction, balking at interruptions and yearning for quietude. The non-spectrum partner is equally frustrated by endless misunderstandings and feeling ignored or unappreciated.

But it is possible for the non-spectrum partner to learn how to respect autistic ways of feeling, thinking, and communicating, and it is possible for the autistic partner to learn how to respect what matters to the non-spectrum partner. Both partners can learn skills and tactics to bridge the gap. Some of these will now be discussed.

Flash Cards and Other Visual Aids

Using index cards and magic markers, both partners can make flash cards to address each other's concerns during regular conversations. The flash cards explain what is happening for each of you and validate each partner's needs. For example, when your partner asks a question and does not receive an immediate answer, she may feel ignored or disrespected. Similarly, you may feel rushed to answer. You could flash a card that says, "Processing." This indicates to your partner that you have heard her question and that you are paying attention but that you need time to process and gather a response. Your partner may feel awkward the first time you flash your "Processing" card. But at least she'll know that she is not being ignored and that she will receive your answer in due time.

Your partner can make her own flash cards. For example, on one card, she could draw a stick figure and a conversational balloon with a prompt word such as "I______." After she asks a question, she could hold up her card to visually prompt you to answer or she could make a "My Turn" card to indicate that she would like a chance to respond or would like to discuss a new topic. Remember to decide together beforehand what the flash cards mean and why you are using them. And make the cards together.

You can also use symbols and icons as visual clues. For example, your partner could hold up a large question mark to alert you that she is asking a question. Or either of you could hold up a red octagonal, just like a stop sign, as an emergency stop signal to indicate it is time to stop talking or doing some behavior.

The possibilities are endless. Just keep in mind that your flash cards will be unique to your circumstances. In my family, the "Processing" flash card has been a life saver. My wife is no longer completely frustrated because I'm "not answering," and I no longer feel pressured to answer before I am ready. Your family may come up with different cards to meet different needs. Whatever works is good.

Over time, you may notice you need to rely on flash cards and visual clues less, perhaps because you've had a chance to practice. You may also notice that eventually you can just say what is written on your flash cards instead of holding them up. That is fine, too. But if you do use flash cards and visual aids the rest of your life, there's no shame in that. Visual cues are communication tools.

Hand Gestures

You can use finger signs and homemade sign language to regulate interaction in a non-hurtful manner. For example, a flash of the "V" symbol, using two fingers to form the shape, can indicate the need for voice volume modulation. Hand signals are extremely useful in public where it would be humiliating if your non-spectrum partner turned to you and said, "Honey, you're talking too loud." Flashing the "V" indicates the need to quiet down quickly and discreetly, without interrupting the flow of conversation to discuss the problem and without hurting anyone's feelings. Hand gestures also produce immediate results.

If you have trouble regulating emotions, occasionally expressing a feeling at the wrong time, in the wrong place, or in the wrong way, your non-spectrum partner can flash an "X" made with two criss-crossed fingers to indicate that it is time to stop your behavior. You don't have to completely understand why, but the "X" indicates it is time to be quiet until you get home or get to a private spot, even if you are very pissed off or upset. Similarly, pointing at the wrist where a watch usually lays can indicate, "I'm taking some time out." These gestures are for everyone in the family, so you can also flash the "V" or the "X" or any other sign you and your partner make up if your non-spectrum partner is being too loud or expressing herself in a way that makes you extremely uncomfortable.

You can create hand signs to explain your needs from an autistic perspective to your non-spectrum partner, too. For example, you could make a sign to indicate that you are overwhelmed by too many questions at once and need time to think and answer. Or you could agree on a sign to indicate to your partner that you are paying attention, even if you have to look at the floor or out the window while she talks to you. You could develop a sign to indicate you are having a sensory emergency so your non-spectrum partner knows instantly why you have to leave the room. You can make hand signs for any situation that you find difficult to explain verbally, but often must explain so as not to confuse your partner or hurt her feelings.

Say you come home from work exhausted from an awful commute, your eyes still hurting from being under fluorescent lights all day and your head spinning from all the socializing. You step into your house only to hear the TV blaring and the dog barking. Your wife asks you how your day was and if you can take out the trash. All of this happens in the span of about 10 seconds.

A typical autistic response is to shut it all out and retreat to a quiet area to focus the mind. But if you just ignore your wife, her feelings will be hurt. You can't ignore the fact that you are too overwhelmed to answer her questions immediately or to get to the trash right away either, but you could flash your hand sign for "Sensory Overwhelm." This way, your wife can rest assured she isn't being ignored and that you will deal with the garbage at some point. She'll also know to expect that you will probably take a few minutes alone to calm down before doing anything else.

Direct Statements

Our spouses and partners who are not on the spectrum communicate a lot of information indirectly or nonverbally. They are somehow able to "tell" what another person wants to communicate by looking at posture, facial expressions, and other subtle gestures. Your partner may incorrectly assume that you can read nonverbal language, too. But facial expressions and body language are foreign languages that those of us on the spectrum typically do not speak. I heard at an autism conference that people not on the autism spectrum use 10% words, 90% nonverbal gestures to communicate, but people on the spectrum use 90% words, 10% gestures!

This area may be one of the biggest sources of miscommunication between spouses when one is on the spectrum and one is not (or between any autistic/non-autistic pair). Your non-autistic spouse may assume that you should be able to "tell" what she means simply by decoding her nonverbal language. Explain to your spouse that this is next to impossible. If she walks in the room upset, but doesn't say so, you won't be able to decipher her emotional state just by looking at her (at least in most circumstances). You need to ask her to state her emotions and anything she wants you to do about the situation with clear Direct Statements.

For example, let's say she is very angry because you forgot to buy cat food on your way home. Maybe she makes an angry face, sighs, stomps around the house, or puts her hands on her hips. Most likely, none of her behaviors will indicate to you that she is angry. She needs to say unequivocally and as simply as possible, "I am angry because you forgot the cat food." Then she needs to state what you should do about it. "Please apologize to me and then go back out and get some."

NOTE: Sometimes those of us on the spectrum are aware of what is expected but are simply unable to respond. For example, I tend to lose the ability to answer questions when I am under stress, even though I know an answer is called for. If this is the problem, check Reaction Rules on page 228.

The same goes for positive emotions. When your partner is happy, she probably wants to share with you what is making her feel so good. Maybe she smiles in a way that indicates she wants you to ask why she is smiling. Maybe she bounces around or makes a bright facial expression. If you don't read these signals, she could incorrectly assume you don't care about her feelings. She'll be disappointed when you don't ask her, "Why are you so happy today?" You need to ask her to say, "Honey, I'm really happy today. I want to share with you what happened." Then she should proceed to tell you. Her request should provide enough information for you to realize that she wants your undivided attention for a few minutes.

When you ask your non-spectrum partner to use Direct Statements for emotional communication, she may be uncomfortable with the notion, assuming that everyone in the world could tell if she were upset or angry or happy from the look on her face. But the fact is most autistic people cannot.

This does not mean we do not care about other people or that we have no capacity for empathy. Some spectrum individuals can decode nonverbal body language through practice or by rote. But most nonverbal signals are delivered rapidly, change constantly with mood and context, and are very subtle. Therefore, the non-spectrum partner needs to do the bulk of the adjusting in this area. The onus is on the non-spectrum partner to verbalize feelings and needs with Direct Statements.

If your non-spectrum partner asks you when she should use Direct Statements, go by this rule: *Always assume everyone in the room is blindfolded.* Would others still get the message? Pretend your wife is carrying in an enormous load of groceries from the car, the bag is about to break, and she really needs help. Maybe she looks concerned or anxious. Maybe she's juggling the bag. Maybe she says something indirect and subtle like, "Gee whiz, this is heavy!" Now ask her to imagine that some other person in the room is completely unable to see and does not understand English. Would he understand what she is trying to indicate? Should he be considered rude because he can't tell she is struggling? No.

The most damaging stereotypes about autistic people probably stem from autism-related nonverbal communication deficits. But if your wife were to state plainly and clearly, "I am having trouble carrying the bags of groceries. Please take the bags from my arms and place them on the kitchen counter for me," most autistic people would be glad to help, including you. Just as some non-spectrum people wouldn't get off the couch to help, some autistic people wouldn't either, but that is due to immaturity, laziness, or an obnoxious personality. Autistic people are not intrinsically uncaring or unempathetic.

Direct Statements can enhance the feeling of emotional connection in an unusual way. When you have to have an intense talk with your partner, sit in a dark room facing in opposite directions. You may feel weird the first few times you do this, but not being able to see each other levels the playing field. Talking in the dark strips away the non-verbal layers and requires each partner to explain feelings in direct, clear terms that both can understand.

Interaction Schedules

Create a weekly Interaction Schedule with slots for time off from socializing. Autistic people tend to enjoy and need time away from what seems like ordinary socializing to the non-spectrum partner. If "regular" socializing causes you incredible pressure and stress, the Interaction Schedule allows you to set boundaries without being rude. Certain blocks of time can be set aside where no interruptions other than dire emergencies are permitted. Your non-spectrum partner needs to understand that these blocks of time may be sacred to you. She can cooperate by ensuring that no disruptions occur.

The Interaction Schedule can also be used to block out social times that are important to the non-spectrum partner. With forewarning and by periodically checking the Interaction Schedule, you will know when you are expected to join certain activities. This advance planning will enable you to schedule special projects and alone time around blocks of family time and other social obligations. You will also be able to schedule enough time to recuperate or to be alone after particularly intense social interactions.

Your non-spectrum partner can relax, knowing that special social time together is on the schedule and will happen. You can relax, knowing what is expected of you socially speaking and when you will have breaks from interaction. You can easily put your Interaction Schedule onto a Weekly Easy Chart, a visual planning aid described in Chapter 2: *Maintaining a Home*.

Reaction Rules

When it comes to an intimate relationship, not reacting to your non-spectrum partner's feelings is bound to cause tension. Therefore, it is a good idea for the two of you to create a list of rules to guide responses to certain feelings or situations. Both partners must agree to the rules in advance. Don't try to come up with rules in the middle of live action. Discuss appropriate responses to different feelings during a calm time. Use visual clues and charts as necessary. I call these rules of response, Reaction Rules.

It is often stated that people on the autism spectrum lack compassion. This is not true. The stereotype comes from two major characteristics: One, autistic people have difficulty flowing from one social interaction to the next smoothly, since social interactions tend to be viewed and interpreted in distinct segments unconnected to each other, like snap shots. Two, autistic people don't automatically absorb and learn the appropriate way to react, which most non-spectrum people do unconsciously.

For example, it may be completely obvious to your partner that if a friend is crying, you stop what you are doing, look at her, and listen to her feelings. The friend may need a hug, some advice, or a box of tissues. Your partner would offer reassurance. What is a simple reaction to her friend's emotional state that nobody had to teach her is a complex tangle of responses to those of us on the spectrum. How do you determine what to do if someone you love is crying? How do you adjust your response as your loved one's mood shifts to worse or better? How do you respond without ignoring your own needs and boundaries? The sheer enormity of responding to someone crying can be so overwhelming to those of us on the spectrum that sometimes we withdraw or do something totally unplanned by accident – like laughing or waving. But this does not mean we do not care.

For you, Reaction Rules will simplify the process of responding emotionally. For your non-spectrum partner, Reaction Rules ensure that her needs are taken care of at the same time. In your house, the Reaction Rule for crying might be: Ask if the crying person wants to talk. The Reaction Rule should go on to explain the basic permutations. If the crying person says yes, then stop what you are doing and listen and help. If the person says no, ask if she wants a hug instead. If physical touch is difficult, perhaps an alternative is to sit down near the crying person to show you are close by and that you care.

You can make Reaction Rules for all types of emotions and situations. For example, say you do not respond when your spouse calls your name, either because you are concentrating intently or you are unable to shift your focus from inside your mind to an interaction with another person. Your spouse is likely to become frustrated because she is calling your name for a reason. It is important for you to answer.

You could create a Reaction Rule requiring all family members to ask, "What?" and then investigate when called by name. This may seem harsh. You could counter with a hand sign or visual aid to indicate your inability to be interrupted at the moment. But even a hand sign or visual aid is, ultimately, a response. In other words, people in our society have an unspoken agreement that when your name is called, you find out why or you let people know you can't interact at the moment. Reaction Rules created in a spirit of cooperation with your non-spectrum spouse will enable you to learn all the unspoken agreements that guide interaction in our culture.

With this in mind, it is true that Reaction Rules will be somewhat different for everyone. The key to making Reaction Rules work is that they are rules. It may seem disappointing to relegate emotional life to

The key to making Reaction Rules work is that they are rules. It may seem disappointing to relegate emotional life to a set of rules, but rules delineate what is expected. Rules can be pre-determined to meet the needs of both partners.

a set of rules, but rules delineate what is expected. Rules can be pre-determined to meet the needs of both partners.

Another example will further illustrate this point. Your non-spectrum partner may need comfort when she is bothered by something. She has a choice: She can remain frustrated her entire life because you never notice the nonverbal clues that indicate her need for reassurance and incorrectly conclude that you are an insensitive jerk. Or, the two of you can create a Reaction Rule to handle the situation such as, *When you see me pacing back and forth through the kitchen, you should give me a hug and ask me what's bothering me. Then listen and hold my hand while I explain my feelings.*

Through the process of creating Reaction Rules together, you have a chance to learn the emotional signs and signals that warrant responses and she has a chance to practice using Direct Statements to state clearly what her needs are.

Write the rules down on paper. Post them in a convenient spot, if necessary. Use visual aids, too. For example, if your Reaction Rule is to place a hand softly on the shoulder of someone crying, cut a photo of this out of a magazine. Run through the Reaction Rules when no one is under stress. Remember that those of us on the spectrum may not know when a response is called for or what would be a typical or acceptable response to a feeling. Therefore, you may have to defer to your non-spectrum partner's experience and knowledge in this area. Non-spectrum spouses and partners can help those of us on the spectrum learn about expressing and sharing feelings.

Nobody on or off the spectrum should have to respond to another's emotions in a way that is uncomfortable, so make sure both partners are comfortable with the requirements of your

Reaction Rules. For example, it is not fair to make a rule requiring a hug from someone with tactile sensitivities, but neither is it fair to deny someone the comforting affection she needs. If hugs are too difficult, compromise and come up with a special gesture that is more comfortable. If you can't look in someone's eyes to show you are paying attention, come up with a hand sign that lets your partner rest assured that you are listening to her. The goal is to come up with a response that lets the receiving partner feel cared for and the giving partner feel capable of caring.

How to Create Reaction Rules

Reaction Rules should be a cooperative effort between you and your non-spectrum partner or spouse. Sit down together and follow these basic how-to steps to come up with Reaction Rules you both agree to.

1. ***List your emotions.*** Make a list of emotions you experience frequently. Have your partner make a list of emotions she experiences frequently.

2. ***Describe what each emotion looks or sounds like.*** Be brief, but provide each other with one or two clues that indicate which emotion is being experienced.

3. ***Ask each other what you like or need for each feeling.*** For example, maybe your partner likes a hug when she is sad. Perhaps you prefer time alone when you are sad. Everybody is different.

4. ***Discuss what an appropriate response to the emotion could be based on personal preferences and needs.*** Throw out any notions of what the response should be. Instead, think of a response that the receiver needs and would like and that the giver can give without distress.

The chart on page 232 shows three Reaction Rules that a hypothetical person on the spectrum might use when responding to his spouse, who is not on the spectrum.

If you look at the emotion sadness on this chart, for example, the non-spectrum spouse has indicated that sometimes she likes physical contact because it reassures her. Our hypothetical autistic person has indicated that hugging while someone is crying causes him to go into sensory overload. Therefore, the two of them have compromised: He will use a soft touch on her shoulder or a gently placed hand on her knee if she requests more contact. Respecting the fact that he does not usually

Sample Reaction Rules – Three Emotions

Emotion	*Looks like*	*Reaction Rule*
Sadness	My spouse cries, changes voice.	Approach and ask, "Are you O.K.?" Listen carefully. Put my hand on her shoulder. If she asks for something like tissues or a glass of water, get it for her. If she requests more physical comfort, place my hand on her knee.
Anger	My spouse's voice volume or speed increases. Sometimes her face gets red.	Say in a calm voice, "I see you are angry. What is the problem?" Listen to the reason. She may be angry at me. Stay calm (or ask for a time-out and make a plan to finish talking later). Reiterate the reason for her anger. Then discuss what can be done to resolve the situation. If she is angry at me, apologize. Then discuss how to avoid the situation in the future.
Happiness	My spouse smiles a lot and "bounces" when she walks.	Ask her why she is happy. Listen carefully to the reason. Show her I am paying attention using our special hand sign. Ask her a few questions to show I am interested in her feelings.

pick up on nonverbal signals, his spouse agrees to state clearly if she needs this additional level of affection.

Some people wonder if a response prompted by a concrete rule is genuine. Reaction Rules are not indicative of a lack of caring or spontaneous mutual interest. But the fact remains that partners on the spectrum may not pick up emotional signals in the first place. Even if an emotion in another person is noticed and recognized, the appropriate response may be a mystery.

Rules clarify appropriate behavior and provide a map for sharing feelings. Additionally, emotional engagement can be chaotic and stressful when you do not know if, when, or how to respond. For this reason, some people on the spectrum prefer to stay within the comfortable confines of their own minds and need a trigger to emotionally engage with another person. Reaction Rules clarify when partners need to engage, what both partners want when certain feelings arise, what each should do to be the most nurturing partner they can be, and what is expected in terms of a response.

With practice, strict adherence to Reaction Rules usually gives way to more flexible and natural responses. Following Reaction Rules over time will give you the vocabulary, the skills, the prompts, and the options you need to respond more spontaneously to your partner's feelings, and, hopefully, receive her responses to your feelings. It is rarely the case that someone on the spectrum just doesn't care. It is almost always a case of not knowing how to respond or that a response is called for.

NOTE: Having Reaction Rules ready and in place will give you a framework for exchanging and expressing concern for your non-spectrum partner's feelings. Your confidence at responding to and sharing feelings will grow. You may notice that you even start coming up with appropriate reactions on your own that reflect your unique style. You won't always need to rely on your sheet of Reaction Rules. But creating Reaction Rules is the first step, and they may always be needed. That is O.K., too.

It is probably an unrealistic expectation that spouses automatically know how to respond to each other emotionally all the time. Your non-spectrum partner may have entered the relationship assuming you would be able to read her mind and react perfectly to her emotions. While that dream is probably not going to come true, both of you can take responsibility for your own feelings and explain yourself in plain language.

Developing rating scales to measure the "amount" of feelings in a given situation can provide both partners with clear clues and can help each one tailor responses to the correct intensity of the moment.

Saying to somebody, "I'm upset right now. Please do something from our list of Reaction Rules to show me you care," is a lot easier and healthier than feeling misunderstood or unloved.

Emotion Rating Scales

Another area of conflict in spectrum/non-spectrum relationships is holding different expectations for how to demonstrate feelings and to what degree a feeling should be expressed. Both partners may view the other's emotional expressions as hypo or hyper, depending on the circumstances. Autistic people tend to have strong feelings with little gradation, so that even minor problems can cause great stress. Those not on the spectrum tend to have feelings about everything, which can seem lacking in purpose to an autistic person. Because those of us on the spectrum are generally not relying on nonverbal information, the extent or depth of our non-spectrum partner's feelings may not be obvious to us. On the other hand, your non-spectrum partner may have few clues regarding your emotional life precisely because autistic people tend not to use tone of voice, inflection, facial expressions, and body language to convey inner emotional states.

Developing rating scales to measure the "amount" of feelings in a given situation can provide both partners with clear clues and can help each one tailor responses to the correct intensity of the moment. Kari Dunn Buron invented a system and explains how to use rating scales with children on the spectrum in her book *The Incredible 5-Point Scale – Assisting Students with Autism Spectrum Disorders in Understanding Social Interactions and Controlling Their Emotional Responses*. The concept of scaling feelings is useful for adults, too, because the scales allow you to vary the expression of a feeling in subtle ways that may otherwise be impossible.

For example, if the store is out of someone's favorite ice cream flavor, you could use an Upset Scale to rate

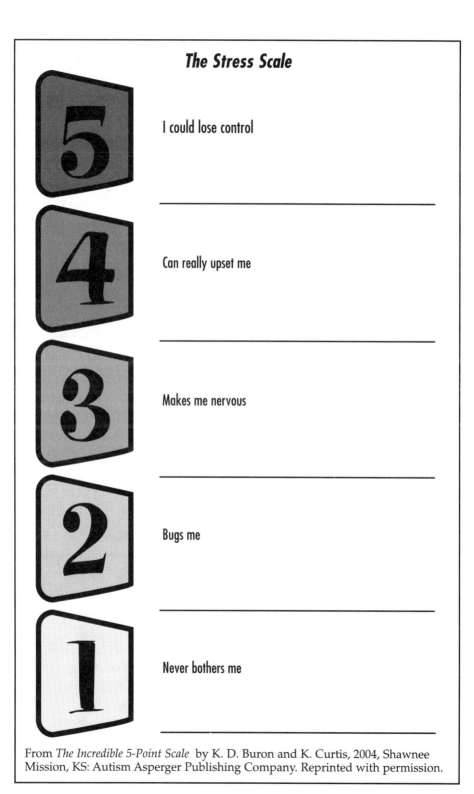

The Stress Scale

5 I could lose control

4 Can really upset me

3 Makes me nervous

2 Bugs me

1 Never bothers me

From *The Incredible 5-Point Scale* by K. D. Buron and K. Curtis, 2004, Shawnee Mission, KS: Autism Asperger Publishing Company. Reprinted with permission.

the incident. On a scale of 1 to 10, with 10 being the worst, most people would rate this problem about a 1 or a 2. Your Upset Scale could include visual aids or written clues that give you an indication of how to react to a Level 1 or Level 2 situation.

What makes one person very upset may not bother another, so it is difficult to make a universal Upset Scale. But you can make scales for any emotion using incidents and problems that occur in your life. Perhaps a Level 1 on your Upset Scale might be dropping a paper clip, a Level 5 might be breaking your foot, and a Level 10 might be experiencing a terrible tragedy. People on the spectrum tend to have a hard time rating emotions – we are either upset, or not. Scales can help us cognitively recognize where an incident lies in the grand scheme of things.

Your scales can include Reaction Rules, too. For example, on your Upset Scale, a Level 1 incident, perhaps dropping all your paper clips off your desk, warrants a curse word or two, but nothing more than that. Level 2, perhaps getting to the store and discovering they are out of Double Mint Fudge, warrants a few minutes of being upset and filing an official complaint with the manager, but a Level 2 situation shouldn't ruin the whole night.

Practice matching situations to levels on the scale. In time, it becomes easier to handle emotions simply because it is suddenly clear how "big" the feelings are. You can make scales for any emotion – negative or positive. For example, a Happy Scale may show a range of happiness from enjoying your glass of orange juice in the morning to winning the $50 million lottery jackpot. Each person's scales will use different incidents to demonstrate levels or amounts of the emotion on the scale simply because we are all different.

The main purpose of these rating scales is to help you gain an emotional octave and a wider choice of responses to the world. But scales also enable your non-spectrum partner to understand you better. For example, your non-spectrum partner may be shocked to discover on a scale of 1 to 5 that eating in the local diner is a Level 3 for you on a Stress Scale. Because autistic people often do not display the extent of a feeling – looking totally calm when terrified, for example – pointing to a number on the rating scale can enhance emotional communication and create dialogue that may otherwise never happen. Your non-spectrum partner may delight in discovering the breadth and depth of your emotional life.

Rating scales can also be used to sort out multiple or subtle emotions. The autistic tendency is to have one feeling at a time. Therefore, it is often disconcerting when multiple feelings are happening at once, and the pressure is on to sort out conflicting emotions. The rating scales can help you realize that you can feel two feelings or even more at the same time and still be able to decide what to do by weighing each to see which weighs the most.

Imagine a balance beam scale in your mind if this helps. For example, say you are out to dinner with your spouse. The lights and music of the restaurant are annoying you at about a Level 3 on an Annoyed Scale. But you are enjoying going on a date, which the two of you haven't been able to do in a very long time. Perhaps you are enjoying your spouse's company at a Level 10 on a Happiness Scale. In this case, the feeling of happiness is outweighing the annoyed feeling. Therefore, you may want to put up with the lights and the music, perhaps using items from your Sensory Emergency Kit, instead of bolting out of the room, which would likely cause the night to end in disappointment for both of you.

Sometimes it helps to visualize this process of sorting multiple feelings by making the motion of a balance scale with both hands. For example, taking your left hand and mimicking a scale, you might say, "I am annoyed by the lights and music in this restaurant at about a Level Three." Then take your right hand, and again mimicking a scale, you might say, "But I am having a lot of fun with my wife and we are enjoying our night out together at about a Level 10!" Using the balance beam analogy can really help sort out "amounts" of different feelings to see which one "weighs" more and to gain perspective on the overall situation.

How to Create an Emotion Rating Scale

1. Label the emotion you are scaling. Include a picture from a magazine or a picture of someone you know experiencing the emotion if visual examples help you.
2. Label your scale from 1 to 10, with 1 being the least emotion and 10 being the most.
3. Fill in examples along the scale. Include pictures, icons, or graphics of your scale examples if visual clues help you, and add Reaction Rules if necessary to guide you in expressing your feelings at the different levels appropriately.
4. When you feel a certain emotion, you can use the scale to determine "how much" of the feeling you are experiencing and tailor your responses and reactions accordingly.

Sample Upset Rating Scale

10 – ***A terrible tragedy happened.***
(This is the greatest "amount" of upset. Ask yourself what would be the most upsetting thing you could imagine.)

9 –
8 –
7 –
6 –

5 – ***You got a very expensive parking ticket and your car was towed.***
(This is the middle range of the chart. Fill in examples to match the different levels. If you are having a hard time, ask family and friends for suggestions.)

4 –
3 –
2 –

1 – ***You dropped a box of paper clips and they landed all over the floor.***
(This is the least "amount" of upset. Think of what is upsetting, but not a big deal.)

Color Codes

Kari Dunn Buron's rating system also employs the use of color, either by itself or as part of a rating scale. Color codes yield emotional information that may be hard to communicate effectively in other ways and provide clear clues to guide appropriate behavior. For example, you could color the shades of increasing frustration according to intensity, with Code Yellow meaning mild frustration, Code Orange meaning frustration is building rapidly and may cause a serious problem, and Code Red meaning you are now so frustrated you need an immediate time out or you will have a meltdown. (This book is printed in black and white, but you can use your imagination to visualize the color blocks.)

Frustration Color Scale

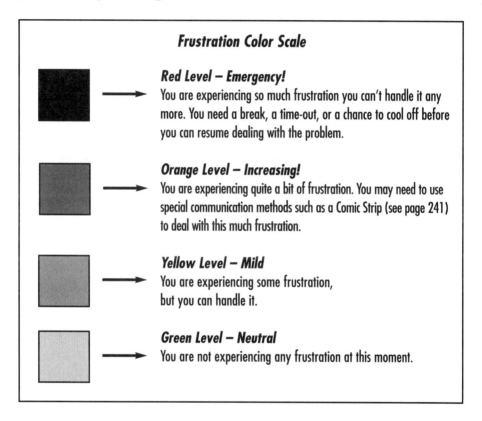

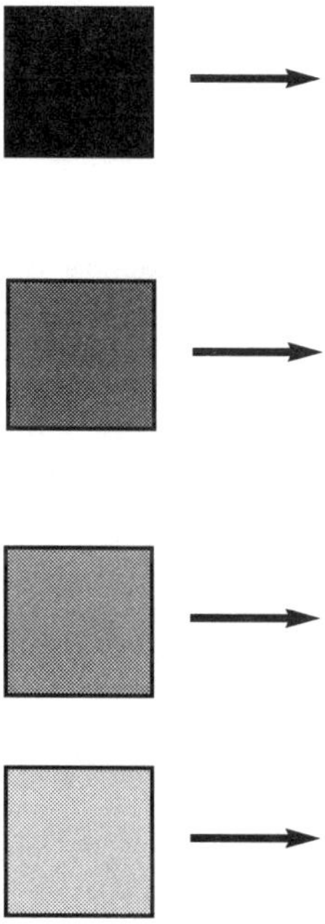

Red Level – Emergency!
You are experiencing so much frustration you can't handle it any more. You need a break, a time-out, or a chance to cool off before you can resume dealing with the problem.

Orange Level – Increasing!
You are experiencing quite a bit of frustration. You may need to use special communication methods such as a Comic Strip (see page 241) to deal with this much frustration.

Yellow Level – Mild
You are experiencing some frustration, but you can handle it.

Green Level – Neutral
You are not experiencing any frustration at this moment.

You can also add Reaction Rules to help you and your partner guide your expression of any emotion. Using the Frustration Scale example above, for example, you might agree that at Code Yellow, both partners can expect dialogue and compromise. At Code Orange, the Reaction Rule might be to try a different method of communicating, such as using a Comic Strip (see page 241) or agreeing to email each other about the issue, which can be easier than talking. Concerning Code Red, you might have determined in advance that at this level, no dialogue or compromise can be expected. The fuse has blown. The frustration level is too high so the interaction should not continue under any circumstances. The Reaction Rule could state that everyone should take a break and resolve the issue later on when you are no longer at Code Red.

Color codes enable each partner to gauge the stage where the other is emotionally. For example, Code Red for anger indicates intense anger – even if you are talking in a monotone voice. Code Yellow for anger indicates only mild irritation – even if you are pacing around, waving your arms, or using an extremely loud voice. Using the color codes can help both partners adjust to the amount of an emotion. For example, if both of you realize that you are at Code Yellow for anger, you can modify your voice volume accordingly.

Color codes are useful for sensory overload as well. For example, you may not be able to indicate to your spouse that you are about to experience a meltdown because you are at maximum sensory overwhelm, but you may be able to say you are at Code Red for sensory issues or to point at code red on a sensory overwhelm chart. This avoids the need to verbalize at an intense moment and allows your partner to understand your behavior more clearly.

Visual aids are useful and flow nicely with color codes. For example, your chart can show what a person might look like at different levels of anger, happiness, frustration, or sensory distress. Put Reaction Rules right onto the color code charts if this would help you. Color codes are not just for you. Both partners can use color codes and associated visual aids to stay at a constructive and effective level of emotional communication or take time out when that is not possible.

Emotion Cards: Draw It Out

Some people on the spectrum find it next to impossible to explain verbally what they are feeling. Others on the spectrum tend not to display feelings physically (i.e., they may be sad, but don't shed tears). To facilitate emotional communication, try drawing the feelings. For example, you could draw yourself crying. Since it is difficult to stop in the middle of an interaction to draw your feelings, draw Emotion Cards for the basic emotions – sadness, fear, happiness – in advance. A simple statement like, "This is how I feel," plus showing the Emotion Card that matches the feeling, can enhance emotional communication and intimacy without requiring a verbal report on your inner state or nonverbal signals like facial expressions.

Emails, Journals, and Comic Strips: Write It Out

Some find writing a useful tool. When writing a letter or composing an email, you do not have to worry about eye contact, tone of voice, sensory distractions, or nonverbal language. Writing gives both partners a chance to develop their thoughts carefully, avoiding harsh words hurled quickly in the heat of an argument.

Journals and even a collection of emails serve another purpose: You can go back and look at how your feelings have changed over time. Do certain issues keep coming up? Is one problem never resolved? Has communication actually improved through the use of visual aids, hand gestures, direct emotional statements, and Reaction Rules? What seems to be working, and what is not? Both partners can use journals for self-reflection and assessment.

Many books explain how to use Comic Strip Stories™, invented by Carol Gray (see the References section at the end of the book). Usually used at school with children, Comic Strip Stories are an excellent tool for adults as well. Comic Strips are especially useful for sorting out mixed or subtle feelings. They break down a social interaction into comprehensible steps. You can draw out Comic Strips to explain your perspective on what happened where you might otherwise be at a loss for words.

Use of a Comic Strip to Decode Social Behavior at Home

My wife came home with the groceries. I was busy on my computer.

I didn't realize she was struggling with the packages because she didn't say so. Her feelings were hurt that I didn't rush over to help, but how was I supposed to know?

Then she used a Direct Statement. She said, "Honey, the bags are heavy. Please help me carry them to the kitchen."

I was glad to help.

When my wife comes home from the store, she needs help with the bags.

We talked about it briefly. My wife will keep using Direct Statements. I will try to remember to help automatically next time.

Emotions Notebook

You can also create an Emotions Notebook. Inside, list signals and facial expressions your non-spectrum partner uses for certain feelings. Take photographs of your spouse or partner modeling faces – a sad face, a happy face, an anxious face, etc. – and then compile the photos into your Emotions Notebook for future reference. The Emotions Notebook can hold flash cards, a sheet of hand gestures, Reaction Rules, a weekly Easy Chart with an Interaction Schedule, rating scales, color codes, Emotion Cards, and Comic Strip blanks, too.

Some people may balk at this suggestion: Does an adult really want to spend time putting together an Emotions Notebook, reviewing it frequently for information, pulling it off the shelf in the middle of an argument to check a Reaction Rule or a facial expression? If you were sent by your corporation to work on an alien planet, would you consider it foolish to stock up on a few books that not only taught you the alien language, but also clued you in on how the aliens greet each other, say goodnight, express their feelings, and conduct themselves in public? Probably not.

Managing Sensory Issues: Creative Compromises

As we have seen in Chapter 1, sensory issues can cause conflicts in several areas of domestic life. Activities like meals, cleaning, organizing the home, decorating, shopping, going to restaurants, or attending social events can pose special challenges. Sensory issues will never go away. Couples can manage these issues best with honest dialogue and creative comprise.

For example, you may have difficulty sitting down to family dinner because of sensory issues with food smells and food sounds. Perhaps you could join your spouse for salad and appetizers, but leave during the main course if that is the biggest source of discomfort. Another suggestion is to join your spouse for tea and dessert at the end of the meal. Or maybe you just need to switch to plasticware to reduce scraping noises that send you over your auditory limit. While your spouse may be disappointed that you can't sit through the entire dinner or need everyone to use plastic forks, your needs and your spouse's desire for you to join her at the meal can both be validated by reaching a compromise.

The autistic style of communicating holds secret blessings. There is a hidden gift in allowing thoughts and ideas to develop as they will, without the pressure to mold them into a specific conversational timeframe and format.

If you are unable to tolerate the plethora of sounds emanating from the TV, try watching on mute, with the captioning on the bottom of the screen. Or perhaps just muting out the commercials, laugh tracks, or clapping will reduce the worst auditory assaults. Compromises such as this can enable you and your spouse to enjoy watching TV together.

If you and your spouse have to go shopping, find the quietest, calmest time of day for the particular store you are going to. Again, bring your Sensory Emergency Kit, including a walkman, sunglasses, a book to occupy your mind, or a hand toy to ease your stress level. Prepare a list of what has to be purchased so you have a clear mission. If shopping is out of the question for you, but your spouse does not want to feel like all the shopping responsibility is placed on her, divide the chores: Perhaps she will do the shopping, while you sit with the car, entertain the kids in the lobby, or take over one or two tasks at home that she hates such as setting out the garbage or vacuuming.

The sensory situations that can come up may seem overwhelmingly numerous. Your non-autistic partner or spouse may feel it is hard to compromise one more time when she has done so 80 times already. But stewing in frustration and dissatisfaction is worse. With a little imagination, you can reach a compromise about most things. And remember, when you start thinking that other couples do not have all the crazy problems you do – guess what? They do. All couples struggle to accommodate the needs and preferences of each partner. Because your spouse or partner loves someone autistic, she gets to make compromises and solve problems she never would have imagined even existed if she hadn't met and fallen in love with you.

Autistic Strengths

Autistic partners can provide a stabilizing force in a relationship. We are often adept at balancing emotional extremes with intellectual insight and objective analysis. When it seems as if the rest of the world is falling apart, we are plodding away, one task at a time, putting one foot in front of the other until we reach the goal. We value logic and can check overwhelming feelings with a rational approach. We can be wholly unaffected by chaos, concentrating instead with our gift of intense focus on the main thing that has to happen next.

Some of us enjoy creating lists, charts, and rules. These skills can be tapped into to develop systems to keep the home running smoothly. We also tend to be good at categorizing. Most of us enjoy putting similar things together or separating disparate items. This aptitude can come in handy when it is time to sort the laundry or the recycling, to organize the medicine cabinet, or to match all the loose socks.

Autistic people are also known for original ideas and novel conceptualizations. For example, we may come up with something much more interesting to do on a holiday than eat dinner. So while the world can think it is an awful fate that we cannot stand the clink of forks on the plate during the Thanksgiving feast, we may be having a better time anyway dressing up as pilgrims, reading an early history of the United States out loud with our loved ones, or enacting the Mayflower landing using the jungle gym in the back yard as the boat.

We have unique ways of assessing and resolving problems, and when we are allowed to apply this skill, we navigate through the world better, regardless of what others think of us. I am reminded of the time my father had to get a haircut, but couldn't stand the barber shop air conditioners blowing on him. He convinced the barber to cut his hair out on the sidewalk in the quiet and comfortable July sunshine. The barber found it quite fun and now profits handsomely from offering the only novelty outdoor summer hair cuts in the whole state, as far as I know!

The autistic style of communicating holds secret blessings. There is a hidden gift in allowing thoughts and ideas to develop as they will, without the pressure to mold them into a specific conversational timeframe and format. Sometimes it is O.K. for somebody not to answer a question, right away or ever. Try letting the question float around the room and see what happens naturally. Make room in your relationship so that sometimes a conversation can go according to autistic standards.

Autistic people may be able to teach the world that quiet and calm are good things. Why do we have to suffer through blasting music just to shop? Why can't we make garbage trucks out of plastic polymers to reduce clanking noises in the middle of the night? Why do supermarkets have to turn the lights up so high? Why can't malls and airports have quiet waiting rooms? Why do taxis have to smell like toxic flowers? How can you have a real conversation with the TV on?

Conclusion

Autistic people have the potential to bring to the world new ways of connecting intimately. We show through the very way that we are that the typical non-spectrum modes of displaying intimacy and connecting intimately are not the only methods. Love can be delivered and expressed in a variety of surprisingly effective and refreshingly creative acts that a non-spectrum person may never otherwise have thought of or previously have valued. Hoping and betting on a Prince Charming who can guess your mind and who always knows exactly what to do may not be the healthiest relationship ideal anyway.

We bring an opportunity for direct and honest communication, clear expectations, and realistic boundaries. All people can benefit from these gifts and from a wider range of options for sharing feelings and expressing closeness, which is something unique that we bring to the world.

■ ■ ■

Chapter 10

Keeping Ourselves Safe

The statistic most often quoted at autism workshops and conferences is that 80% of women on the spectrum will experience sexual abuse and/or violence in their lifetimes, 65% at the hands of men they know or who are entrusted with their care. I have no idea where this statistic comes from. Although I lack statistics for autistic men, anecdotal evidence suggests that they also find themselves at greater risk for danger than the general population. Autistic men and women who know the facts of life and who have been told what is safe – and what is not – still often find themselves in harm's way. Women and men on the spectrum tell stories about trusted teachers, friends, co-workers, bosses, officials, and even partners, taking advantage of them in very similar ways. Inadvertently running right into trouble is a common theme in our lives.

Our trusting nature and our autistic way of thinking are some of the reasons why we are at greater risk. We don't see hidden intentions. We are likely to miss any forewarning of danger expressed nonverbally or via body language. Clues from tone of voice or posture are likely to go unnoticed. Generalizing is another problem. We may understand a large, broad rule such as, "Don't go home with a stranger," but may not be able to apply this to a slightly different situation such as going home with someone *you just met*. If you've met, then the other person is no longer a stranger, literally speaking. Making deliberate, conscious choices in open-ended situations can also be challenging because we can't rely on concrete answers to our present dilemma. Lastly, we may have a hard time interpreting and expressing our own feelings and motives, which can cause us to make poor decisions, react too slowly, or unintentionally encourage others to take advantage of our vulnerability.

Four Reasons Why Autistic People Are at Greater Risk of Social Danger

1. We miss social clues hidden in tone of voice, body language, and innuendo that could forewarn of danger.

2. We can't generalize to a new situation well, especially a situation that in our minds is unique.

3. We have a hard time deliberating over choices, especially those that do not have concrete or obvious consequences.

4. We have trouble determining our feelings and motives, especially if we must do so quickly, making it hard to decide what to do in many social situations.

We do have to go out into the world. Even in relatively "safe" locations you will be approached by others – some familiar, some who are strangers – often close to home, in the usual places like school, the movie theater, the store where you work, the swim club. Sometimes you will want these exchanges; at other times, you won't. Take care of yourself physically and sexually. You have the right to say no to unwanted affection or sexual activity and not to do dangerous things like going home with somebody you just met who is no longer a stranger per se but who is still completely unfamiliar.

Those of us on the spectrum have to make our own choices and mistakes when it comes to relationships, dating, and sexuality. We can't stay sheltered forever. Other people can't make choices in life for us. Unless we lock ourselves indoors, we're bound to experience the normal hurts and bumps and bruises and heartaches and mistakes that everyone – off and on the spectrum – goes through to learn what – and maybe who – we really want in life. No one can take this volition away from us just because we have a disability. That would violate our dignity. But what is true volition and what is a consequence of special challenges stemming from the way we think?

While those not on the spectrum can use the safety strategies in this chapter, the suggestions described below are designed to address the core autistic trait that can make it challenging for autistic people to avoid serious social danger: a deficit in interpreting and responding to social language. Unfortunately, I do not have a magic formula or an easy way to stay safe all the time. But I can share my experiences and what I have learned from them. The suggestions and strategies can help you navigate through a world that is dangerous enough – and all the more so when you have the kind of social skills deficits that go along with autism. While most of these strategies may be used by both men and women, two sections at the end of the chapter address some of the unique issues women face.

Understanding Emergency Services

You may be asking, what does getting familiar with emergency services have to do with keeping ourselves safe? The answer is *everything*. The goal in life is to avoid getting oneself into emergency situations in the first place. But emergencies do happen. As with all things social, practice is important for those of us on the spectrum. We need to know how to avail ourselves of the help emergency departments can offer and how to respond to emergency personnel as part of protecting ourselves from potentially dangerous situations.

Police

You are more likely to call the police if you understand what they do and why they exist. Most people "get" it automatically that if you have a problem, you call the police. They show up in a special car, then they get out and try to help you. Most autistic people, on the other hand, do not automatically "get" anything about society. In addition to potentially not realizing that you can call the police when you are in trouble, some of us may have absorbed negative images of police officers from TV shows and movies. You're not likely to call the police department if, from all you can tell, they will show up and possibly hurt you. But TV is not reality. Police exist to help everyone and anyone when you are facing a dire emergency.

Because unfamiliar places and unfamiliar routines can cause great anxiety for some on the spectrum, it is wise to gather as much knowledge about true emergency situations as possible before an emergency happens.

You may not know that police can help in other ways, too. If you are lost, a police officer can give you directions. If you are walking home at night on a college campus or from work and someone is following you or bothering you, a police officer can escort you home. These extra roles police officers play are not always obvious, but you can approach an officer with your problems and he will help you.

Because unfamiliar places and unfamiliar routines can cause great anxiety for some on the spectrum, it is wise to gather as much knowledge about true emergency situations as possible before an emergency happens. Visit your local police station or precinct. See what it looks like. Watch what happens so the scene is not totally unfamiliar if you should wind up there for some reason.

Do you have to stop at a front desk first? Do you go right to a police officer who takes down your complaint? Do you have to wait a long time for someone to answer your questions? Is it crowded or noisy? Is there a bathroom? Are the police officers and other people who work there friendly? Know how to walk there. Know how to call the police at the local precinct in addition to calling 911.

Since you usually can't just walk right into a police station and look around, explain that you have a disability and that you want to be familiar with the police station in case you have an emergency. Tell them that unfamiliar locations can cause you incredible stress, so you want to gain familiarity with the environment. If they say they are too busy to show you around, agree to come back when it isn't busy. You don't want to be rude or get in the way.

Fire

Just as it is important to gain familiarity with what police officers do and what police stations are like, you should also know what firefighters do. Fire stations usually have community days when you can see what a firefighter looks like in uniform. Any person in his or her right mind who woke up in the middle of a crisis to find somebody dressed in bright yellow clothing carrying enormous tubes, shouting instructions, and wearing a scary rubber mask would be terrified beyond belief. Now imagine trying to cope with sensory overload, unfamiliarity, and confusion on top of the terror of a dire emergency. Finding out what firefighters look and sound like in advance could be the crucial difference between cooperating or dying.

Along these lines, listen once to what your fire alarm sounds like. Fire alarms are an absolute autistic nightmare, sending almost all of us way beyond our sensory limitations. But better to hear it once when not under stress, with ear plugs and a friend who can shut it off right away, than not recognize the sound in a crisis and collapse in sensory distress because you don't realize the significance of the noise. If you live in a place where the alarm automatically notifies the fire department, call first to tell them you're just doing a test.

Also, if someone is trying to hurt you or follow you, or otherwise bother you, while you are on the street, you may not be able to get to a pay phone or use your cell phone to call for help. But almost all street corners have a fire alarm that you can pull. You may hesitate to pull an unfamiliar alarm that is going to hurt your ears terribly, but these alarms summon help quickly. You may be able to save yourself from being stalked, mugged, or raped by pulling one.

Ambulance

Get familiar with medical emergency responders, too. Again, most hospitals or ambulance corps hold "open house" or community days when you can see and hear an ambulance, see what a paramedic looks like, and watch what paramedics do if you are hurt. You can touch the equipment so you know what a stretcher feels like or what an oxygen mask feels like against your skin. Being familiar with ambulances will come in handy should you ever need assistance. Instead of running from the horrible noise and the strange people, or resisting medical equipment that is hard to deal with on a sensory level, you'll know that the intention is to help you. Familiarity may ease some of the initial panic.

Responding to Emergency Officers

While familiarity with what police, fire, and medical emergency people do, what they sound and look like, and what equipment they use is absolutely essential for people on the spectrum, a balanced approach is necessary. Autistic people need to know how to respond to emergency personnel and how to handle their demands. See the boxes below and on the following page for information on how to respond to police officers and what to do if you are questioned by the police.

Police officers are usually helpful and friendly. The information to follow in this paragraph is not intended in any way to disrespect police officers, the vast majority of whom are honest people who want to help all members of society. But it is true that those of us on the spectrum are particularly vulnerable to the one or two officers who unfortunately are not morally scrupulous or helpful. If you don't have a friend with you and an officer seems to be yelling at you or being mean to you, try to move into view of other people. If others can see

How to Respond to a Police Officer

If a police officer shouts at you, "Don't move! Police!" immediately put your hands in the air and face him. If you are on the spectrum, you are likely to take the command, "Don't move!" literally, freezing in place, with your back still to the police officer, which can be viewed by the officer as non-cooperation.

Several youth in American cities have been shot by police officers due to confusion regarding police orders. If a police officer has told you not to move but then requests your I.D., your driver's license, or your wallet, tell him where it is – don't reach for it under any circumstances! If you reach into your pocket or purse to get the requested item, the police officer may think you are reaching for a gun or a weapon and shoot you to prevent danger to himself. Say, "Officer, my wallet is in my pocket. You can reach into my pocket and get it." Or, "Officer, my license is in my purse, which is on the ground over there. You can get the purse and take the license out of it." Stand still, keep your hands in the air, and don't change your mind.

What to Do If You Are Questioned by the Police

You also need to learn when to tell the police what's going on versus when to stay quiet. Usually, the only answer to any questions from the police should be, "I have the right to talk to a lawyer first." Because autistic people are particularly vulnerable, a police officer may press incriminating statements out of you even if you are completely innocent. We do not understand subtleties, "double meanings," implications, or ulterior motives. If you look different from most people or if you have a strange voice, you will stand out. Stay quiet unless you must tell the police officer that you are injured, need help, or are being attacked by someone.

If the police officer says things like, "You have to tell me right now or you'll be in trouble," or "It's the law – you have to say what you saw," remain firm. Repeat over and over, "I have to talk to my lawyer first."

The law and your rights are very confusing. Don't get in trouble just because you say something by accident. Keep quiet. You may balk at this suggestion because you don't have a lawyer, you did see what happened, the police seem to need your help to catch the crook, etc., etc. But it must be drilled into your head as an absolute rule that you should say nothing until you have a chance to talk to a lawyer or a family member.

If you keep saying, "I have a right to talk to my lawyer first," the police officer will stop trying to make you answer questions. He will either let you go, or he will put you in handcuffs and take you to the police station. He may read you a list of your rights, called "Miranda Rights." You may wait at the police station for a very long time, sometimes in a room by yourself. But eventually you will be allowed to talk to a lawyer, your parents, or your spouse. Since most of us do not have lawyers, the police station will provide you with a volunteer lawyer, at least until you decide if you want to hire your own. I cannot repeat this enough – you need to keep quiet until you get a chance to talk to your family or a lawyer.

you, the officer is less likely to threaten you or your possessions. If nobody else is around, tell the police officer that you want another officer present. Explain that you will cooperate with him when the second officer arrives. Be polite but firm. A police officer is less likely to hurt you or be mean to you if another police officer is on the scene.

It is unfortunate but true that we have to learn how to defend ourselves in cases of fraud or abuse. Several cases have been reported of women being raped and murdered by criminals in fake police uniforms driving fake police cars, who ordered the women to step out of the car for a drunk driving test or some other fraudulent reason.

Whether you are a man or a woman, if a police officer walks up to your car and says you must step outside, call 911 on your cell phone first and ask if the county or town has sent somebody out from the local police force.

Whether you are a man or a woman, if a police officer walks up to your car and says you must step outside, call 911 on your cell phone first and ask if the county or town has sent somebody out from the local police force. If not, stay in the car despite what the person tells you and ask 911 for immediate assistance. If you don't have a cell phone, stay in your car no matter what and ask the officer making the request to send out a second patrol car. Tell him you will cooperate when the second patrol car arrives. If he is not a legitimate officer, he won't be able to do this, so you'll know it's time to drive away quickly. Drive to the nearest busy street, supermarket or other location and honk excessively. This will alert others that you are in trouble. Stay in your car and wait for legitimate police officials to arrive.

Women have also been molested by criminals in fake firefighter uniforms who insist they must inspect the house because a neighbor reports the smell of smoke. Some men have been robbed in the same manner. If any emergency official shows up at your home when you did not call for help, tell the person to wait outside for a moment, close and lock your front door, and then call your local police to find out if indeed emergency personnel are supposed to be at your home and for what reason. The police will either confirm that emergency personnel are supposed to be there or they will say they don't know why this official has shown up. If they don't know, insist that the police come to your home to investigate before you open the door again.

Another possible tactic if this unannounced official is acting like his mission is urgent and he must inspect your home immediately, which may be true if there is a fire, is to call a neighbor or knock on a neighbor's door. Have the neighbor stand with you while the official begins his investigation. Still call the police and confirm the legitimacy of the visit. It is unfortunate that we have to be on guard. Your safety is very important. While your instinct is to trust uniformed officials, be careful if someone makes a surprise visit.

Lastly, the issue of body searches must be addressed. A woman who must undergo a body search has the right to demand that a female police officer conduct the search. Do not agree to be searched on your body by a man. Even when a woman is going to search you, make sure at least one other police woman or official is in the room with you or standing nearby. Do not give in if the police tell you there is no police woman to do the search. They have to find a female officer or an equivalent female official to do the search. Men, too, should complain if a search ever makes them feel uncomfortable.

Explaining Your Disability to Emergency Personnel and Emergency Service Centers

If you display certain behaviors that could be confusing to others in emergency situations, notify your local 911 control center that you have a disability and explain what may happen when you call them. I learned about this from a friend who lives in upstate New York. In my friend's case, if a 911 call is placed from his phone, the 911 department knows that sometimes he loses his voice in a crisis. They know they should send emergency personnel, even if they don't hear anything on his end of the line. They also know that they may find him hiding in a dark confined space, unable to talk, or very slow to answer questions, particularly if he is traumatized or overstimulated. They are instructed in advance to take the situation seriously even if his behavior appears confusing or unusual to them.

Along these lines, it is a wise idea to carry an Emergency Card in your wallet that you can give to a police officer, a paramedic, a firefighter, or some other official if you've called for help and suddenly find yourself unable to talk, unable to process questions, or whatever else happens to you. The card should briefly explain that you are autistic and then describe what accommodations you require or what behaviors emergency personnel may see. The card should also list the things that help you calm down and communicate.

Sample Emergency Card

Hello, my name is Beatrice. I am autistic. I have an extreme sensitivity to light. Please do not remove my sunglasses under any circumstances.

Also, when I am under stress, I rock back and forth. If I seem unable to answer questions, give me a few extra minutes to answer.

Thank you for your understanding. If you would like more information about autism, just ask me.

Also, always carry a Safety Tool Kit with you. The items on the list below will help you in a variety of emergency situations. Most of the items are small and easy to carry around in a large pocket, a purse, a backpack, or your briefcase.

Safety Tool Kit

- A cell phone to make calls in an emergency
- Lots of quarters or a prepaid phone card if you don't have a cell phone
- A whistle to blow if you are in danger and can't get to a phone or can't talk
- A flashlight so even if it is dark, you can see where you are going (you can buy very small flashlights)
- Your Safe Activities List – a list of alternative activities you know are safe that you can steer people toward if you are invited to do things you aren't sure about (this will be explained on page 257)
- Your Buddies List – a list of Buddies, even just one or two, who will join you for activities (see page 262)
- Your Helpers List – a list of a few trusted Helpers you can turn to for advice (see page 263)
- A Personal Information Card with your name, your address, and the phone number of a family member or friend, in case you find it difficult to remember under stress or can't talk
- Your Emergency Card (see pages 255-256) – you can combine this with your Personal Information Card
- Some cash in case you have to take a cab, buy emergency medication like aspirin, or purchase food during an unexpected delay in your plans

In addition to being familiar with emergency services and carrying a Safety Tool Kit, you can use certain strategies to stay safe when socializing with friends, going on dates, or just going about your usual activities. Because those of us on the spectrum tend to have trouble decoding social nuances and generalizing rules to unique situations, the strategies I invented and included in this chapter are designed to create a safety system you can rely on even without strong social skills.

Using a Safe Activities List

Make a Safe Activities List of dating or friendship activities. Then if you are approached by someone who suggests doing an activity you are not sure is totally safe, pick one from your Safe Activities List and invite him to do this alternative activity instead. Review your Safe Activities List frequently. Carry it with you in your Safety Tool Kit. Add to it or change it as your life changes. Friends and family can offer suggestions, too. Everybody's list is going to be different. Make sure the things on your Safe Activities List are things you like doing, in addition to being safe. When making your Safe Activities List, use your imagination. You can always find something fun to do that is also safe, depending on where you live and what your interests are.

Be sure to practice offering to do things from your Safe Activities List with family and friends first. Once you get the hang of it, you'll be able to respond with more ease to social invitations you aren't so sure about.

Sample Safe Activities List

- Invite the person to watch my basketball games on Friday nights. The gym is crowded and all my friends are around.
- Walk to Dave's Ice Cream Shop from the college campus if it is still daylight. The road is busy, and Dave's Ice Cream Shop has a pay phone in case I need to call someone to pick me up if things go bad.
- Invite the person to go for a swim in the community pool. The pool is always full of people, including a lot of moms and kids, and the lifeguard is always there.
- Invite the person to go to the library. It's well lit, it's quiet, and it's fun to look for books together.
- Invite the person to come over to my home for a snack, to study for a test together, or to play video games, but only when other family members are home.
- Invite the person to go to my favorite after-school club.
- Meet at church/synagogue services or get-togethers.
- Have lunch together in the college cafeteria.
- Ask the person to go to a coffee shop for coffee.

Spotting Bad Maybes

In any given situation, you can create a quick list of things that might happen, both good and bad. These are your "Maybes." If you can think of even just one single Bad Maybe – get away. You don't need to be sure! As long as you see one single possible negative Maybe, leave the situation or get help immediately.

Listing your Maybes is not that hard. In your mind, run through the things that might or could happen. Using three hypothetical situations, I will demonstrate how listing Maybes can be used as a safety tactic.

Spotting Bad Maybes: Example 1

You're getting ready to leave school at the end of a long day. A boy you don't know comes up to you and introduces himself. He seems very friendly. You chat with him for a few minutes. He's cute. He asks you if you would like to go downtown and get a soda. Run through the Maybes in your mind and list them:

- Maybe you'd have a lot of fun.
- Maybe you'd really like each other and fall in love.
- Maybe he could help you with your stupid French homework, since he said he's good at languages.
- *Maybe walking to town you'd be all alone on an empty stretch of road, and he would try to hurt you. No one would be around to help.*
- Maybe he's a nice guy, and you'd wind up being friends.
- *Maybe he's just trying to lure you out of the school building, when his friends will jump on you and steal your wallet.*

Can you spot the two Bad Maybes in this example? (They are in italics.) As long as you have one Bad Maybe, don't do it. That is the absolute rule. You do not need to interpret his behavior, his body language, the innuendos in his statements, or his tone of voice. You spotted a Bad Maybe. That's all you need to know to make your decision. You can offer to do something with him from your Safe Activities List that you made in advance. Instead, you could tell him, "Gee, I'd love to, but I can't today. Would you like to meet me for lunch in the cafeteria tomorrow though?" You don't have to be mean or ruin your social life if you do like him. You can use your Safe Activities List to engage in activities you know are safe. But you spotted a Bad Maybe, so don't go get that soda.

Spotting Bad Maybes: Example 2

Your science teacher invites you to stay after class to see his special experiment in his private lab down the hall. You really like your science teacher. You're majoring in biology, and you look up to him. He has always been very fair. You think he is a nice guy too. You'd love to see his lab. Quickly go through the Maybes in your mind and make your mental list:

- Maybe his experiment would be really cool, and you'd have a good time checking out his lab.
- Maybe he's inviting you to see his lab because he thinks you are the best student in the class.
- Maybe he'll offer you a job as lab assistant.
- *Maybe once alone in the lab he will try to kiss you and you won't be able to get away.*

Can you spot the one Bad Maybe? Your science teacher might be a great guy. His lab might be really cool. He might want to offer you a job or collaborate with you because he thinks you are a genius. He might want to kiss you against your will and no one would be around to help. DING! One Bad Maybe and that's your cue: Don't go. You can still be polite if you like your teacher. You could say something nice like, "I'd love to see your lab. Maybe you could show us your lab during normal class time. I'm sure some of the other kids would like to see it, too." But as soon as you spot a Bad Maybe, leave – even if you think he is the nicest teacher in the whole world.

Spotting Bad Maybes: Example 3

You are in a bar. A nice man comes up and sits next to you. You start talking. You like each other. He buys you a beer. You wind up talking practically all night, you dance to a few songs, and you are really attracted to him. He invites you to spend the night at his place. It sounds romantic and fun. People on TV have affairs all the time, right? Well, list the Maybes:

- Maybe you'd go back to his house and have a wonderful night of romance.
- Maybe he would be great in bed.
- *Maybe he would force you to do sexual things you don't like to do.*
- Maybe he would turn out to be the sweetest guy in the world and become your husband.
- Maybe it would turn out he loves *Star Trek* as much as you do, as evidenced by the giant Spock poster in his kitchen.
- *Maybe he would hurt you physically or rob you.*
- *Maybe he is married and is cheating on his wife.*

Run through your list of Maybes. Obviously, you can see a few Bad Maybes. That's it. Don't go home with him.

Again, since you do like him and you want to be nice, you can ask him to do something fun from your Safe Activities List. You could say, "I'd love to. You are really cute. I'd like to get to know you. Since we don't know each other that well yet, would you like to meet me for coffee at Starbucks tomorrow?" But don't take chances with your life. It's not worth it.

By now, you see how listing your Maybes works. Making a mental list of your Maybes only takes a split second. Practice until you are really good at listing the Maybes for all sorts of hypothetical situations. Try listing Maybes for things you see on TV, things you hear about in the news, situations you read about in books and magazines, things that happen around you, and situations that could come up in your life. You can practice by yourself, with your parents, or with a trusted friend. Ask your family or friends to help you list Maybes for pretend situations so you'll be an expert when it comes time to do so in a real-life moment. Even if you can't

Make a list of Buddies you can trust. If you don't really have any friends, you can ask your parents or siblings to help you locate one or two classmates or neighbors who would be willing to do the Buddy System with you.

list every possible Maybe, you will be able to come up with the basic Maybes, like *Maybe he would hurt me and nobody would be there to help me*. That's a very understandable possibility and doesn't require a lot of contextual understanding or abstraction.

NOTE: Remember the important rule: As long as one Bad Maybe shows up on the list, it's time to get out, go away, say no thanks, or offer something from your Safe Activities List instead. That's the rule. Don't second-guess yourself. Sometimes, you will have a few Good Maybes and a few Bad Maybes. What you are doing is protecting yourself against future possibilities. So you might spot a few Good Maybes, but don't take a chance if there is even one Bad Maybe.

Developing a Buddy System

Bring a friend. It's that simple. Chances are if someone asks you to do something but you can't bring a friend, it is not a situation you want to go into. Even if you think your gym teacher, your neighbor, your boss, or that cute guy on the football team is really cool and you are excited to be invited to do something, be on the safe side and bring a Buddy.

Remember Example 1 where a boy you just met asks you to join him for a soda downtown? Ask him if your friend can come, too. You could say, "Do you mind if I ask my friend Sara to come? She and I walk home together sometimes." If the boy says he doesn't want your friend along, that's weird. Why does somebody you just met want to be alone with you so quickly?

And remember Example 2 where your science professor invites you to see his private lab? Ask him if your best friend Sue, one of the Buddies on your list, can see it, too. You could say something like, "I know Sue would love to see your lab, too! Can we see it during break tomorrow?" If your science teacher says your friend can't see his lab or acts terribly disappointed that you won't go with him alone, that signals a problem.

Make a list of Buddies you can trust. If you don't really have any friends, you can ask your parents or siblings to help you locate one or two classmates or neighbors who would be willing to do the Buddy System with you. Carry a list of the phone numbers of your Buddies. If you are all alone and somebody asks you to do something you aren't sure about, you can always say, "Let me call my friend Tina and see if she wants to join us!" Usually if the person has bad intentions, he won't want Tina to come and that's a clue to get away.

Turning to Others for Help

In addition to familiarizing yourself with emergency responders and always using specific safety strategies such as the ones outlined above, another very important practice that can help you remain safe is to share what is going on in your life with one or two people whom you trust. You can get advice and input from these people. They can help you steer clear of unhealthy dating situations or awkward social mishaps. By sharing your life with others, you'll also learn to recognize and explain your feelings, which can help you when it comes time to make important life decisions.

Because connecting to others is usually not a strong instinct for those of us on the spectrum, we may not realize we can turn to other people – even in moments of crisis. We may want to turn to somebody for help or support, but not know how. Rules can act as a guideline for when and why to talk to someone else. It may seem crazy to form rules about getting help, something most people do naturally without a thought. But the social exchange of giving and taking help is not an obvious or intrinsic activity for most of us on the spectrum.

The following rules of turning to someone else are only a starting point. They fall into two broad categories: Some rules cover when to turn to people; some cover what to turn to people about. Modify the rules to fit your life situation. Post the rules in an obvious spot if necessary. The purpose as outlined above is to encourage the kind of dialogue and sharing that can help you avoid common social pitfalls and navigate away from bad situations and bad choices.

Rules for When to Turn to Someone Else

Generally speaking, it is a good idea to turn to someone you trust when you experience new feelings, new situations, or unexpected social events. The following list is only a guide for when it is important to turn to someone. You will have to modify it according to situations that occur in your life or that make more sense for you.

When to Turn to Somebody

- Tell somebody when something bad happens to you, or if you aren't sure whether it's bad.
- Tell somebody when something good happens to you, or if you aren't sure whether it's good.
- Tell somebody when a stranger or acquaintance is requesting social or sexual activity that you do not want.
- Tell somebody when something happens to you that is confusing or making you feel bad.
- Tell somebody when you experience intense, new, or special feelings such as worry, fear, confusion, excitement, or romantic interest.
- Tell somebody when you are feeling great or feeling really awful.

Rules for What to Turn to People About

Most people turn to each other to discuss relationships, social life, and emotions. Turning to people about the following list of subjects will help you beyond just getting advice. You can learn a lot by watching a person's reaction to what you share. Is the person you turn to surprised? Happy for you? Concerned? Because those of us on the spectrum sometimes have difficulty realizing what is expected or reasonable when it comes to socializing and relationships, the reaction of the person you turn to can provide important clues as to what is healthy or typical.

What to Turn to Others For

- Tell someone what is happening in your romantic relationship. Are you happy, or are you having trouble?
- Tell someone what is happening at work or school. Are things going well, or are you running into difficulty?
- Tell someone what is going on with you emotionally. Are you satisfied with your life, or are you very lonely, bored, or frustrated?
- Tell someone what things confuse you.
- Tell someone what things you enjoy.
- Tell someone what problems you are working on or trying to overcome.

Sharing these topics with somebody you trust, or other topics you might think of that are more applicable to your life, will also give you practice discussing your inner life. You might be thinking, what does this have to do with safety? The answer is that when you can communicate how you feel, how you are doing, what you want out of life, or which areas of life you need help with, you will be better prepared to navigate social issues as they arise. For example, if a stranger approaches you for a date, you will recognize this as a slightly uncomfortable situation that warrants checking in with someone you trust first. If you fall madly in love with somebody at work, this is also something that would be good to discuss with a trusted family member or friend before acting on the feeling.

Learning when to talk to somebody and what to talk about can increase your emotional communication skills, in turn preventing you from making hasty social decisions and reducing the risk of winding up in an unsafe or awkward social situation.

How to Ask for Help

Turning to others is a vital skill that we need to acquire through practice. The rules outlined above, modified to fit your situation, suggest when it is a good idea to share what is going on in your life with somebody you trust and what topics are good to discuss with them to make sure you are doing O.K. But it may not be enough to intellectually understand when and why to seek the advice, opinions, and help of others. You may not know *how* to do so.

Very young autistic children don't seek out adults when they hurt themselves on the playground, get teased, can't tie a shoe, lose a pencil, or don't understand the rules of a game. They tend to withdraw or act out. It is absolutely critical to figure out how to ask for help because we do not magically acquire these skills by osmosis like other people.

The best way to learn how to ask for help is by observing the process in action. In your daily life, watch closely and observe people asking for help. Then practice yourself. Make a game of it. For example, you can go to a local store and watch people asking the clerks for help. Then try it yourself. If you're buying soap and can't find the price, say clearly to a clerk, "I can't figure out how much this soap costs. I need help." Keep practicing until you are comfortable going up to someone and stating that you require assistance to deal with some problem.

If other members of your family are amenable to this, ask them if you can watch them asking for help. Also ask them if you can watch them helping each other when it comes to personal issues. For example, if your mother is going to have a talk with your sister because she got into a huge fight with her best friend, ask if you can sit in on the discussion. You can even ask them to point out what is happening along the way. For example, your mother could say, "Now your sister is describing what happened. This will give me a better idea of what went wrong and why they had a fight, so I can offer better advice." If necessary, break down the steps of asking for help and make a poster for your room or carry the steps on a small piece of paper in your pocket.

Steps of Asking for Help

1. Approach somebody to ask for help.
2. Tell what happened.
3. Ask questions.
4. Listen for advice.
5. Ask more questions if necessary.
6. Come to a conclusion.
7. Make a decision for the future.

Make a list of people you can go to for help and advice. Try to think of two or three people you trust the most in the whole world. These people will be your Helpers. They will listen to you when you come to them to discuss your life. If a Helper is doing something or she is busy, she will stop to listen to you. You do not have to be afraid to go to your Helpers with questions and issues. Write down the names and phone numbers of your Helpers on a piece of paper and carry the information with you if necessary.

Let your Helpers know that they are on your list so they will always be prepared to listen to you. Helpers need to recognize the monumental conscious effort it takes for an autistic person to reach out. Therefore, ask your Helpers to be receptive. Again, remind your Helpers that certain truths about a social situation that are completely obvious to them may not be obvious at all to you. That is why you are turning to them!

Sometimes you may know that you need help, or you may recognize that it is time to turn to somebody, but you can't figure out what questions to ask. Or maybe you are under too much stress to formulate questions. Making a list of basic questions in advance can be useful. If you are having trouble forming questions or talking, you can bring your question list to one of your Helpers and point to questions to jump start the discussion.

Also remember that sometimes, when you ask somebody you trust for advice, you may not like what they say. Yet, the response or advice

Sometimes in life it is a good idea to listen to other people's advice, even when to do so is difficult.

could be very important. Let's say you really love a certain guy. You think he is the coolest person on Earth. You've told a few people you trust so they can help you sort out your feelings. Things go well for a while. But then suddenly the guy stops calling you on the phone. You call him and leave messages but he never calls you back. You are very upset. You recognize that it is time to turn to your Helpers again.

In this case, your best friend, your mother, and your sister are your Helpers. All three of them keep telling you that his behavior is inappropriate. He should call you back. If he loves you, he should call you to say hello, see how you are doing, make plans with you, and chat. If he doesn't love you, he should still call to say he doesn't want to be your boyfriend right now. So, your best friend, your mother, and your sister try to explain to you that something is wrong with his behavior. They advise you to break up with him and move on.

This kind of news is difficult to handle. But if several people you trust are saying the same thing, they may be right. Sometimes in life it is a good idea to listen to other people's advice, even when to do so is difficult. Your family and friends care about you. You may disagree with them or you may not like what they have to say, but listen carefully. They probably have good advice that can protect you.

How Not to Talk to Others

It is just as important to figure out what things you do *not* talk to others about. Most people do not tell others the details of their intimate relationships. Society does not appreciate people who describe the private things they do in bed, for example. Society also discourages people from telling their partner's secrets. While it is just as vitally important that we learn to confide in someone regarding social experiences and relationships precisely because it is so difficult for us to gauge somebody else's behavior, it is just as important to protect our privacy and the privacy of our partner or spouse.

You can distinguish between what is O.K. to talk about and what is not O.K. to talk about by analyzing the method and purpose of the discussion. It is considered rude, for example, when someone tells just anybody about their private business. These people use the "blab" method of talking: They tell their neighbors, their friends – anyone who will listen. They often use vulgar language and are sometimes disrespectful and rude. They talk inappropriately about their private lives for negative reasons, for attention, or to show off.

On the other hand, it is completely acceptable to use the "polite" method of talking to turn to a few people you know you can trust – your mom, a best friend, a clergy member. You aren't showing off and you don't use dirty language. You can talk about sex and the body, but your words are respectful. In this case, you talk appropriately about your private life for positive reasons. You initiate a discussion because you need advice, you want to make sure you are doing O.K., you aren't sure how to tell if something is normal or healthy, or you need information to make good decisions.

If possible, a visualization of the difference can be extremely useful. Find a few scenes from bad movies where offensive people show off about their private lives in a negative way. Then find a few scenes from a tender movie where a daughter asks her mother for advice about a boyfriend, or a teenager asks her brother for dating advice. Can you see the difference? When examples come up in life or in the media, capitalize on them. Ask family and friends to help you determine if the examples you see are positive or negative demonstrations of one person turning to another.

Also realize that some behaviors and some words are O.K. in certain situations, but not in others. Every community has slightly different expectations. An acceptable word in one community may be considered vulgar in another, or some language may be O.K. to use with friends, but not at work. As embarrassing as it can be to discuss this with one of your Helpers, it is a lot less embarrassing than saying the wrong word. The only way to figure out what is acceptable is to ask someone you trust, another reason why it is a good idea to learn how and when to turn to somebody else for advice.

Knowing what you feel and what to do when you feel that way will enable you to respond to the social world quicker, more accurately, and with less confusion.

Knowing Your Feelings

Knowing your feelings as an aspect of keeping yourself safe was mentioned briefly in the previous section, *Turning to Others for Help*. Again, you may be wondering what knowing your feelings or sharing them with others has to do with personal safety. Learning how to turn to others, ask for help, and identify your emotions increases your social communication skills and improves your ability to make decisions about your personal life, a crucial component of keeping safe. But determining feelings and acting on them are usually conscious exercises for most autistic people. The following suggestions will help you learn how to identify your feelings and respond to the world appropriately based on them.

- **Begin by noticing carefully what you feel like physically and mentally when you are worried, scared, confused, or upset.**
  Do you cry? Do you get shaky? Do your thoughts race? Do you pace back and forth? Do you start talking to yourself, trying to sort everything out? These are very important signals. When you recognize these signals, you will know whether a given situation is positive or negative.

- **Make a list of your signals and carry it with you so you can check it if necessary.**
  If you are doing one of your worried, scared, upset, or confused signals, it is time to get help. Don't be embarrassed to have somebody you trust assist you in making a list of your signals. We all get upset and confused sometimes. We need to recognize our feelings so we can solicit help, get out of danger, or make healthy social choices.

The reverse is true for positive feelings. What are your signals when you like somebody? What are your signals when you want to be friends with somebody versus when you want to be romantic with someone? Do you smile a lot? Laugh? Get sweaty? Get quiet and shy?

Again, ask for assistance making your list of positive signals if necessary. You need to practice recognizing positive signals just as much as the negative ones. With experience, you'll learn to differentiate between people and experiences that are healthy and make you feel good, versus people and experiences that are unhealthy or dangerous.

Many autistic people say that charts and signs provide visual clues that are extremely useful for recognizing feelings. An Emotions Signal Chart such as the one Teresa Bolick describes and explains in her book, *Asperger Syndrome and Adolescence: Helping preteens and teens get ready for the real world* (see References on page 345), can prompt you to recognize the signals for various negative and positive emotions like fear and discomfort or happiness and romantic interest with words or pictures. The chart can additionally provide written or visual prompts to take specific actions when you feel certain emotions, such as soliciting help if you are scared. The chart could show a heart racing as the signal for fear, plus a telephone to indicate that it is time to talk about it with one of your Helpers. Signal Charts can be carried in your pocket and referred to as necessary. Take a look at the sample Emotions Signal Chart on page 272 and make up one of your own.

As you can see from the sample, an Emotions Signal Chart acts as a visual guide for recognizing your feelings and deciding what to do when they occur. Signals, descriptions, and actions will vary from person to person. Have someone you trust help you make your Emotions Signal Chart if you are stuck. You can also find more information about feelings charts in Teresa Bolick's book. Again, knowing what you feel and what to do when you feel that way will enable you to respond to the social world quicker, more accurately, and with less confusion.

Sample Emotions Signal Chart

Feeling	***Description***	***Signals***	***Action***
Worry	Not sure if everything is O.K., panicked, very anxious	Wave my arms around, pace, think about the issue over and over	Take time out to calm down and think, ask someone to help me, get away if I am too anxious
Fear	Afraid, scared of what might happen, frightened by a situation	Heart races, want to hide or run	Get away, call a Buddy
Confused	Not sure what is going on, not sure what to do, not sure how I feel, can't decide anything	Can't concentrate, too many questions, unable to continue socializing	Use a Comic Strip Story to decipher what happened or what might happen, list Maybes
Upset	Somebody hurt my feelings, plans fell apart, everything went wrong, something is bothering me a lot	Cry, talk to myself to sort it out, can't continue the current activity	Take a break until I feel better, use a Comic Strip Story to figure out what went wrong
Interest in someone for friendship	Want to spend time together, want to learn things about the other person, want to share activities	Happy, talking, having fun, laughing	Ask a Buddy to hang out with me and my new friend at first
Interest in someone for romance	Just dying to see her, can't wait to spend time together	Heart races (in a good way), palms sweat, forget what to say, can't stop thinking about her	Check in with a Helper to go over the situation and discuss safety and other issues

Self-Defense

Because a dangerous situation can happen anywhere at any time, it is a good idea to know how to defend yourself. Self-defense is a non-aggressive way of protecting yourself and heading off danger when you are attacked. In other words, learning how to defend yourself is not about fighting or being able to attack people you do not like. Several methods of learning or acquiring self-defense skill will be outlined briefly in this section.

Self-Defense Classes

One option is taking a self-defense class. At a self-defense class you will learn the best way to respond to an attacker. You might think kicking or hitting would be the best responses in an attack scenario, but that is not always the case. Most communities offer special self-defense courses tailored specifically for women. Men can also take self-defense courses.

Model Mugging Classes

A second option is to take a model mugging class where "attackers" in padded equipment pretend to mug or hurt participants, who get a chance to practice real defense techniques. A model mugging class can be great for autistic people: In addition to experiencing what an attacker looks and sounds like, your ability to identify danger will improve. The class allows you to try out the most effective methods of defense or escape, so you'll know ahead of time what works best for you. By taking such a class, your self-confidence that you can handle even the worst-case scenario increases.

A model mugging class can be scary and intense though. Watch a class once or twice before joining. I recommend explaining to the teacher that you are on the spectrum and what that means for you. For example, you may need special explanations of what is going on. Also, you may be confused by the defensive maneuvers that class members are practicing. For example, because of concrete thinking, you may wonder why a classmate is punching the model mugger if he didn't "pretend hurt" her yet, he only threatened to do so verbally. You may need the steps and reasons behind actions explained one at a time, broken down into sequential order, and repeated several times.

Martial Arts Classes

A third option is to take a basic martial arts class. Look for martial arts classes that include self-defense techniques. Knowing martial arts will help you learn more about your body's capabilities in addition to providing you with a self-defense method. Because so many different kinds of martial arts exist, watch a class or two before you sign up to make sure you want to join. You can always try a different style if you don't like the first.

Staying in Good Physical Shape

Lastly, staying in good physical shape will help you protect yourself better. Obviously, if you are in shape, you can run from danger. But the benefits go beyond physical feats. You will also feel better about your body and your life. When you are fit and satisfied with your life, you think more clearly and make better decisions. If you can take special self-defense classes or martial arts, that's great. If you can't, at least keep yourself healthy and feeling good.

Pretending as a Safety Technique

Since people on the spectrum have a hard time decoding social reality, the assumption is that it is very difficult for us to "pretend" various identities. But actually, most of us are adept imitators. When I was a child, I could mimic exactly the gestures, intonations, expressions, posture, and vocabulary of my teachers. And if I was around someone from the deep South, or London, for example, I would suddenly be able to speak with the person's accent! I could replicate the sounds, motions, and style of almost anybody. If you can do this, harness the skill and use it to keep safe.

What do I mean by this? For example, if someone is making unwelcome sexual advances on you, pretend you are married. If someone is trying to get you to go out on a date and you feel pressured, pretend you have to walk your dog, even if you don't have a dog. These are overly simplistic answers. But the point is that you can make a list of a few pretend characters and situations to use when you need to get out of a bad moment. You can practice with your parents and friends if this would help you get the hang of it.

One time I was the only passenger on a long-distance bus in the middle of the night. The driver started to chat with me. He was a nice guy, mid 50s, married (at least, he wore a wedding band). We talked about bus routes, bus schedules, and ticket policies. Out of the blue, as we approached my destination in Missouri, he asked me to continue on to Tennessee with him. He promised me a ride back to my city in the morning.

I knew it was too dangerous to go to an unfamiliar city with an unfamiliar person, even though he was in uniform. I told him my father was picking me up and that I couldn't. This wasn't true. But a father carries a lot of authority. If I hadn't known that it was alright to pretend and make up a fake story, I might have wound up in a lot of trouble. Autistic people tend to communicate directly. We say what we think. We tell the truth. We don't always see why it could be necessary to lie. Somehow, without becoming a dishonest person, it is important for you to figure out how to pretend to get out of difficult situations.

Safety Tools and Methods – A Review

Using the above example where a bus driver tried to get me to drive through the night alone with him to a place I had never been, ostensibly just to chat, all of the safety strategies and tools explained in this chapter so far could have been applied and used to stay out of danger. For example, if it turned out that indeed I liked the driver and found him friendly and interesting, I could have used a Safe Activities List and suggested meeting for coffee at a crowded diner the next time he was traveling through my town. Whether or not I liked him, I easily could have listed my Maybes:

- Maybe I'll get to see Tennessee, a state I've never been to.
- Maybe he is really just trying to be friendly and we'll have a good talk on the drive.

- Maybe he is going to pull over on the side of the road and try to hurt me, and I'll have no way to get help.

- Maybe he has a bad reputation I don't know about, despite being a professional in uniform. I could list more, but I already spotted at least two Bad Maybes. Remember the rule: If you have one Bad Maybe on the list, it's time to get away.

I could also have checked my Emotions Signal Chart. My heart was racing just slightly and I had a little anxiety in my stomach, clues that something isn't comfortable or good. These signals tell me to back away from the situation and get help. I could have called a Buddy or a Helper. In those days, cell phones were not popular yet. But today, it is easy to carry a cell phone. If you are on a low budget, consider getting a cheap, pre-paid cell phone that comes with a block of minutes you can renew. You'll at least be able to use it in an emergency.

I did consider calling the police. But the town I was going to is extremely rural and at least at that time there were no local police stations. I knew the county had a sheriff, but I did not know the number of the sheriff's office. With hindsight, it would have been a good idea to have brought that number with me. If you are planning a trip to a strange place, call the city government in advance and get a list of emergency numbers in addition to 911 that you can call if you have trouble.

Even if I had called the county sheriff, it would have taken him over a half an hour to arrive. This is why alternative skills – recognizing danger, making decisions, using pretend stories to get out of a bad spot, lying to save yourself, and realizing your feelings and acting on them – are crucial survival skills in addition to knowing how to summon the police. People won't always be around to help. Somehow, without destroying what is positive and good about our autistic way of being, we need to learn these concrete methods of keeping safe.

Media vs. Reality

I hear over and over again from autistic people that they have taken cues about the world from TV and movies, especially when it comes to romance and dating. It is true that certain TV shows and certain movies can provide you with some useful social information and visual examples of how people interact in different scenarios. But to somebody with a literal mind, concrete thinking, an inability to generalize, and trouble with abstraction, TV is just about the worst place imaginable to pick up your dating lessons. People on TV have affairs, lie, and hurt each other all the time – sometimes with no consequences. Love on TV seems so easy – meet, fall in love, live happily ever after. Romance is exciting and dramatic. Family life is condensed and simple. Nothing on the TV can really prepare someone for the reality of dating, relationships, and family responsibilities.

At the age of 15, about when I began to go into the world seeking adult social interaction, I had absolutely no clues about dating or love. By comparison, my middle sister somehow knew what the lingo meant, what the different levels of dating were, what the different stages of a relationship entailed, how to tell if someone liked her, how to tell if someone was worthy of liking in a romantic sense – in short, how to navigate through the world as a social person. I have no idea how she knew so much. Granted, she still had to go into the world and test out what would work for her and what wouldn't. But she still had an inner sense of what it was all about.

The first time a boy asked me out, I couldn't figure out why he wanted to go outside – it was pouring rain. Children not on the spectrum absorb a lot from their environments, from their parents, and from the couples and families in the community surrounding them. But autistic people do not learn by osmosis.

I had very vague notions about friendship and love. Because I heard people talking about loving each other forever and most songs on the radio echoed this sentiment, I assumed in a literal way that being in love was a feeling you felt all the time. This made no sense to me. I knew that

I wasn't happy 24 hours a day. I also knew that sometimes I was sad, but the sad feeling dissipated – usually within a few hours or a few days. So if you were in love with someone forever, did you ever get a break from that feeling? How could you have a feeling 24 hours a day? And what if you got mad at the person – would you still have the "in love" feeling in addition to the pissed-off feeling?

I could see from watching other teenagers at school that people could date casually or seriously. Some were "seeing" each other, some were "going steady," and some were "involved." What was the difference, if each case had to do with one person liking the other in a romantic way? Did you talk about different subjects if you were dating casually as opposed to being involved? Did you do different activities? Did you call them on the phone every day or once a week? Where could you get this knowledge?

I also did not understand what two people in love actually did with each other that was any different from what two people ordinarily did together. Sure, people who were in love had sex, or at least this was the standing assumption. But so did people who weren't in love. Whether or not you were in love, you could still go to the movies with somebody, go to dinner, or live in the same house, I reasoned. So perhaps the difference was that the two people in love just felt special toward each other. But this led in a circuitous route back to my first dilemma – how could you have a special feeling for somebody every single moment of your entire life, forever?

As I mentioned, TV and movies were fairly useless sources for obtaining information to clarify my confusion. The only thing that ever helped me understand the different kinds of social or romantic connections people make with each other was watching and observing the real lives of real people around me like a keen scientist. I had the amazing fortune of winding up in situations where I got to see first-hand the more intimate and complex details of people's lives. How did they talk to each other? How did they react to each other? How did they share themselves? How did they deal with different feelings? How did they deal with changes?

Try some of the suggestions below to gain a firmer understanding of social reality.

- **Quiz the people in your immediate life,** if they are open and willing to divulge the answers. For example, ask a parent, a sibling, or a friend how she feels about her spouse. Does she feel this way 24 hours a day? How does she know she still loves him if sometimes she gets angry at him? What does she do when she has these types of negative feelings toward him? How long do the negative feelings last in different cases? How do they negotiate what to do each day? Does she know everything about her husband, or do people keep some things private? Does he tell her every single thing that happens to him while he is away from her? How does he know which things to share, how much to share, when to share? In short: How do you have a life with somebody?

  Keep going: How did they meet? Did bells go off and the whole city light up – the way it does in the movies? Or did they have to get to know each other over time? Did they ever hurt each other's feelings? How did they make up? Did they love every single thing about each other (rare) or did they have to learn to accept the not-so-great parts of each person's personality? Did they automatically know they would get married? Even if they were sure, didn't they also ask someone for an opinion? How did they make the decisions that led to a life together?

- **Consider asking somebody you trust to break "dating" and "love" into concrete steps across the lifespan for you,** again always citing specific examples. See if you can find someone to outline the types of interactions you can expect at different ages. Practice the language. Ask for a description of what people do on dates – assuming different levels of involvement. What does it mean to make a commitment to someone? What does that entail? What actually goes on between the two people who are romantically involved in different scenarios and contexts?

Sure, dating and relationships can be lots of fun, but relationships also entail a lot of work. They take time to develop, and the fun is usually a lot less racy than the fun you see in the media.

- **Be sure to ask about the "ins and outs" of relationships if you find someone who is willing to talk to you.** Relationships take a lot of work. An actual example of relationships in different stages, at different points of responsibilities and decisions, with different styles of communication and effectiveness, is crucial for gaining a sense of what *really* goes on in life. The only way you can find out for yourself is by asking others and by observing closely how people interact with each other.

Again, the point isn't to find abstract information about the facts of life. We've all seen plenty of people on TV falling in love, having sex, and going on dates. The point is to make real what it is *actually like* for average people in daily life. It's not like on TV, when everything is fun and groovy and life is worked out by the end of the show. It's not like on TV, when you can be dating three different people and just see your kids every other weekend. It's not like in the movies, when cute boys ask you to surf and then you're the most popular girl on the beach. It's not like in the music videos, when you can just ring someone's doorbell with a surprise bouquet of flowers and then all your problems are solved.

People have real responsibilities that match real feelings. We need images, words, and examples. Sure, dating and relationships can be lots of fun, but relationships also entail a lot of work. They take time to develop, and the fun is usually a lot less racy than the fun you see in the media. The goal is to provide a framework for life, a context for feelings and decisions that is grounded in reality as opposed to the two-dimensional world of the media. You need to know and see what is usual, what is not usual, what is acceptable in your community and what is not, and what actually goes on when two people interact with each other.

Real-Life Relationships

Most people are happy if they find someone friendly who shares their values, interests, and dreams, and if the two of them can carve out a little life for themselves. They usually wake up in the morning, help each other get ready, and go to their jobs. They come home after work and have dinner. Then at night or on the weekends, they relax at home or do hobbies, watch TV, hang out with friends, visit family members, or plan a special night out, either together or individually. Some couples join clubs, play sports, or volunteer, again either together or separately. They may or may not decide to raise children, in which case most of their time will be devoted to the children's needs.

Being in love with somebody is not a big, exciting, never-ending drama. Being with someone romantically is not fantastical or super-ordinary. For most couples, it is about quiet days at home, taking care of each other, helping each other with the basic activities of life, having fun or going on vacation once in a while, sharing emotions, and sharing values. These simple days together are what the big deal is.

The being in love part of the equation is the bond that forms over time, not a feeling that goes on 24 hours a day, though the love is there all the time as the two people do things together, take care of each other, share daily life, and share each other's feelings and concerns. You may have to learn all of this consciously and come to your own conclusions based on your experiences. Knowing what life is all about – and not from the TV– is crucial because only when you are armed with a sense of what real people do, what real people say, what ways real people enjoy themselves, how people get to know others, and how people "do" their lives will you be able to make solid social decisions.

Again, the more you know about social life, social expectations, and social reality, the less surprised and confused you will be. Ultimately, when you have a clear sense of what goes on in life, you'll be able to protect yourself better from poor social decisions and social danger.

Other Learning Tools

Don't hesitate to use other methods of learning about social reality that have a proven record of being beneficial. For example, use visual aids of positive friendship, dating, and relationship behaviors. Make charts and posters that demonstrate good methods of dealing with various social situations. Watch scenes from movies and break down what you are seeing: Is it realistic? Positive? Or not? Do people really say those things? Do they really do those things? What would you do if somebody acted that way around you?

Comic Strips and Social Stories, two methods developed by Carol Gray, are used with children to spell out or break down social situations that have occurred or that may occur in the future. Adults can use them to deconstruct social situations, display different social possibilities, and plan appropriate responses in a visual manner. Several books widely available describe how to construct and use Comic Strips and Social Stories effectively (see the References section at the end of the book for more information).

Two sample Comic Strips that I created follow to demonstrate how you can use these tools to improve your understanding of the social world and to reinforce the safety concepts explained in this chapter.

Example 1: Using a Safe Activities List

Today, a girl I don't know asked me to get a soda at the diner after class.

I never met her before. It's a long walk to the diner.

I think she is really cute.

I remembered my Safe Activities List and asked her to meet me for lunch tomorrow in the college cafeteria instead. She said yes!

I'm so nervous I've been pacing around my room. I asked my Dorm Advisor what she thinks. She said I did a good job using my Safe Activities List, and that it's normal to be a little nervous.

I'm really excited I have a date tomorrow!

Example 2: Asking Someone for Help Decoding Social Reality

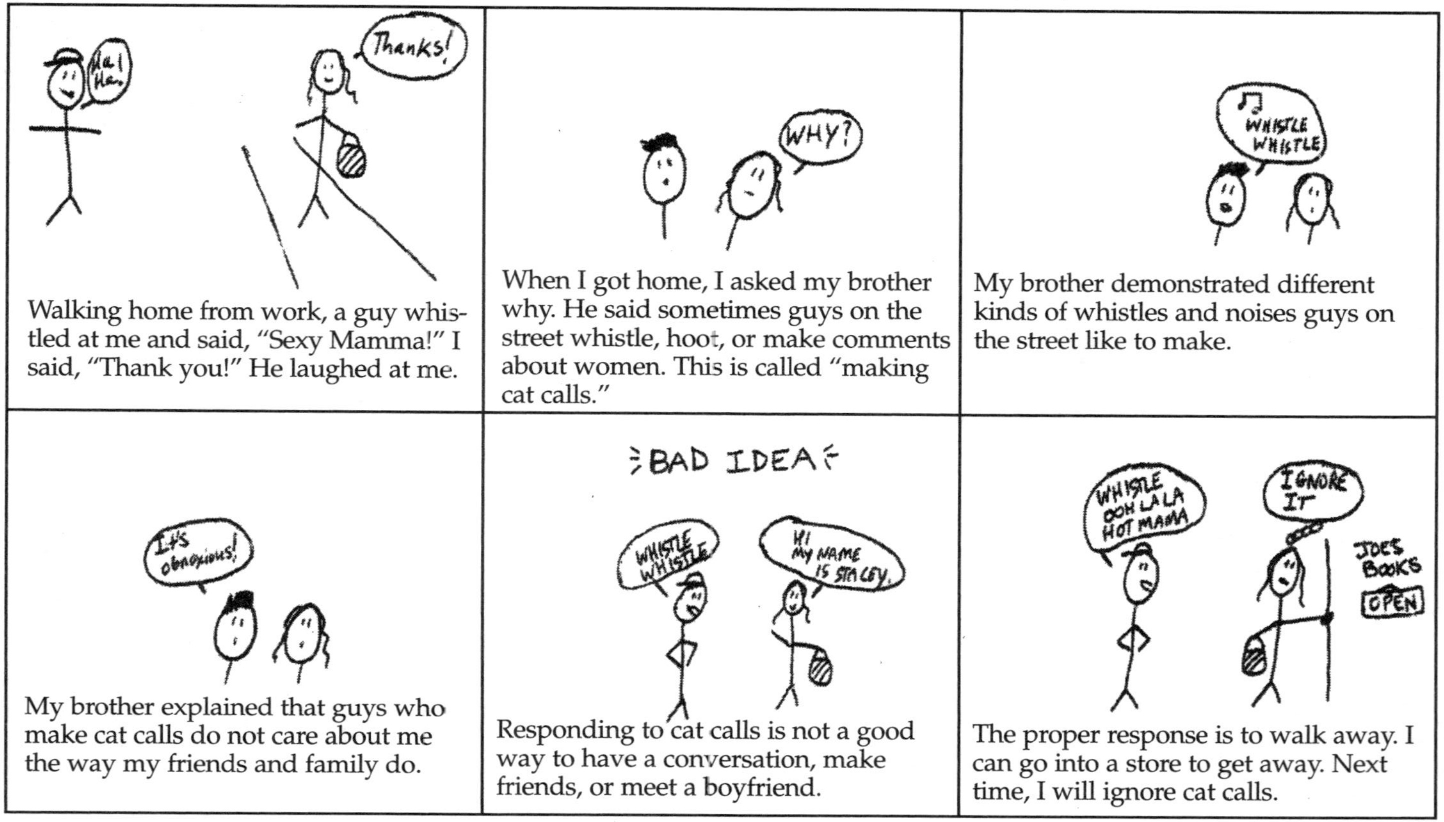

Ha! Ha.
Thanks!
Walking home from work, a guy whistled at me and said, "Sexy Mamma!" I said, "Thank you!" He laughed at me.
WHY?
When I got home, I asked my brother why. He said sometimes guys on the street whistle, hoot, or make comments about women. This is called "making cat calls."
WHISTLE WHISTLE
My brother demonstrated different kinds of whistles and noises guys on the street like to make.
It's obnoxious!
My brother explained that guys who make cat calls do not care about me the way my friends and family do.
BAD IDEA
WHISTLE WHISTLE
HI MY NAME IS STACEY.
Responding to cat calls is not a good way to have a conversation, make friends, or meet a boyfriend.
WHISTLE OOH LA LA HOT MAMA
IGNORE IT
JOE'S BOOKS
OPEN
The proper response is to walk away. I can go into a store to get away. Next time, I will ignore cat calls.

Additional Issues Women Face in the Autism Community

Privacy of Information

When I first thought that I might have Asperger Syndrome, I did an Internet search and found a support group. I wanted to learn about Asperger Syndrome and find out if my issues were similar to those of others. I took the subway uptown eagerly. The meeting was O.K. Indeed, many of my issues were shared by members of the group. I learned more about the "spectrum" concept. Overall, I considered the meeting useful.

Unfortunately, toward the end of the meeting, the leader urged me in front of the whole room to sign a contact sheet. He wanted me to write down my name, phone number, and address. Immediately I hesitated. I was living alone at the time. I didn't want a bunch of strange guys to know my number and where I lived. I told the leader of the group that I wasn't comfortable signing the contact sheet, but he continued to pressure me to sign it. Eventually, I just walked out feeling humiliated and upset.

If you are a woman, whether you live alone or not, it is risky for you to disclose personal information. Ask the leader of your support group if you can give an email address instead of a phone number or your physical address. If the leader says he needs your phone number or address for calls and mailings, but promises to keep your information confidential, email your contact information to him privately. Don't succumb to pressure to divulge your personal information. This is true not just at autism support meetings, but at any meetings, social events, clubs, or other activities you join.

Travel Safety Issues

While men can also encounter trouble in transit, it is a fact of life that it is more dangerous for women to walk or take public transit through certain neighborhoods, especially after dark. If you are a woman and you want to go to an evening autism support meeting, or any other activity for that matter, ask the leader in advance if it is safe for you to travel to the location. Are the streets lit? Is it a long walk to the bus or subway station? Can the leader assign you a designated Travel Buddy

You could have a rule requiring a person to ask somebody first if she wants to talk or be social before launching into a conversation.

to travel with to and from the meeting? Or does the leader know somebody who could give you a ride if other options aren't safe?

Romantic Pressure at Support Meetings

While both men and women can experience uncomfortable romantic overtures at autism support meetings, this advice is in this section because, unfortunately, it is another fact of life that women are at greater risk for sexual harassment and sexual violence. While it is true that support groups can be a safe autistic space to meet other autistic individuals, and while acknowledging that positive healthy friendships and romantic relationships have grown out of introductions made at support groups, it is equally important to make sure everyone in attendance feels safe.

Ask the leader to make rules for everyone's benefit if you are ever confused by a social exchange or if you have received unwelcome social advances. For example, you could have a rule requiring a person to ask somebody first if she wants to talk or be social before launching into a conversation. Or you could make a rule reserving romantic approaches for events specifically tagged as social in nature – picnics, field trips, holiday dinners, social time at conferences, meetings announced in advance as specifically for socializing, or at optional social times after the support meeting. If you experience extreme or ongoing social or romantic pressure at a support meeting, speak to the leader in private. Explain what happened and how it made you feel. Further action beyond creating social rules may be needed. You shouldn't have to sit through a support meeting feeling anxious about your safety.

Autistic Women With Children

Many women have children. This includes autistic women. Unfortunately, the attitude toward parents with disabilities is not often positive in this society. Several women on the spectrum have expressed to me privately their concern that their rights to parent their children could be threatened if it is publicly known that they are autistic. The court system can be increasingly hostile if a disabled mother is also divorced, low income, or gay.

If you are comfortable discussing your diagnosis at a meeting, workshop, conference, or informal get-together, but do not want your diagnosis made public, you need to let others know. Request that all information about you remains strictly confidential. You also have the right to refuse to give out your real name. If you want privacy when it comes to the newspapers, an interview, photography, or videography, tell the person from the media that you do not give your consent to be included in the material or footage. According to media law, if you are in a public domain such as a hotel lobby, a sidewalk, or a restaurant, someone filming does not need to secure your permission first, but you do have the right to go up to the person and request that you be excluded if this is your preference.

Additional Information for Women Regarding Sexual Violence

While acknowledging that boys and men unfortunately also experience sexual violence, it is an undeniable fact that in our society all women are vulnerable and at great risk of experiencing all types of sexual violence. If you experience romantic or sexual pressure, sexual harassment, or sexual violence of any kind, it is not your fault. Get help right away. You must tell someone. Schools and colleges usually have a staff member who handles complaints of sexual misconduct. If you are young, turn to your parents for advice and for protection. If nobody in your family believes you, or if somebody in your family is violating you sexually, you will have to turn to outside authorities at school or in the community.

NOTE: Whatever your age or circumstances in life, you must tell the police if a crime has been committed against you. Go to a hospital or police station right away. Don't be ashamed and don't delay. In situations like these, you need immediate assistance.

Recovering from sexual violence takes years. You may also realize only years after an incident that someone took advantage of you in ways that were inappropriate. Perhaps you didn't recognize the situation was

Those of us on the spectrum seem to have a higher incidence than the general population of being taken advantage of socially and sexually.

dangerous at the time precisely because you are on the spectrum. Talking with a professional therapist who specializes in this area is an important part of the healing process (see Chapter 6, page 133, for more information on finding a therapist). You may also find support groups and self-defense classes specifically tailored for women who have experienced sexual harassment or sexual violence useful. Again, don't blame yourself or feel ashamed and be sure to reach out for the help you need.

Conclusion

Those of us on the spectrum seem to have a higher incidence than the general population of being taken advantage of socially and sexually. When I hear story after story from people on the spectrum about running into social danger, some kind of response from the autism community is called for. To assume that we have the same level of risk as all members of society is to deny our unique set of social and linguistic challenges. Our situation is different and compounded by the way we think about and react to the world around us.

This doesn't mean that because of our issues, we can never be safe. I am suggesting that additional layers of training in special policies and techniques, such as the ones outlined in this chapter, are necessary. I suspect that those with more advanced qualifications will be able to refine and fine-tune my suggestions as the discussion regarding safety for autistic people is opened and continued. If nothing else, I have at least posed a question that deserves an answer.

■ ■ ■

Chapter 11

Gender Issues on the Spectrum

As a woman with Asperger Syndrome, I am often asked if things are different for me because of my gender, and if so, how? Certainly not all, but a lot of the literature on autism is about boys and men and the experience of autism from their perspective. While writing this chapter, I realized just how much women and men on the spectrum have in common and these commonalities will be highlighted in the first section. But while acknowledging our similarities, it has been my experience that males and females on the spectrum manifest autistic behaviors differently and have different social problems as a result of being autistic. As well, the social consequences of being on the spectrum may be different for women than men. Therefore, in the second part of the chapter, I explore differences that may be due to gender.

When discussing how things are different for females than for males, one must keep in mind that, ultimately, people are individuals and rarely fit into neat categories. Some girls and women may not have had experiences similar to mine. Some boys and men may disagree with my opinions based on their unique experiences. My concern is that, because society raises or views girls and boys differently, at least to some degree, girls may be under-diagnosed or misdiagnosed and thus at risk for not obtaining needed services and interventions. A discussion of gender differences is a step toward rectifying this situation.

Both autistic males and females exhibit communication challenges as part of the picture of autism. People on the autism spectrum understand language literally.

Similarities Among All People on the Spectrum

Communication Skills

Both autistic males and females exhibit communication challenges as part of the picture of autism. People on the autism spectrum understand language literally. This can lead to many misunderstandings, some funnier than others. For example, asking someone on the spectrum for coffee with milk may result in being served two drinks. We may be confused by statements such as, "Throw your coat on!" or "Grab the newspaper." I have to remind myself of the true meaning or purpose of statements like, "His ears are on fire."

Autistic people have a tendency to rely strictly on the verbal information presented, without picking up subtleties, innuendos, emotional cues, humor, sarcasm, or nonverbal body language. Because of this challenge in decoding nonverbal language and figurative meaning, we may have trouble deciphering social and emotional clues exchanged in conversation. For example, it may not be readily apparent to us that another person is just joking, is annoyed, finds the topic boring, wants to change the subject of conversation, or vice versa, is extremely interested in or excited by the content. Additionally, it may not be obvious that the other person is trying to convey emotions behind the words. Skills like adjusting tone of voice, taking turns, regulating body posture, and modifying the length of responses may have to be learned by rote. This is true for both autistic men and women.

Socializing

Again, all autistic men and women by definition experience challenges when it comes to social interaction. We have trouble deciphering common rules of interaction or knowing what is socially appropriate. Certain expected social behaviors such as eye contact, gestures, hand-shaking, or answering questions may not be done properly, at the right times, or at all. While the desire for friendship and social interaction exists, the ability to engage successfully is compromised by misunderstandings and sometimes eccentric mannerisms.

This can lead to intense isolation. Some on the spectrum prefer or get used to the solitude, but others experience great sadness or even depression as a result. Both men and women are at risk for loneliness and low self-esteem. The pressure from the social isolation may be a factor in the high incidence of poor decision-making when it comes to relationships and the social world. Many on the spectrum report that at least at some point in their lives they took great risks, consciously or not, for the sake of companionship and acceptance. Based on anecdotal evidence, this is true for both men and women.

Executive Functioning

Executive functioning is another area that both men and women on the spectrum often have trouble with. Executive functioning can be thought of as the ability to execute a plan and carry it from the idea stage to a completed goal. For example, to do something as minor as combing your hair requires

1. realizing your hair is out of place
2. knowing where the comb is kept
3. gathering the comb and a mirror (or standing in front of a mirror)
4. doing the combing, and
5. putting away the comb.

Most people do many daily tasks without a conscious thought. But for people on the spectrum, all the little steps involved in even minor actions and operations can be overwhelming and fraught with difficulty, making it hard to achieve basic goals like taking a shower. It is as if the autistic mind cannot put the different steps of an activity into a linear string *and* attach required actions to each segment of the string *and* gather and deal with disparate objects and tools *and* remember all the social and practical rules of the activity in question – all at the same time. An executive functioning problem can also be thought of as a global action-mapping deficit.

Puberty for both men and women on the spectrum may be the time of greatest challenge when it comes to executive functioning. Parents tend to monitor younger children, but once a child is a teenager he is expected to care for himself for the most part. A whole new roster of executive functioning skills is required to accomplish all the self-care tasks an adult must do for himself, by himself.

The tasks of caring for oneself as an adult on top of the psychological adjustment to a new body can pose stressors beyond what all adolescents deal with to some degree. In other words, while all teenagers struggle to deal with growing up, it is more difficult when you add in executive functioning issues, difficulty recognizing body signals, sensory issues, and possibly a low tolerance for physical discordance. Also, some adults may view young men and young women on the spectrum who express a great dislike for the changes they are going through as wanting to stay children or not wanting to face growing up, when in fact they may be inundated with executive functioning issues that are going unrecognized.

Executive functioning issues usually continue throughout adulthood. As we have seen, it can be a challenge to get ready for work in the morning, to handle tasks on the job, or to manage caring for a home. Some of the topics covered in different chapters of this book are really suggestions on how to circumnavigate the greatest challenges posed by executive functioning issues. While steps can be taken to reduce the difficulty with planning and executing tasks at home, at school, and at work, both men and women on the spectrum report a common feeling of physical and mental exhaustion. Again based on anecdotal evidence, executive functioning challenges do not appear worse for men or for women.

Other Commonalities

In addition to core challenges in communication, socializing, and executive functioning, men and women on the spectrum have other issues in common. Both experience sensory issues. The degree to which someone has sensory trouble varies from individual to individual and is not gender correlated. This is also true for common autistic traits like intense passion about our favorite topics. In other words, many characteristics and behaviors associated with the autism spectrum, including an uneven profile of skills, motor issues, intense interests, extensive knowledge of special subjects, and sometimes excellent memory are equally seen in men and women.

Gender-Based Differences in the Expression of Autistic Traits

Aggressive Behavior

A girl on the spectrum is more likely to withdraw, take out her frustrations on herself, or become depressed when faced with various challenges, whereas boys more readily act out, cry, or otherwise display frustration. Because girls are usually culturally influenced from birth to "be nice" and to "be good," they may be less likely to act aggressively.

This is not to imply that girls on the spectrum never have meltdowns, tantrums, or outbursts. "Rage control" is an issue for some girls, or is more of an issue at certain ages. But in general, girls and women have a much greater tendency to become depressed or withdrawn when upset. For this reason, the extent of a woman's frustrations and limitations may not be readily apparent. Because many women can control their anger, rage, and frustration, or feel enormous pressure to do so, loved ones and professionals may not realize just how upset or confused a woman feels.

Obsessions

Sometimes the obsessive interests of girls on the spectrum are more palatable to society than the obsessions of boys on the spectrum. A little boy on the spectrum who desperately seeks to talk to people for hours on end about the different kinds of toasters manufactured around the world may be discouraged from his obsession. This is unfortunate, since such an interest could translate into a decent career in electronics.

On the other hand, I was obsessed with the *Little House on the Prairie* series of books and the heroine Laura Ingalls. I wore prairie dresses just like she did. I made my mother find true bonnets at a costume shop. I insisted that I had to have my hair in two braids just like Laura. I had a wooden structure in the backyard that was my cabin and I spent extraordinary amounts of time out there eating, sleeping, and living on the prairie. My *Little House on the Prairie* obsession was viewed as cute and did, in fact, lead to a life-long interest in the history of women. People enjoyed my precocious knowledge of history and thought my prairie dresses were a creative expression, if a bit eccentric.

I was also obsessed with ballet. I knew about every single ballerina that ever existed. Again, my interest in ballet was considered healthy and constructive. My knowledge of historical ballerinas was viewed as a good opportunity for healthy role models. And ballet classes were good exercise. While people thought I was a bit weird because of the intensity of my interests, nobody thought I had a typical autistic characteristic.

Math and Memory Skills

It has been my experience that autistic women less frequently have the kind of instant math skills that autistic men sometimes have, and that fewer women on the spectrum than men have the ability to memorize loads of data in an exact manner. Nevertheless, I do have a better memory than most people and I can hold large quantities of data in my mind. For example, I really liked flags when I was a child. I had a poster in my room from the U.N. of all the flags of all the countries in the world. I can still recognize most of them. But I have no knack for memorizing train schedules, doing great math problems in my head, or knowing every single kind of airplane every built. And although I knew what happened in all of the *Little House on the Prairie* books and TV episodes, I did not know long tracts verbatim.

Differences Likely Due to the Effects of Gender Socialization

The Effect of Gender Socialization on Communication Skills

Little girls are usually instructed and expected to talk in a pleasant manner, so girls on the spectrum may be more sensitive to criticism regarding voice and conversation skills than boys. For this reason, a boy may be more likely to jump into a conversation, not sensing he is interrupting, too loud, or missing the point. Conversely, realizing a deficit in this area, a girl may decide the best tactic is to be quiet rather than cause a scene. As a result, her conversational issues may go undetected. A girl may also be more likely to act like she "gets it" to avoid conflict, ridicule, or danger.

At home, I was constantly prompted to use my "polite voice." So if I had an issue with regulating my voice volume, it was not addressed. I was also constantly interrupting people without meaning to, probably because I couldn't decode conversational turn-taking signals. But I was reminded often that "nice girls wait their turn." Yet, without gaining the conversational skills I needed, I was still able to figure out strategies to keep myself in the "nice" category: I kept quiet or I asked if it was O.K. to speak. In other words, a reduction in my episodes of interrupting did not correlate to an increased understanding of social cues, but was actually an indication of withdrawal due to frustration.

I was completely confused in group conversations, especially when I couldn't decipher the humor or determine the sequence of a story. With familiar people like my parents and my teachers, I would demand the details and explanations I needed in order to understand. My mother taught me to persevere until I was confident that I understood. But I was acutely aware that my peers – and people in society in general – were not so patient. Because of this unique socialization picture, a girl may be more likely to hover on the outskirts of

Perhaps because girls are primed from an early age to be sensitive to other people's feelings and are expected to achieve social adeptness, we may inadvertently gain skills or absorb lessons on social interaction that help us avoid embarrassing blunders and manage ourselves socially.

the interaction, pretend that she understands to avoid being singled out, or just keep to herself. No one in my elementary school saw any value in being the rude, loud, clueless girl.

The Effect of Gender Socialization on Social Skills

Perhaps because girls are primed from an early age to be sensitive to other people's feelings and are expected to achieve social adeptness, we may inadvertently gain skills or absorb lessons on social interaction that help us avoid embarrassing blunders and manage ourselves socially. When I was little, I had the common autistic problem of not being able to match my feelings to the correct verbalization or the appropriate facial expression. For example, I could be feeling fine but look upset. Vice versa, I could be terrified and look normal. I also laughed by accident if I meant to cry. It was as if my signals were haywire.

Because I received enormous negative feedback from my peers for these sorts of misfires, I would practice over and over and over in front of the mirror how to look and how to sound in different scenarios so that I wouldn't stand out as a freak. I was not overwhelmingly successful in this area, but I managed to squeak through enough social moments to survive.

Further, because girls are encouraged from a very early age to be responsive to other people's feelings and moods, we may notice the reactions of others in conversation, even though this is atypical for autistic people. For example, a girl may notice that the girls in her class find her boring, weird, excessively talkative, or not talkative enough, and then take the rejection by her peers very hard. She may notice her failures more than a boy of the same age. She may also try to avoid conflict or disruption at all costs, to smooth over the problems she believes she is causing, and to appear to be a "nice" girl anyway, despite her perceived or real deficits. This effort soaks up an enormous amount of mental and physical energy.

I was extremely sensitive and received much praise from the adults in my environment for this trait. For example, when a mouse died in our summer camp cabin, I insisted that it needed a proper funeral. I felt terrible about the famine in Ethiopia and sent all my allowance to help. Whenever I saw old people trying to cross the street, I made sure they got across, standing in the crosswalk to hold up traffic if necessary. I considered it my civic duty to volunteer at our local hospital and to play violin at the nursing home once a week. And I had a club – membership of one – whose purpose was to pick up trash along the side of our road.

Whenever a girl acts in a sensitive manner toward the people around her and her community, she is praised and her behavior is reinforced. This served as another chance social lesson: People liked me when I was kind, when I did a favor, when I volunteered, when I helped, when I asked if there was something I could do. So I built more successful experiences on the last. I discovered early that I could "win" people over and that they would assume I was a good girl with no problems – if I did nice things.

While I would hope that parents encourage and praise boys when they do nice things – and most parents do – it is also true that a very sensitive boy is often unfortunately ridiculed. It is a big shame in our culture that a boy's instinct to care, to worry, to help, to serve, or to be emotional is sometimes discouraged by teasing from peers, by lack of reinforcement from parents, and by counter-images in the media. A boy on the spectrum may discover that he is praised and rewarded by the culture when he is tough, when he does not display his vulnerability, when he appears independent at all costs, and when he defends himself and his own interests strongly.

This cultural standard can inadvertently reinforce for a boy on the spectrum that it is better to shout, to be rude, to run roughshod over others, to be big and macho, and to avoid affection and tears. In other words, "typical" spectrum behaviors, like not showing affection, not acknowledging other people's feelings, not engaging emotionally, and using aggression to assert needs may, in fact, be an autistic boy's desperate and misunderstood attempt to be male, to fit in as a male, and to copy what he perceives to be the ideal male mode of being in his society. On the flip side, a girl may not appear autistic because she emulates, practices, and copies to survive the highly valued stereotypically un-autistic-like female traits of caring, empathy, and sharing to fit in as a female and to match the ideal female mode of being in our society, with varying degrees of success depending on her circumstances and opportunities.

Different Consequences of Social Challenges for Men Versus Women

Precisely because girls are primed to care and to share feelings with other girls as a method of getting along and fitting in, girls on the spectrum may gain sufficient skills in displaying emotions or socializing successfully to slide by or to get along. But failing socially is more common, resulting in high rates of low self-esteem, depression, and anxiety. I know boys on the spectrum experience this as well and can feel both fatigued by the effort to join in and depressed or lonely by the inability to make friends. Yet a crucial difference between boys and girls may be in this area of friendship and social development because social failure has a different meaning and consequence for women.

For example, when the other little girls on the street were around, I would insist we play *Little House on the Prairie* and that I be Laura. This was O.K. with them. But then as we started to pretend, they would do things that never happened in the TV shows or the books. I would throw up my arms, "But Ma NEVER did that!" They didn't seem to care. I would get so frustrated with them that the game would disintegrate. What I didn't understand was that they didn't care how things went in the game per se, or what the rules were per se.

Something else was more important to them. I just couldn't figure out what this secret was. They cared much more about being with each other, about sharing each other's experiences of the world, and about having fun. Rules, what actually happened in history, and creating a logical sequence of events in the game were only secondary to the main point of interaction and were easily abandoned by them in favor of their main priority – each other's company.

Boys are more likely to value the actual games: If you agree to play by the rules, you can join. Acceptance depends in great part on a boy's willingness to follow the rules. Girls value rules less and emotional and social exchanges more. Gender studies have shown, for example, that boys will hash out the rules at all costs, but girls will abandon a game when they disagree about the rules because the game is less important than being together (see Carol Gillagan's book, *In a Different Voice: Psychological Theory and Women's Development,* page 355).

Boys definitely experience loneliness, and it is no easier for autistic boys to find friends than for girls. But a boy *may* be able to gain some respect from his peers if he knows everything about the Yankees, or if he can fix things. He may gain some recognition from his peers if he has every single *Star Trek* collector's card. He may be able to join games if the rules are clear. He has avenues in a boy culture that he can, with adult guidance and input, use to make a bridge to the other boys.

These options for boys can be built on autistic strengths – enjoying collections, having a great memory or knack for facts and figures, appreciating and relying on rules to govern interaction. But the options are not going to work for girls. Girls form friendships through *sharing their identities* and *relating to each other's emotions.* Since most autistic girls struggle with the nuanced rules of emotional and social exchange, the priorities and values of the other little girls may not be understood. In other words, it is not just that girls on the spectrum struggle, like boys, to understand how to navigate the social landscape. It's that in our society, girls form their very identities based on how well they navigate.

The result of failing at navigating socially for an autistic girl can have an impact on her identity development that ripples into her adult life. Succeeding at relationships – at least somewhat – is a key developmental phase for girls in this society that becomes a crucial bridge to adulthood. Without some social achievement and connection, a girl's identity can falter and suffer. If every single effort she makes to identify herself positively through her relationships with those around her ends in failure or social disaster, her concept of self is in jeopardy.

None of this denies the social trouble autistic boys encounter, nor the deep feelings of isolation an autistic boy can experience. Boys on the spectrum often mention the pressure to be athletic as one of the only means of creating social connections to other boys. This can be intensely difficult for a boy who is uncoordinated or otherwise completely uninterested in sports. Some men on the spectrum look back to their boyhoods and only remember social failure because they couldn't hit a ball. As adults, some say they don't know how to make friends with other men because sports – something they know next to nothing about – forms the bulk of conversation and recreation among men.

But whereas boys in this society may be able to develop self-identities based on a set of skills, a hobby, a favorite pastime, or success in an activity, girls tend to develop their self-identities based on their ability to relate to other people and how well they do this. Boys will often say during middle school, "I'm a good basketball player," or "I'm a train expert." Girls will say, "I'm Lucy's best friend." This is not to say that girls never identify themselves in other ways, or that boys never define themselves in terms of their relationships. But these general tendencies and their implications cannot be ignored.

I have met some girls on the spectrum who are content to delve into an activity of strong interest, who feel no strong proclivity to bond with other girls, and who could care less what the other girls think. But in my experience this is the exception. Women's lives in our culture tend to form around concentric rings of friendship. Failing to grasp the core essence of female social life as a girl – caring, sharing, and identifying with other girls – leaves a woman without the skills or experience needed to join the friendship networks that are a crucial element of adult female life in our society. Some women on the spectrum have expressed deep frustration about this. Because adult women often base their sense of self on who they relate to and how well they do so, another layer of risk develops: They may accept less than desirable relationships, sometimes but not always for the sake of succeeding socially as a woman, occasionally putting themselves in serious danger. (Check Chapter 10: *Keeping Ourselves Safe,* for more information about this issue.)

The Impact of Executive Functioning Challenges

Another area of autistic life that is probably different for girls than boys, at least to some degree, is physical appearance. Physical appearance tasks are heavily dependent on executive functioning skills. Both women and men can face challenges in this area. For example, some men find shaving a challenge because the task requires a person to monitor when a shave is necessary, to purchase and replenish needed supplies, and then to actually do the shaving. Some women have similar challenges with their self-care. But men and women are judged differently when it comes to personal appearance.

While the world often tolerates a little sloppiness from men, women are under pressure to look attractive. Hundreds of magazines and tons of media bandwidth are devoted to hair, make-up, color, style, and fashion for women. Men who appear grungy, archaic in their fashion sense, or just eccentric are usually excused for this shortcoming. It is assumed that such a guy works in a messy occupation, doesn't have a girlfriend to fix him up, or is just – simply put – being a guy. But a grungy, unkempt, or strange-looking woman is a spectacle. Even in casual circles women feel pressured to look a certain way. Women on the spectrum who cannot or choose not to put themselves together in the way society expects are often viewed as childish, disorderly, or rebellious and not accorded respect or taken seriously.

Women who are having trouble managing their lives, engaging socially, or functioning at work may be viewed differently by mental health workers than men with the same problems.

The Consequences of Gender Difference: Double Standards

Women who are having trouble managing their lives, engaging socially, or functioning at work may be viewed differently by mental health workers than men with the same problems. Many mental health professionals are still prone to assume that a woman's problems are self-created.

I've heard of a man and a woman going to the same psychiatrist to determine if they are on the spectrum. The man is given a proper diagnosis of autism. He is referred to support groups and agencies. The woman is told to stop feeling sorry for herself and receives a prescription for antidepressants to help her fit in better. She is told that self-pity will get her nowhere and that she shouldn't create problems that don't exist. Because the underlying assumption is that her problems are her fault, she may not receive the help she needs.

This double standard begins in childhood when girls are held to different behavioral expectations. For example, if a boy is very hyperactive, his parents are apt to bring him in for diagnosis and treatment. If a boy has trouble controlling his temper, modulating the volume of his voice, sitting in his desk and cooperating with the teacher, or getting along with his peers, his parents bring him in to see a specialist promptly.

But if a girl acts hyper, the adults in her life leap to the conclusion that she is obstinate. They admonish her to listen to the teacher and stop acting like a bad girl. If she doesn't get along with her peers, it must be because she won't play nice. If she is loud, if she interrupts, or if she can't maintain a polite conversation, she must be irritating people on purpose for attention. If she cries because she has no friends, she must have PMS.

This carries over into adulthood. A woman's autistic symptoms may be seen as emotional issues that need to be addressed as such. The mental health community must understand that women are not overreacting when we say we don't fit in or we are overwhelmed by sadness because of our perceived or actual social ineptitude. The inability to make friends, form relationships, or otherwise get along in society can't be chalked up to moodiness or hormones. A serious investigation into the reasons why a woman is having difficulties in life is warranted. Everyone has a turn being depressed. We all go through rough spells. That is not the same thing as a chronic struggle due to a developmental disability.

I am convinced that girls on the spectrum fly under the radar far too easily, getting by until survival techniques no longer work. Most little girls try hard not to interrupt, they want to look pretty and well groomed, they tend to stay in their seats, they tend to withdraw instead of acting out, and they may stay quiet instead of making a scene. As adults, autistic women may seem weird, lost in their own worlds, unusually withdrawn or alone, rebellious or wallowing in self-pity, while the true struggle – dealing with the challenges of autism – goes unrecognized. Again, I'm not a scientist, but even if more males than females are autistic, I think many women are missing from the count and losing out on valuable chances to learn skill sets that can be the difference between healthy self-esteem and confidence or trouble and danger.

Conclusion

In short, males and females on the spectrum have the same core challenges. But females may display different behaviors due to socialization factors. The challenges associated with social deficits may have a different meaning for women and may impact the lives of women differently because of societal structures and expectations. Society's response may affect a woman's ability to find the help she needs.

These issues need to be addressed however uncomfortable it may be for us to make generalizations based on gender. The special needs and problems of autistic women can't be ignored, incorrectly demoted to a refusal on our part to be what a woman is supposed to be. Only when issues of gender are addressed can we be sure that women are being accurately diagnosed and that they are receiving help and support tailored to their unique position in life and in society.

■ ■ ■

Chapter 12

Friendship

Many autistic people are socially isolated. While some truly prefer being alone, others report an interest in making friends and interacting with peers. Even if you enjoy time by yourself, can amuse yourself with your own activities, or feel no strong interest in social contact with others, you may still feel lonely. The complexities of friendship and social engagement may not be easy, but even so, people are usually comforted by the presence of others. It is safe to say that social isolation is not always indicative of a preference for solitude.

It can be difficult to make friends and then maintain a friendship. Since the very nature of friendship involves social exchange between at least two people, understanding concepts of friendship can be like trying to figure out life on an alien planet in a distant galaxy. Unfortunately, those of us on the spectrum are often easy targets for maltreatment, teasing, and other forms of victimization well past childhood. We are at risk for making naïve social decisions because of the very nature of the challenges we face.

People tend to gravitate toward what they are good at doing, favoring activities that produce the least friction. So if every attempt you make to approach other people and join them in friendship ends in disaster, you may very well sit in your room alone playing video games or reading up on your favorite topics for hours. Does this mean you truly prefer solitary activities? Maybe. But maybe not.

If you knew how to make and keep a friend, if you tried to make a friend and you were successful, you might still choose to spend most of your time alone. But at least this would be a free choice. You could choose to be with your friends when you wanted companionship or you could decline social invitations when you preferred to be by

Though ultimately you may choose to avoid most forms of social contact, having certain information about friendship will help you make sure that being alone is a true choice rather than a default option.

yourself. You would have a variety of pursuits – some solitary, some social – that you could engage in depending on your mood. Though ultimately you may choose to avoid most forms of social contact, having certain information about friendship will help you make sure that being alone is a true choice rather than a default option.

Casual Friends

Casual friendships are often called "superficial" friendships because the topics that casual friends discuss and the amount and type of emotions casual friends share usually stay simple or "at the surface." In other words, with casual friends you only share the top layers of yourself. Casual friends are people you are friendly toward when you see them, but you probably do not spend much time together. You may not even do any activities together. Or, you may share time together but only because you must. For example, usually your co-workers won't know all about your life, or visit with you in the evenings, even though you spend large amounts of time with them on the job. One or two co-workers may turn into intimate friends (see page 308), in which case you would share more activities and more knowledge about yourself, but the process of going from casual friend to intimate friend usually takes time.

Examples of Casual Friends

The postal person who delivers your mail is a good example of a casual friend or "acquaintance" you meet around the neighborhood. You probably see him or her delivering the mail a couple of times a week. You say hello. Sometimes if neither of you is busy, you stop and talk about something such as the weather or the neighbor's dog for a few minutes. But you don't invite the postal worker over for dinner or tell the postal worker about your personal problems.

Another good example of a casual friend is someone you meet in a class at college. Perhaps you are both very interested in the class subject. Therefore, you decide to meet after class in the cafeteria to talk about the teacher, your homework, or ideas shared in class. This type of friend can easily become a more intimate friend if the two of you discover that you love talking to one another and visiting with each other. But this would happen only after meeting at least a few times and realizing that you would like to get to know each more intimately.

Conversations With Casual Friends

Casual friends usually talk about "safe" topics like the weather, a sports team, TV shows, maybe a recent concert or show that came to your town, movie stars, or something you have in common. For example, at work, casual friends discuss what's going on in the office, such as the new coffee machine the boss just purchased for everyone or how many days until the next vacation. Look in your local newspaper for things to discuss with casual friends if you can't think of good conversation topics. For example, you may find an article about a new type of salad that is popular, a movie star's latest film, or a storm that is due to hit later in the week. These are all topics that are safe to discuss with a casual friend.

Avoid talking about topics that might be offensive or cause a fight. Most people don't talk about politics, religion, the body, sex, or family life with casual friends. What do you think would happen if you went up to your neighbor and said, "This president stinks!" What if your neighbor likes the president? How do you think your neighbor would feel? Sometimes it is O.K. to talk about an unsafe topic on very special occasions. For example, in the weeks before Election Day, people discuss the positive and negative aspects of presidential candidates, at least as they see it. But if you are ever in doubt, stay away from unsafe topics.

Once in a while, you will be in a conversation with several people and two or three of them will begin discussing unsafe topics. It is possible that they know each other better than they know you and that you just happen to be around. Or maybe they are rude and don't care about other people's feelings. Because it is very difficult to determine when it is O.K. to discuss unsafe topics with casual friends, the best policy is talk only about safe subjects.

Close Friends

Close friendships are more intricate and intimate than superficial friendships. Sometimes a close friendship is described as an intimate friendship for this reason, but the word 'intimate' does not imply romance. Close friends know each other fairly well. They spend a good amount of time together and enjoy seeing each other. They like to do many things together. Most people call their intimate friends "my close friend," "my best friend," or "my good friend" as a way of implying that the other person is not a casual friend.

The Nature of Close Friendships

Close friends like each other and feel very comfortable around each other. This means that they can be themselves fully. A casual friend, for example, probably does not know what makes you angry or what you like to do first thing in the morning, but a close friend usually does. A close friend knows many things about you that you wouldn't share with just anyone. Because you are good friends and you trust each other, you have the freedom to expose more of your personality. Unlike casual friends, close friends talk about anything on Earth. If they disagree strongly about a passionate subject such as politics, they agree to respect each other's differences and move on to the next topic.

How People Become Close Friends

How do two people become close friends? People can become close friends in a variety of ways. Sometimes casual friends turn into intimate friends over time as they discover how much they enjoy each other's company. Once in a while, people will "click" right away – this means they become close friends almost instantly from the very first moment they meet. Usually people make close friends in specific settings. For example, you may become close friends with your college roommate or with someone from your photography club.

The process of becoming somebody's close friend usually happens naturally. This means you do not go up to somebody you like and ask, "Would you like to be my best friend?" While children do this sometimes, adults don't. The only way you can become someone's good friend is by inviting the other person to share activities and conversations, spending time together, and seeing if the other person enjoys your company as much as you enjoy his.

Advantages of Close Friendships

If someone is a close friend, she should be tolerant of your eccentricities and should never make fun of you. She may also advocate for you. For example, if you are in a group of people and find yourself unable to do group behaviors but you are still enjoying yourself, a close friend can act as an interpreter and explain your behavior on your behalf. A lot of people on the spectrum like to be present among others but keep to themselves at the same time because group interaction can be overwhelming. In other words, you may want to just sit and listen or watch everybody. Your close friend knows this about you and can make sure you are still included and invited along even though you socialize in a special way.

In the right situation, a close friend can be a very valuable source of social information. When information is delivered out of genuine concern for your well-being, a good friend can share enormous amounts of important "life" advice that you just can't glean from parents, casual friends, or books. Especially because those of us on the spectrum tend not to learn about social things unconsciously and effortlessly, a good friend can be a useful social teacher of sorts. Unlike social skills training, which is abstract and practiced only periodically, a friend is there during live action and understands life as it is. You may do eye contact perfectly in a social skills session where you know what the therapist expects, but while hanging out on the football field you may not be able to maintain proper eye contact. A friend can prompt you naturally: "Don't forget to look at Sally this time when you ask her out for hot chocolate after the game!"

Another advantage is that a good friend will probably learn that you are on the autism spectrum at some point (disclosure is discussed in greater detail in Chapter 13), developing a special understanding of your issues and making accommodations for you. For example, your good friend may be willing to hang out with you "side-by-side" while you work on one of your projects and she does something that she enjoys. This may seem odd, but it is possible. A true close friend is someone who is just as happy to let you sit quietly, think to yourself, "space out," or take a break from chatting as she is to interact verbally and socially. All three of the above examples – advocating for you, providing you with special social information, and accommodating your special needs – are what close friends do for each other.

Friendship Rules and Expectations

So, whether you are talking about a casual friend or a close friend, what is friendship based on? Do friends help each other? With what? Do friends do activities with each other? What sort? What is expected of a friend? Can you ask a friend to help you make more friends? And what is different about hanging out in a group versus hanging out with just one person?

These concepts, and the values most people base friendship decisions on, are not obvious to autistic people. In this part of the chapter, I will attempt to answer these and other questions. Not wanting to clog my sentences with awkward pronoun combinations, I randomly use the feminine or masculine.

Casual and Close: The Two Basic Types of Friends

Casual Friends	*Close Friends*
Who	***Who***
Neighbors, co-workers, familiar people such as mailcarrier, classmates	College roommate, best friend from *Star Trek* club, maybe a casual friend over time
Characteristics	***Characteristics***
• Share just a few layers of yourself	• Share a lot about yourself
• Spend a little time together (possible exception: co-workers)	• Spend more time together
• Maybe do some light activities together	• Do some activities together
• Talk about safe subjects only	• Talk freely, even about difficult topics
• Don't share much about your personal emotions	• Share some things about your personal life and your emotions depending on how close
• Help with basic problems: loan a pen, give directions, carry something	• Help with a range of problems depending on how close: move furniture, watch a pet, share dating advice, sort through personal issues
• Usually won't know about your autism (possible exception: co-workers)	• Probably will find out about your diagnosis and probably will be willing to make accommodations
• Can make a casual friend quickly	• Usually takes time to become close friends

If you do not understand how or why you would choose to be friends with someone and have limited or no experience in choosing friends, building bonds, or breaking up the friendship when necessary, you are susceptible to making poor social choices.

What Friendships Are Based On

As a child grows up, concepts of play and social life develop in tandem with all other developmental stages. It only makes sense then that those with developmental "delays" or challenges may have a circumscribed understanding of broadening social relationships. For example, I was startled when someone told me I was lucky to have sisters because then we could be friends and go out together – I didn't play with my sisters. My middle sister (two years younger) was often irritated with me because I was less interested in drawing with the crayons than putting them back into the box in an exact rainbow order. Or if we were playing with a board game, I was more preoccupied with the position of the plastic pieces than with playing the game. I was aware of a huge gap between me and my peers as early as age five.

Since those of us on the spectrum figure out what friendships are about at a much slower pace than our peers, or never figure it out, we tend to come up with some interesting substitute ideas. For example, in high school, it appeared to me that if you wore certain clothes, you would automatically be friends with and included in the social circle that also dressed in that style. So I would mimic the clothes, mannerisms, and style of a certain group – the preppies, the popular girls, the nerds – one by one. I would organize outfits for my mission, then wear them, expecting automatic entrance into the associated group. When I did not make friends, I would realize my effort had failed somehow. But then I would try with a different group!

If you do not understand how or why you would choose to be friends with someone and have limited or no experience in choosing friends, building bonds, or breaking up the friendship when necessary, you are susceptible to making poor social choices. You are also at risk of being taken advantage by others who are more astutely aware of social nuances and who can sense your vulnerability. Therefore, it is important to understand why two people become friends, but the logic is very subtle and may be hard to grasp.

People usually decide to become friends because they are interested in each other. This means the other person is interested in the things you know and the things you do, and he hopes and anticipates that you will be interested in him. People also become friends because human beings have an internal capacity to connect. For example, somebody may want to share or try an activity you are doing. A friend wants to connect his life to your life by sharing.

Friendship is based on this sharing that goes back and forth. You listen to your friend; she listens to you. You say hello to your friend when you see her; she asks you how you are doing. Your friend wants to try watching your favorite TV show; you try eating at your friend's favorite diner. Your friend wants to talk about the homework assignment you both have to do because he is sure he has the perfect answer; you discuss the assignment with your friend and offer a few ideas of your own.

What two friends do together depends on the depth of the friendship. You might just say hello. You might have a very complicated discussion. You might go somewhere interesting. You might do something fun. You might just "hang out" or spend time together relaxing. You might want to spend all your free time together. It depends. As long as both people agree, two friends can share any activity on Earth.

Sometimes friends dress in a similar manner or live in a similar way. But this is because they have common interests and values. In other words, you don't pick a friend just because she looks, dresses, acts, or lives like you do. When you do find someone who is interested in connecting and sharing with you, and whom you are interested in connecting and sharing with in return, the two of you could have *some* similarities, but the similarities are not exactly what you base the friendship on.

To phrase it differently, two people become friends because they have parts of themselves that they want to share. With this concept in mind, you can judge more clearly whether or not somebody else has something to share that is worthwhile to you. If somebody wants to share doing drugs, being promiscuous, ignoring responsibilities, stealing, or teasing and hurting other people, it would be unwise to befriend this person. But if somebody wants to share activities, hobbies, special interests, conversations, and feelings with you, whether yours are the same or extremely different, it can be fun to try being friends.

Again, the two of you do not have to like the same things, wear the same clothes, read the same books, enjoy the same hobbies, live the same way, or even speak the same language. You may discover that you have things in common, but this is not a requirement to be friends. In fact, since the whole point of being friends is to share unique aspects about yourself and enjoy unique aspects about your friend, differences between the two of you can be a source of enjoyment and inspiration.

Be wary of people who want to be your friend, but never want to share anything with you. They may be using you for their own purposes. Also realize that if someone wants to be your friend, but she only wants to share what she enjoys and never wants to experience what you like, or vice versa, if you want to be someone's friend but you always have to pick the activity or topic of conversation, this is a lopsided friendship and it almost never lasts.

Friendships are also not based on pay-offs. Nobody should say to you, "I'll be your friend if you do me a special favor." Friends are friends because they want to be. You can't force or bribe somebody to be your friend, nor should somebody else force or bribe you into a friendship. If someone tries to, avoid any further contact with that person. Friendship is a voluntary act. It is considered cruel to induce or extort somebody to be friends or to place conditions on the friendship.

As two friends share conversations and activities and exchange information about themselves, they almost always begin to care about each other – sometimes a little bit, sometimes a lot. It is as if sharing is the recipe for a special cookie. After you put all the special sharing ingredients into the bowl and mix them up, you get caring. This is why friends like to be together. Additional sharing leads to even more caring. If you bake the sharing cookies for some time, the caring can turn into a very loving friendship.

Helping

Don't be afraid to ask a friend for help. Friends almost always like to help each other. The problem is in knowing which friends to ask for what type of help. Helping ranges from very simple to very intense. For example, a casual friend can help you by loaning you a pen. A good friend can help you by babysitting your dog when you go on vacation. Your very best friend in the whole world will stick up for you if someone tries to tease you or hurt you.

If you ask a friend to help you and she can't, maybe she is simply too busy. On the other hand, you may be asking her to help you with a very big problem that she isn't ready to help you with because she doesn't feel like she knows you well enough. A good rule to follow: *The bigger the problem you need help with, the closer your friend should be.* Don't ask somebody you just met to help you move to your new house or to run an errand for you when you have the flu.

Also, do not expect your friends to help you with everything. Even a good friend probably can't come over to your house at 3:00 a.m. just because you found a roach in your tub and you're scared. Would you want someone to wake you up at that hour for this kind of problem? Your friends can help you out in a lot of ways, but don't expect them to help you every single second of every single day with every little issue that comes up.

Friends can help each other with problems of a personal nature, not just with moving, watching pets, or giving social advice. With your best friend or one or two really good friends, you can talk about your personal problems as part of sharing your feelings. Very close friends will comfort you and give you suggestions.

But be careful. If you have a lot of serious personal problems that aren't getting better, talk to licensed therapist, not your buddies. Save your friendships for fun times and "regular" problems like fixing your bike, figuring out what to wear or say on a date, decorating your room, moving furniture, or advice on how to be cool. If all you do is talk about your personal problems and ask friends to help sort them out, they will get frustrated. If they feel like they must help you constantly, they may also be reluctant to help when you do have a desperate situation. Friends will help you, but they do not want to provide therapy or spend all their time sorting out your life.

Expectations

As you become friends with somebody, certain expectations start floating around invisibly in the air. Helping, described above, is one expectation of friendship. Nobody talks about these expectations because most people understand the expectations automatically. People on the spectrum may be unsure as to what to expect from a friend. Ask nicely and in a non-critical way. You can start the conversation off by explaining that since you are on the autism spectrum, social expectations aren't always clear to you.

Since almost all friends have some basic expectations, you can follow these as a general guide:

- **Be polite.** Friends do not tease each other or hurt each other's feelings. If you hurt your friend's feelings by accident, apologize.
- **Don't "flake out" on a friend.** This means that if you say you are going to meet your friend at the movies at 3:00 p.m., you better show up. If you say you'll help a friend paint his car on Sunday, don't call Sunday morning and tell him you don't feel like it any more. It's not fair to make plans with your friends and then break them. Of course, there are some exceptions.

- **Call your friend and cancel your plans with as much notice as possible,** if you are sick, if you have an emergency, or if you have to help take care of a family member. Your friend will probably be disappointed, so it is polite to reschedule the activity or to offer to do something else instead.

Keeping or Ending a Friendship

The following information pertains mostly to close friends. With casual friends, you do not put that much energy into the friendship. If you see a casual friend at the grocery store and you wind up chatting, that's great. If you don't see each other, that is O.K., too. But with close friends, the situation is different.

Once you have made a close friend, you need to keep nurturing the friendship. Your friendships are like plants. You have to water them every now and then or they wilt. This means you need to call your close friends once in a while. When you call, all you have to do is chat and ask how your friend is doing. Occasionally, you should also ask your friend if she would like to do an activity with you. This is how you keep a close friendship going. If you neglect to call your close friends, or if you call once in a while but never invite your friends to do an activity with you, they will probably venture off to find new friends.

Vice versa, if your close friend never calls you, or she calls but never invites you to do anything, then perhaps she is no longer interested in being your friend. This can be sad if you care about her a lot. If you are very sad because the friendship seems to be fading away, give your friend a call and double-check before you give up completely. Perhaps she just got very busy with her life. You can say something like, "I haven't heard from you in a while. I'd love to do something with you." Or, "We haven't done anything in a number of weeks. Would you like to do something with me this weekend?" Because people do get busy with school, work, and life, it is O.K. to give a close friend a few chances to keep being friends. On the other hand, if you've tried several times to remain friends with somebody and she *still* never has time to do something with you, or she *still* never calls you, it is time to move on and make some new friends, no matter how sad this situation may be.

Spending time with one friend can be very easy and relaxing, but when you spend time with several friends at once, things may not go as smoothly as you wish.

Sometimes friends "drop off" for a while and then reconnect later. This means you may lose contact with a close friend for a period of time for whatever reason, but not because you don't like each other any more. The friendship may restart again at a future time. Life is unpredictable.

In the event that you are not able to maintain a friendship with someone you care about, or the friendship never starts up again, your feelings may be hurt or you may be lonely. You'll just have to treasure the memories of the good times you shared. Always be polite if you see your old friend again. After all, you cared about each other in the past. And don't despair. You will be able to make new friends eventually.

Friendship Groups

Most people have different kinds of friends. For example, you may have one friend who loves to go swimming with you and another friend who hates swimming but shares your love of everything *Star Trek*. Maybe your *Star Trek* friend will invite you to a *Star Trek* convention where you can meet other Trekkies. Or maybe your swimming friend will take you to his favorite pool and introduce you to his other swimming friends.

Spending time with one friend can be very easy and relaxing, but when you spend time with several friends at once, things may not go as smoothly as you wish. Using the example from the previous paragraph, what do you think would happen if you went with your swimming friend to his pool, and after meeting his swimming buddies it turned out that you liked one of them better? Your original friend's feelings will be hurt. Vice versa, what if, when you get to the pool, he runs off with his other swimming buddies and basically ignores you? How would you feel? Feelings get very complicated in groups of people. This doesn't mean

Basic Rules of Friendship

1. Friendships are based on two people being interested in each other.
2. Friends share conversations and activities. Two friends can share any activity as long as both agree.
3. Friends begin to care about each other through the sharing they do. Sometimes they care a little bit. Sometimes they care a lot.
4. Friends help each other. The help they offer depends on how close they are. Casual friends help each other with basic problems, such as loaning a pen or giving travel directions. Close friends help each other with common situations in life – painting a car, watching a pet during vacation, moving, installing a computer. Very close friends may also help each other with more personal problems such as dating advice or sorting out personal issues. But friends do not provide therapy or spend all of their time helping.
5. Friends are polite to each other.
6. Friends do not hurt each other's feelings. If friends hurt each other's feelings by accident, they apologize.
7. Friends do not cancel plans on each other except in emergencies. If plans do have to change, they call each other with as much notice as possible and reschedule or make new plans.
8. Friends never abuse each other or force each other to do activities they don't want to do.
9. Friends continue to call each other on the phone and invite each other to do activities over time.
10. Sometimes friends drift apart and the friendship ends. People remain fond of their old friends and act polite if they happen to run into each other again in the future. Sometimes they even restart their old friendship. But sometimes they don't. This is just part of life.

you should never meet new people through your old friends or that groups can't have fun together. Just remember it is a bit different than hanging out with one friend.

Developing a Social Persona

When I asked someone about friendship and socializing a few years ago, she explained the concept of having a social persona. Most people on the spectrum are the same person at every moment. Who we are does not change or shift. But most people who are not on the spectrum have lighter versions of themselves for socializing. I was shocked to learn that people change who they are just slightly for different situations. I couldn't relate to the idea that most people have more than one version of themselves for different occasions. This news may be very confusing to you, too.

With very good friends, the social persona issue is less of a big deal. Your closest friends shouldn't mind if you are always yourself, no matter what. They will come to accept you and your quirks. If they don't, they aren't very accepting friends.

But people develop social personas because when they are having fun with casual friends, schoolmates, co-workers, or neighbors, they do not want to be in a serious mood. They want to play and have a good time. Of course, they help each other if a problem arises as already explained, but they focus mostly on enjoying themselves. If you are very serious all of the time, if you can't break your concentration to join in whatever is happening at the moment, or if you can't modify your personality based on who is around at the time, other people may wrongly assume you aren't enjoying yourself or don't want to participate.

Again, it is not necessary to hide anything from very close friends and family. People also develop social personas because it is unacceptable to share private matters with the world at large. In fact, it is considered inappropriate to display your more intense feelings and special personality traits at work or school. This doesn't mean you have to act like a brick with no feelings at all. But, for example, while you can cry in front of your close friends and family members at home or in private, you are expected to control your emotions at work or in public. A social persona is useful in this regard because it enables you to pick and choose what pieces of yourself you will show the world.

Exchanging Social Signals

Many of us on the spectrum have trouble forming or exchanging social signals. For example, you may look upset even if you are feeling quite calm. Or you may smile at someone else too long. You may not look at a friend in the eyes, causing her to wonder if you are interested in her companionship.

Misfired social signals are more of a problem with co-workers and casual friends who do not know you well enough to ask you questions about your signals. For example, if the mail carrier approaches you to chat, but you look away and take a very long time to answer his questions or join the conversation he has initiated, he is likely to assume you don't like him or don't want to be casual friends. He will move on to chat and be friendly with other people.

If you are casual friends with somebody and you care what he thinks about you, or if you have to get along with your co-workers, you may need to provide them with some sort of explanation for your behavior. You do not necessarily have to disclose your diagnosis (see more about disclosure in Chapter 13, *Disclosing Your Diagnosis*). Using the above example, you could say to the mail carrier, "I'd love to chat with you, but it takes me an extra minute to form my ideas." Lots of people think or talk slowly. Another example: You could say to a co-worker, "I appreciate our friendship, even if sometimes I don't seem excited on the outside." Caring, insightful, intelligent people understand that all human beings are different and that diversity is good. A caring person will give you a chance even if she is confused by your occasional signal mix-ups.

Additional Friendship Advice

Even if we are lonely or having trouble finding the friendships we want, it is important to steer clear of certain people. If you make a friend who does not treat you well, break the friendship and move on. Do not make friends with people who force you to do things you don't like to do. Also, your self-worth is not dependent on what other people think of you. In other words, if some people do not like you or do not want to be your friend, that doesn't mean you aren't interesting, fun, or ever worthy of friendship. You just have to keep waiting until you find someone who *is* interested in you for friendship.

If you are extremely lonely and not having much luck making friends, see if a family member wants to be your friend. It sounds strange, but sometimes someone in your family would love to hang out with you if only he knew you wanted to.

If you are extremely lonely and not having much luck making friends, see if a family member wants to be your friend. It sounds strange, but sometimes someone in your family would love to hang out with you if only he knew you wanted to. One "bridge" that helped me enormously was friendship with my father. As a young girl, I thoroughly enjoyed long conversations with him. We would talk about the world, history, politics, current events, math, science, literature – anything. He is brilliant, and we loved sharing our thoughts. He would take hours to explain anything in the world to me. I could always rely on him as a parent and a friend.

My father and I would go out to a restaurant and enjoy a meal together without having to talk. We would watch football games, again without the pressure to chat or socialize, commenting occasionally about the game or the players, but otherwise at ease in our own worlds. Whenever we were on a family trip in the car, he seemed to know just what I would be fascinated to see, waking me up to look at a coal mine or standing with me and watching locks on the Eerie canal slowly fill and raise a ship. To this day, I know I can seek him out for non-judgmental companionship. We understand the world similarly and find the same things funny. A close relationship to a parent or another kind and trustworthy family member may help alleviate your feelings of social ineptitude and isolation.

Conclusion

In terms of friendship, autistic adulthood may be easier than childhood. As children, we had no choice but to go to school and deal with the other children. But as adults, we are free to choose with whom we associate. Most adults have a higher tolerance for individuality that comes with maturity. Usually, adults can find opportunities to befriend others with similar hobbies, values, and interests – either at work, at college, or in the community. While efforts to make friends can still be frustrating, the consequences often feel much less severe than when we were children and it was glaringly obvious that we did not fit in.

You may not want to interact with anybody. You may be totally content with solitary pursuits. But the common autistic trait of mild to severe social isolation is not always a pure choice. Even if you only want to socialize in moderate doses and in certain circumstances, you can still have a friend if you want one. You are not doomed to a life of social isolation and loneliness simply because you are autistic. This is why the issue of friendship should not be overlooked. With knowledge about how friendship works, we can make friends and experience the benefits of friendship – a universal aspect of human culture that has the potential to be very sweet and rewarding.

■ ■ ■

Chapter 13

Disclosing Your Diagnosis

I am often asked by people on the spectrum if I think they should tell others about their diagnosis. My answer is usually yes, but it depends. Obviously, the situation is different if you are talking about disclosing to a boss versus disclosing to a friend or a date. While the issue of disclosure has been discussed briefly in other chapters when relevant, this chapter focuses solely on disclosure, including the potential consequences of disclosing to various types of people in your life and how to disclose your diagnosis as successfully as possible in different scenarios.

Basic Disclosure Information

Disclosure is important because autism is so much a part of who we are. If you were born with only one arm, you would look at your body and know something was different. You would compare yourself to your siblings and peers early on, and the difference would be obvious to all. You would not be able to hide from the fact that you were missing a limb. You would have to learn how to navigate the world with one arm from a young age. You would have to figure out how to explain your needs and issues, plus be able to describe your experiences. You would need the skills to explain your unique situation, to advocate for yourself, to manage your fears, to make the best health decisions, and to get along in life.

Being autistic is no different, except that nobody can tell automatically – at least, not so easily. You do not have something different about your body, but you have something different about your behavior.

Telling other people you are autistic allows them to understand you and help you. But because many people know nothing about autism, you may have to supply some information.

You may have sensory issues. You may not be able to decode and exchange facial expressions well or at all. You may miss the nonverbal expressions of others. You may have trouble with language – innuendos, double meanings, implications, subtleties – all the clues people rely on in social exchanges. You may have no means to decipher humor or deception. You may have little understanding of why people act in the ways that they do. You may rock back and forth or flap your hands, talk obsessively about every capital city in the United States, or prefer sitting in a dark corner. You know deep inside yourself that you are not *trying* to be weird, you are just being yourself.

But people who do not know you and who do not know you are autistic may see your behavior and start wondering about you. When someone is unusual in one way or another, people begin to guess why. If they do not know you have a disability, they may not have any other way to explain your differences than to make negative assumptions about you. For example, if you do not smile cheerfully and greet everybody at your place of work in the morning, your officemates might decide you do not like them or you are a mean person. You probably *do* like your co-workers and you probably are not a mean person. It is possible that you just do not have enough "social energy" on top of work, or you may not understand the greeting rules. To avoid people guessing negative things about you is one main reason why it is important to explain your diagnosis in various areas of life.

General Disclosure Policies

Telling other people you are autistic allows them to understand you and help you. But because many people know nothing about autism, you may have to supply some information. It is usually not enough to just say, "I'm autistic," and then stop there. Because other people will try to figure out who you are and why you do the things you do, you also have to explain how autism affects you. Using the previous example of not greeting your co-workers in the morning, if you were to explain to them that you are autistic but gave no other information, they would still wonder why you do not say hello to them. Therefore, you may need to explain that being autistic makes it hard for you to socialize *and* concentrate on work at the same time, or that being autistic means you don't always know the social rules.

Remember, you do not have to launch into a long explanation about autism. Usually a few sentences are plenty. You can even just explain one or two aspects of being on the spectrum that are most relevant to your case. People are usually not interested in hearing every single fact about autism – they just need to know about you. For example, if you have sensory issues with indoor lighting, just say something like, "I'm on the autism spectrum. This means I have sensory issues with indoor lights. They hurt my eyes. You may see me wearing sunglasses indoors." That is enough information. Or, if socializing is tricky for you, just say something like, "I'm on the autism spectrum. This means I have some social challenges. I may not do 'regular' social things like say hello in the morning because I'm so busy concentrating. I may not even realize some of the social things I'm expected to do. But it doesn't mean I don't like you." That is enough information.

Even when you provide the right type and the right amount of information, the danger in disclosing your diagnosis is that some people will act with prejudice toward you. It is sad but true that some people discriminate against people with disabilities. Or when they hear the word autism, they think this means you can't do a good job or can't get along with people under all circumstances. They may have these negative attitudes because they've never met someone autistic or don't know much about disabilities in general. But it can still hurt your feelings to be rejected. Therefore, it is very important to think carefully about what you want to say and what the consequences might be *before* you disclose your diagnosis.

Disclosing at Work: Dealing With Consequences

Disclosing your diagnosis at work was discussed briefly in Chapter 7: *Vocational Issues*. One reason why it is a good idea to disclose your diagnosis to your boss is that if your boss and your co-workers know that you are on the autism spectrum, they can look at your behavior and think of good reasons why you are doing the things you do. They can try to understand you in a positive way. They may have suggestions to help you when you run into difficulties. They may even include you in the workplace social life, making special exceptions for you because they have learned about your disability. But people on the spectrum face one big problem: As mentioned in Chapter 7, you may not get the job in the first place if you disclose before you obtain the position.

Many people on the spectrum decide to take the honest route, explaining during a job interview that they are on the autism spectrum and that they will require certain physical and/or social accommodations. They want to tell their potential boss upfront that they need non-fluorescent lighting or that it would be hard to go to required lunch meetings, for example. But because of such honesty, you may not get the job. If an accommodation is within reason, it is illegal not to hire a disabled candidate, but unfortunately it still happens.

Others have decided to wait until after they obtain the job. But sometimes the boss will say, "Well, why weren't you honest with me during the interview?" The boss may decide that because she did not know in advance, she cannot make any accommodations now. This is a circular problem for which there is no easy answer. *Only you can decide what the best course of action is.* Some say you should never disclose anything about yourself at work, only addressing problems that arise as anyone else would. I would rather be totally honest and get a job with a boss who is open-minded and tolerant enough to give me an opportunity to succeed and to do my best.

You may find it easier to disclose your diagnosis to your co-workers and work around your problems that way. You could explain to them that you are on the spectrum and then explain what they need to know. For example, if you have trouble with eye contact, they probably want to know why you look away when someone is talking to you. Sometimes your co-workers just need to be assured of your friendliness in cases like this. How can they be sure that you care about them if you don't do the usual greetings, chatting, waving, or hanging out? By explaining the reasons why you behave the way you do, you and the people in your immediate work environment may be able to establish a mutual understanding without ever having to go to the boss.

To disclose or not at work also depends on the type of job you have. If you work in a large warehouse where you rarely have to talk to anybody, you can go at your own pace, and your tasks are easy for you to complete, you may never have to tell anybody about your diagnosis. On the other hand, if you are working in a small office where people are expected to interact a lot, you may need to say something to the people you will be in contact with for many hours at a time. If you work in a corporate environment where roles are highly structured, you may only need to talk to your immediate supervisor. But if you work in a small enterprise with just a few other people, the challenges you face may be more noticeable, requiring at least some discussion about being on the spectrum.

Again, ultimately the choice is yours. Always keep in mind why you are making a disclosure. The only reason to disclose your diagnosis at work is so that others can understand and interpret your behavior positively, and so that you can reach your potential and succeed at your position. With this in mind, keep any discussion about autism related to the job. As explained in Chapter 7, the boss does not need to know you find shopping a challenge. Stick to what matters at work.

Disclosing to Friends and Dates: Dealing With Various Reactions

The key to deciding whether to disclose to a friend or a date is how useful the disclosure would be. And that depends on the nature of the friendship or date. For example, if you have a friend whom you see only once in a while for very brief periods of time, this type of friend is called a casual friend or acquaintance and usually it is not necessary to explain your diagnosis (see Chapter 12: *Friendship*).

If you have a close friend with whom you spend a lot of time and whom you care about a lot, it may be useful to disclose your diagnosis if information about autism would help your friend understand you better. For example, your friend may wonder why you never look at her face or why you take so long to answer questions. Or she may wonder why you refuse to go to loud clubs. In this case, a brief explanation similar to the type you would give someone at work should be sufficient. A friend does not need to hear every single thing about autism, unless she asks you. A friend only needs enough information so she can understand how you behave and how to react to you.

As mentioned in Chapter 8: *Dating on the Spectrum*, disclosing your diagnosis to someone you want to be in a romantic relationship with will probably be necessary at some point. Again, it depends on the level of the relationship. If you are dating someone informally or once in a while, a friendship-style disclosure is probably be enough. In fact, it is only necessary to discuss autism with a casual date if the other person has questions about your behavior, does not understand why you behave a certain way, or can't communicate with you effectively.

On the other hand, if you are dating someone seriously, if you are in love with someone, or if you are considering marrying someone, a more serious discussion is warranted at some point. It is hard to say when. The important thing to remember is that sharing your diagnosis with someone you love deeply (or want to love deeply) should be done in a way that allows the other person to get to know you better. In other words, make sure you want to share this part of yourself because the two of you care about each other and want to be involved in each other's lives. Disclosing your diagnosis just to see how the other person reacts or to test the other person's loyalty almost always backfires.

This leads to an important point: *In disclosing your diagnosis to friends and dates, you have to accept the fact that some people discriminate against disabled people.* However, discrimination is less likely with friends. After all, friendship is about meeting new people and learning about the world from them. It is fairly rare that a friend at school or work or church will outright reject you because you are autistic.

Most people you date will also not completely reject you just because you have a disability. Everyone has some issue to work out, even those not on the spectrum. Your romantic partner may need some time to learn about autism and how autism is going to impact your life together as a couple. But again, as discussed in Chapter 8, anyone who doesn't want to be your girlfriend or boyfriend just because you are on the autism spectrum does not deserve your companionship. This may seem simplistic, but it is the truth. Such a person probably does not have the maturity to accept another person in a tolerant and loving way. Move on and find someone new. (See Chapter 8 for a more detailed discussion on this issue.)

Disclosing to Parents and Relatives: Dealing With Disbelief

An entire generation of people on the spectrum grew up not knowing we were autistic. Some of us were able to disguise just how different we really are and never had much trouble at home or at school. But this is rare. Most of us were obviously different, beyond the regular range of differences among children. Many of us ran into trouble at school and in the community. Some of us had serious difficulty with our parents, siblings, and other relatives. Because nobody had an explanation for our chal-

NOTE: Disclosing to family is very different from disclosing to a boss or a co-worker. Unlike at work, you will be explaining a lot about the autism spectrum and how you fit into it. Go slow. Don't rush. You may have to have multiple conversations.

lenges, others might have assumed we acted eccentric for attention, that we were full of self-pity if we complained about life, or that we were downright lazy and stupid when we failed at usual activities like sports, jobs, or getting along with peers. Many of us spent years searching for the truth, blaming ourselves for problems we couldn't understand, winding up in all sorts of trouble, bumbling into adulthood and adult responsibilities ill prepared to function in the world.

Upon discovering our diagnoses, some of us react with anxiety and new questions, others with relief at a new way to understand life. However you are managing your diagnosis, you will probably reach a point when it is time to tell your parents, your siblings, perhaps old friends, or other members of your childhood community. What do you expect will happen when you tell them? Try to answer this question before you talk to them. You may hope everyone will react positively. But they may not, which can be shocking and disappointing. Be prepared.

Some family members will say, "Ah-ha! This all makes sense!" They will look back in time and finally be able to put all the pieces together. Relatives may feel relief, too. They will now have reasons for the things you did. They may express great compassion, now understanding why you had such a tough time at college or why you've had such a hard time holding down a job. They may see you in a new light, realizing you weren't acting up or trying to cause problems.

But family members could just as easily react the opposite way. Some will deny you ever had any problems. Even though as a child I could not sit comfortably in a restaurant due to sensory issues, even though I was always complaining of eye pain from bright lights, even though I had constant battles with my teachers over wearing sunglasses in class, even though I could barely tolerate most foods and most fabrics, one relative said to me, "I swear you never had any sensory issues, whatever they are. All kids hate to sit in a restaurant for a long time! All kids have little complaints about what they'll eat or what they'll wear!"

Others will insist that your diagnosis is incorrect. Even if you show them materials that describe the autism spectrum, you may be met with comments like, "Autistic people don't talk." Still others will blame you again – this time because they allege you are fishing for excuses. For example, they may say in a very sarcastic manner, "Oh how convenient. Now you don't have to keep trying to get a job because you're disabled." Or they may counter with, "The real reason you have no friends is that you won't get out of the house, not because you're autistic."

Dealing With Negative Reactions

We all expect family members to love us and care about us, so it can be very disappointing and heart-breaking if they don't believe us, they don't affirm our memories and experiences, or they contradict our attempts to understand ourselves. If your family has a negative reaction, be patient and don't give up. Sometimes your relatives just need time to get used to the idea. They may also be having a hard time if, upon hearing about your diagnosis, they begin discovering similar traits in themselves or other family members. Still others may resist thinking of you as disabled because when they grew up, society was very inhospitable for disabled people in ways it is not today.

Ultimately, if you can't find support from your family, you may have to stop talking about it with them. This can be sad. In this type of extreme case, look for support in the autism community. Find solace in new friends and a new support system, which you can begin to build by attending support meetings for adults on the spectrum.

But keep an open mind. Who knows, maybe your loved ones will be ready to hear about your diagnosis later on. Whether you meet stiff initial resistance from your family or complete acceptance and willingness to learn, family members can become valuable "allies" over time, as Phil Schwarz explains in his essay, "Building Alliances: Community Identity and the Role of Allies in Autistic Self-Advocacy." Mr. Schwarz defines an ally as someone non-autistic who tries both to understand autism in new, positive ways and to promote tolerance, acceptance, and this new understanding in society.

Family members are the people who love us the most. They are therefore the most likely to work with us in changing negative stereotypes and misconceptions about autistic people.

Family members are the people who love us the most. They are therefore the most likely to work with us in changing negative stereotypes and misconceptions about autistic people. They may also become your advocate or a general advocate for the autistic community. This is why it is worth being patient with your family and loved ones. Supplying information at a pace they can handle, respecting what they can manage to talk about, and giving them time to learn and to think about your diagnosis is the best approach for reaching a successful outcome to your disclosure.

Disclosing to a Child: Dealing With Insecurity

How to Tell Your Child

A number of us diagnosed later in life have children. This brings up a rarely discussed but important issue: How, when, and even why should we disclose our diagnosis to our children? It depends on the age of the child and the circumstances of your family. Generally speaking, children should not feel burdened or encumbered by a parent's problems. A child should never feel responsible for the parent. Parents take care of children, not the other way around. Otherwise, children can feel very insecure.

But a child will notice differences, both subtle and obvious, in an autistic parent. Why are you wearing sunglasses at the grocery store? How come you don't really chat with the other kids' parents? How could you forget that guy is your next-door neighbor? Why are you looking at the wall when Mommy talks to you? A child may never ask you these types of questions directly, but you can be sure your child notices everything – positive and negative – about you.

Direct factual statements are usually the best approach with very young children. Leave out social complications that could worry a child. For example, regarding the sunglasses at the grocery store, the fact is the lights bother your eyes. A small child can accept this: Some people in the store are cold and wear sweaters; others don't mind the chill and are in shorts. People are all different, and this is the easiest way for a young child to understand you.

When a child is older, she begins to realize that your differences aren't just a matter of personal preference. This is when disclosure becomes more important. But disclosure must be done in a way that does not leave the child worried about you or worried about your ability to care for her. Again, simple facts with whatever amount of detail the child can handle usually suffice. Analogies are helpful. For example, a blind person can still play basketball if he puts bells in the ball so he can hear where it is. A disability doesn't mean you can't do something. It just means that you sometimes have to find new ways of doing things.

Also point out your strengths. For example, maybe you aren't a great socializer, but you are great at finding places on a map or organizing the family's recycling. Teach your child how to use an atlas or take him on a special trip to the county recycling center. Emphasize the things you like to do. Maybe you hate going to restaurants because of sensory issues, but love going to the nature center or the library. If your child complains about the things you can't do, compromise: Order take-out from the diner for a picnic if you can't stand sitting inside. Your issues do not need to be your child's issues. But by elementary school, children are ready to learn and to accept that the world requires a degree of compromise and tolerance for people's varying abilities. Even "regular" parents can't promise everything.

When your child is older, you can begin to bring in more of the social information about your situation. A small child just doesn't have the capacity to understand the complex relationship between society and peer rejection, or the intricate relationship between failure and personal choice. Nor do most small children have the maturity to understand that positive things can come out of times of trouble. They learn these subtleties as they grow older and gain the capacity to reflect on their own expanding life experiences.

Before you have any discussions about your autism, review your goals: If you are aiming for sympathy, if you want to get your child to see things your way, or if you think you can steer your child clear of some activity you disapprove of, chances are any discussion about your autism will break down and you won't get what you hoped for out of the talk. But if you are answering a child's natural curiosity, if you yearn to share more about yourself, if you hope to pass on some bit of wisdom you've gained through your experiences, or if you genuinely must put an issue into context, then a careful discussion about your autism can be beneficial.

NOTE: Even if your children are young adults or full-grown adults, it is still important to tailor your discussions to take into account what they can handle. Many people view their parents in an idealistic way well past childhood. Therefore, the news that a parent has a disability can be troublesome.

Disclosure When Your Child Is on the Spectrum, Too

Another case in which it is obviously beneficial to discuss your autism is if your children share your diagnosis. Who could be a better role model and advocate for them than you? Again, tailor what you say to the child's age, ability to understand, and sensitivities. Keep in mind that in this case, the child is also learning about himself through your experiences and reactions. In other words, if your child is not on the spectrum, she is learning about you and learning about tolerance and compromise in a general way, but if your child is on the spectrum, she is additionally learning how to move through the world as an autistic person based on your methods.

Do you advocate for yourself in positive ways? Can you compromise with the world politely without sacrificing your needs or jeopardizing your physical and mental health? Have you found ways to reach your potential, despite the challenges you face? You have a wonderful opportunity to become the role model and advocate you wish you had when you were growing up.

While it is important to disclose your diagnosis when your child is also on the spectrum, be careful that the diagnosis does not become an excuse or a technique of "dividing and conquering." For example, you don't want a situation where your child says, "Daddy and I don't have to go to the restaurant because we have Asperger Syndrome." Either find a restaurant the whole family can enjoy, involve all your children in planning a picnic instead, or pack a Sensory Emergency Kit with your autistic child and teach him how to survive this type of unavoidable social situation by asking politely for breaks during the meal or whatever other positive strategies you use to take care of yourself. If restaurants are out of the question because of sensory or other issues, teach your child how to explain this challenge to other family members and how to compromise by inviting family members to do some other fun activity that is acceptable.

Disclosing to Other Children in Your Life

What about other children in your life, such as nieces and nephews or grandchildren? The same general principles apply, but always follow this rule: *Talk to the parents first.* Parents have the right to make decisions on behalf of their children. A parent may think it is unnecessary or perhaps even damaging in some way for you to discuss your autism with the child in question. Ultimately you must go along with the parents' wishes even if you disagree. The child's parents are going to want to know why you think it is necessary to tell the child. Unless you have a very good reason – for example, the child asked you point blank, or the child has some other question about your behavior – it probably isn't, especially if the child is young.

The hardest situation you may encounter is when you are pretty sure a relative's or friend's child is on the spectrum and you see the child suffering or not getting services and interventions that you know could make a big difference in his life. Don't approach the child. Turning to the child thinking you will help him discover his place on the spectrum will backfire; you won't achieve the goal of getting the child proper help. If anything, you'll confuse him or make him wonder why his parents never told him these things about himself.

Instead, talk to the parents and let them take it from there. It is the parents who will decide to bring the child in for an assessment or for treatment and is the parents who know the child the best. Most par-

People You May Disclose to and Why

Person	*Reasons to Disclose*
Boss	• Request accommodations • Provide an explanation for any atypical behavior at work
Co-worker	• Provide an explanation for any atypical behavior at work • Reassure them that you are friendly and cooperative, just different
Casual friend	• Usually do not disclose • May disclose only to explain an immediate issue • May "disclose" without mentioning autism
Close friend	• Provide an explanation for any behavior that might be confusing • Share more about who you are with a tolerant, loving friend • Provide information so your friend can advocate for you
Parent	• Discuss unresolved childhood issues • Provide an explanation for problems in childhood or adolescence • Get along better
Other relative (sibling, grandparent)	• Discuss issues from childhood • Resolve any misunderstandings • Get along better
Your child	• Learn about differences, tolerance, and acceptance • Show positive aspects of autism • Inspire to overcome challenges
Your autistic child	• Same as for a child not on the spectrum, plus: – Provide a role model and a positive example of self-advocacy – Demonstrate ways of getting along with the non-autistic world
An unrelated child (talk to the parents)	• Provide an explanation for your behavior • Advocate on behalf of a potentially autistic child in need of services

ents are going to resist the idea that their child has a disability, especially if they know next to nothing about autism. Additionally, if being on the spectrum has been difficult for you, the parents probably don't want to think their child could have the same problems. You are most likely not a trained diagnostician, so you could be wrong. If you do have a strong feeling that a child you know is on the spectrum and disclosing your diagnosis to his parents could open up a discussion that might help the child in the long run, it may be worth trying. Just remember you are probably going to meet some degree of resistance.

Conclusion

Disclosure is not a matter of yes, you should disclose, or no, you should not disclose. When and how you disclose the fact that you are autistic depends on many factors: What relationship do you have to the person who will receive this information? Is it someone who really has to know, like a spouse or a parent? How will it help the other person to know this bit of information about you?

It is also very important to consider how the person may react. Do you think they will still accept you? Do you think they will want to help you? Or do you think they will lose respect for you, treat you differently, or reject you? You may still need to tell. In that case, how will you handle your feelings of disappointment?

Because disclosing your diagnosis depends on so many social factors – the type of relationship, the depth of the relationship, the social context – and because disclosing can bring up a lot of emotions, it is important to talk to someone you trust first. See if you can role-play with this trusted person what you will say when disclosing and what you will do if the other person reacts negatively or in a way you do not expect.

Remember also that other people are not perfect. The first time someone hears you are autistic, he or she might be very surprised. It may take time to digest this new fact about you. If after you have disclosed your diagnosis the other person asks for some time to think about it, this does not mean he is rejecting you. Family members, especially, may have lots of feelings about you being autistic. When you disclose your diagnosis, you are providing an opportunity for both you and the other person to learn and to grow in ways you may not have thought of before, or in ways that may not be obvious. Learning and growing takes time. Give others a chance, and you may be amazed at the new ways they can care about you and help you, once they understand.

■ ■ ■

Chapter 14

Invisibility and Self-Esteem in the Autistic Community

What all the chapters in this book have in common is an attempt to help fellow members of the autism community find strength in the way we are. We may experience challenges in areas of life, ranging from shopping to holding down a job, but this is no reason to stop us from doing anything we want to do. Autistic traits such as visual thinking, ability to categorize, and appreciation for rules and systems can be used to overcome difficulties and even to excel at our endeavors. The way we think, feel, and communicate can also enhance relationships of all sorts, especially relationships with friends and family. Contrary to society's perception that our lives are fraught with struggle or the common assumption that we tragically go from disappointment to disappointment, our lives can be full, happy, and rewarding as we bring the world our gifts.

Unfortunately, for the most part, those of us with autism remain fairly invisible. In discussing potential role models from history for people on the autism spectrum, Valerie Paradiz says in her book *Elija's Cup* regarding Albert Einstein, whom many people believe was autistic, "Had he been born in our contemporary era of learning disabilities and special education, young Einstein would most likely have been identified for an early intervention program … But this was not the paradigm of the 1890s when Einstein was a boy. What has remained, however, is the legacy of autistic invisibility" (p. 125). In other words, while educators, doctors, clinicians, and parents are skilled these days at recognizing autistic behaviors and diagnosing

When others cannot see that we are disabled but sense that we are different in some fundamental way, their tendency is to immediately make negative assumptions about our behavior.

children, autistic people still remain an enigma, an invisible group that the world barely realizes exists.

Over and over again, I hear people on the spectrum express a looming sense of failure. Chronic low-self esteem appears to be prevalent in the community. I am not a scientist. I do not have statistics, nor have I done methodical research in this area. But I can say with a degree of anecdotal surety that in the autism community, depression, suicidal thoughts, low self-esteem, lack of confidence, loneliness, and a lack of self-worth at times seem epidemic. Is this due, in part or in whole, to our invisibility? And why are we so invisible?

When others cannot see that we are disabled but sense that we are different in some fundamental way, their tendency is to immediately make negative assumptions about our behavior. As Valerie Paradiz writes in a different part of her book:

> The … autistics I have met … describe what neurotypicals perceive as a withdrawal as a partial shutdown of the senses, as a busy cataloguing of events around them, or as a stimulating fascination with a nearby sensory experience. Sometimes there are just too many social cues to read and interpret all in the same moment … One thing is certain: the apparent distancing is a necessary safety device, a way of navigating through neurotypicals waters, even though it's wrongly read as shutting out, as a puzzling lack of social grace, or as just plain bad behavior. (p. 163)

With no word for me, with no word for my behavior, with no other way to understand my wavy eyes and expressionless face and my dark shades and my strange posture and my wool ponchos, it is easy for others to assume I am a disinterested eccentric lost in my own world, unconcerned about something as complex as socializing or contributing in a broad sense to all sorts of human endeavors.

Imagine these scenarios for a moment: Every time you go out into the world and try to befriend the other children, you are rebuffed. You have no idea why. Also inexplicably, you are often chastised for sounding rude, for not choosing the correct words, for using the wrong tone of voice, for missing the point completely. As an adult, every time you try hard at work, your efforts are misunderstood. You are "over-focused" and don't handle disruptions well. You stumble over yourself when you try to interact socially with other adults. What is going to happen to your soul?

Because our disability is hidden, nobody reacts to us with an "Ah ha – I understand." We need to start asking ourselves what we can do to make autism recognizable. Some people are very uncomfortable with this idea. Autism is still a painful and big question mark in certain circles, not something to flaunt. When these people hear the "A" word, they shudder. Some will accuse me of being in denial because autism can present extreme challenges. But the risk of invisibility is too high. Autistic visibility is crucial to fixing the dilemma of sagging mental health in our community.

Autistic children and adults need to see reflections of success and achievement, no matter how small the increments or how much learning is left to do. In my opinion, the only way we can collectively address the intense moods of failure and loneliness in the autistic community is by consistently accentuating what is worthy and noble in even the tiniest effort or the greatest "blunder." Mistakes, especially social ones, may stem from traits and values that could actually benefit the world.

From the very beginning of life, positive autistic behaviors need to be valued and put to good use. Intense focus, thorough knowledge of special subjects, visual thinking, simple and direct emotional processing, plain and honest language skills, ability to remember and repeat, sincere curiosity, and innocent fascination are necessary components of many human activities and are often sorely lacking in society. Autistic people have much to contribute to life. I do not live in a fantasy world of eternal patience or presumed facility, but I believe firmly that all autistic people have capacity and potential, even if that capacity and that potential is just to exist and to experience life, valuable traits in and of themselves.

We need to find a way to move us from the stigma of behavioral problems or social deviance to the healing light of neurological diversity.

The seeds for a positive understanding of autism have been sown in the Autism Self-Advocacy Community and little plants are already flowering. Though it may not seem so on very bad days, society has changed a lot. All the efforts to normalize us are slowly being questioned by a world that is growing in its awareness of diversity's value. Even the severely disabled are gaining a voice, some chances here and there, to explain how it feels on the inside and to claim recognition for their different experiences of life and love.

I'm not suggesting that we all start wearing letter "A"s on our shirts. But until we become clearly visible through pride and acceptance, existing everywhere just like everybody else, we will remain marginalized, our behavior questioned for what it is not. If people said, "This person's behavior is different from what I expect, but difference is a good and interesting thing," what would be the result?

We need to find a way to move us from the stigma of behavioral problems or social deviance to the healing light of neurological diversity. All the suggestions, tips, and advice offered in this book are like lampposts on that path. The only way we will get down the path is if we stop the legacy of autistic invisibility by living our lives fully and with a deep sense of pride and purpose.

■ ■ ■

REFERENCES

Below is a list of references that I used as I wrote this book. Including a reference does not mean that I agree with the author or authors or concur with all or any of the opinions and conclusions they express.

Reference Material Used for All Chapters

Adams, C., Green, J., Gilchrist, A., & Cox, A. (2002). Conversational behaviour of children with Asperger syndrome and conduct disorder. *Journal of Child Psychology and Psychiatry, 43*(5), 679-690.

Atwood, T. (1998). *Asperger's Syndrome: A guide for parents and professionals*. London & Philadelphia: Jessica Kingsley Publications.

Barnhill, G. P., Cook, K. T., Tebbenkamp, K., & Myles, B. S. (2002). The effectiveness of social skills intervention targeting nonverbal communication for adolescents with Asperger's Syndrome and related pervasive developmental delays. *Focus on Autism & Other Developmental Disabilities, 17*(2), 112-119.

Beglinger, L. J., & Smith, T. H. (2001). A review of subtyping in autism and proposed dimensional classification model. *Journal of Autism and Developmental Disorders, 31*(4), 411-422.

Blakeslee, S. (November 19, 2002). A boy, a mother, and a rare map of autism's world. *The New York Times*, F1.

Bledsoe, R., Myles, B. S., & Simpson, R. (2003). Use of a Social Story intervention to improve mealtime skills of an adolescent with Asperger syndrome. *Autism, 7*(3), 289-295.

Bolick, T. (2001). *Asperger Syndrome and adolescence: Helping preteens and teens get ready for the real world*. Gloucester, MA: Fair Winds Press, a division of Rockport Publishers, Inc.

Bowman, E. P. (1988). Asperger's Syndrome and autism: The case for a connection. *The British Journal of Psychiatry, 152*, 377-382.

Brownell, M. T., & Walther-Thomas, C. (2001). An interview with Steven [sic] Shore: Understanding the autism spectrum – what teachers need to know. *Intervention in School and Clinic, 36*(5), 293-300.

Burgoine, E., & Wing, L. (1983). Identical triplets with Asperger's syndrome. *The British Journal of Psychiatry, 143*, 261-265.

Chen, P. S., et al. (2003). Asperger's disorder: a case report of repeated stealing and the collecting behaviours of an adolescent patient. *Acta Psychiatrica Scandinavica, 107*(1), 73-79.

Conner, M. (1999). Children on the autistic spectrum: Guidelines for mainstream practice. *Support for Learning, 14*(2), 80-86.

Dyck, M. J., Ferguson, K., & Shochet, I. M. (2001). Do autism spectrum disorders differ from each other and from non-spectrum disorders on emotion recognition tests? *European Child and Adolescent Psychiatry, 10*(105), 105-116.

Else, L. Opinion: In a different world: Interview with Simon Baron-Cohen. *New Scientist, 170*(2286), 42-45.

Fine, L. (November 21, 2001). Cracking the shell. *Education Week, 21*(12), 22-27.

Freeman, B. J., Cronin, P., & Candela, P. (2002). Asperger Syndrome or autistic disorder? *Focus on Autism and Other Developmental Disabilities, 17*(3), 145-151.

Ghaziuddin, M. (2002). Asperger syndrome: Associated psychiatric and medical conditions. *Focus on Autism and Other Developmental Disabilities, 17*(3), 138-144.

Grandin, T. (1996). *Emergence: Labeled autistic*. New York: Warner Books, Inc.

Grandin, T. (1996). *Thinking in pictures and other reports from my life with autism*. New York: Vintage Books, a Division of Random House, Inc.

Gray, C. (1994). *Comic strip conversations.* Jenson, MI: Jenson Public Schools.

Gray, C. (1997). *Social stories and comic strip conversations: Unique methods to improve social understanding*. Jenson, MI: Jenson Public Schools.

Greenway, C. (2000). Autism and Asperger syndrome: Strategies to promote prosocial behaviours. *Educational Psychology in Practice, 16*(3), 469-486.

Gross, J. (April 13, 2003). An answer to autism – nudging toward normal. *The New York Times Education Life,* 27.

Harmon, A. (December 20, 2004). How about not 'curing' us, some autistics are pleading. *The New York Times*, A1.

Holland, O. (2003). *The dragons of autism: Autism as a source of wisdom.* London & Philadelphia: Jessica Kingsley Publishers.

Howlin, P. (2003). *Autism and Asperger Syndrome – Preparing for adulthood.* London & Philadelphia: Jessica Kingsley Publishers.

Howlin, P. (1998). Practitioner review: Psychological and educational treatments for autism. *Journal of Child Psychology, 39*(3), 307-322.

Jackson, L. (2002). *Freaks, geeks and Asperger Syndrome.* London & Philadelphia: Jessica Kingsley Publishers.

Kiln, A., et al. (2002). Defining and quantifying the social phenotype in autism. *American Journal of Psychiatry, 159*(6), 895-907.

McLaughlin-Cheng, E. (1998). Asperger Syndrome and autism: A literature review and meta-analysis. *Focus on Autism and Other Developmental Disabilities, 13*(4), 234-246.

Meyer, J. A., & Minshew, N. J. (2002). An update on neurocognitive profiles in Asperger Syndrome and high-functioning autism. *Focus on Autism and Other Developmental Disabilities, 17*(3), 152-160.

Nash, J. M. (May 6, 2002). The secrets of autism. *Time, 59*(18), 46-56.

Osborne, L. (June 18, 2000). The little professor syndrome. *The New York Times Sunday Magazine*, 54-59.

Ozonoff, S. (2001). Advances in the cognitive neuroscience of autism. In C. A. Nelson, & M. Luciana (Eds.), *Handbook of developmental cognitive neuroscience* (pp. 537-548). Cambridge, MA: The MIT Press.

Ozonoff, S., Dawson, G., & McPortland, J. (2002). *A parent's guide to Asperger Syndrome and high-functioning autism: How to meet the challenges and help your child thrive*. New York: The Guilford Press.

Paradiz, V. (2002). *Elijah's cup: A family's journey into the community and culture of high-functioning autism and Asperger's Syndrome*. New York: The Free Press.

Prior, M., et al. (1998). Are there subgroups within the autistic spectrum? A cluster analysis of a group of children with autistic spectrum disorders. *Journal of Child Psychology and Psychiatry, 39*(6), 893-902.

Rapin, I. (2002). The autistic-spectrum disorders. *New England Journal of Medicine, 347*(5), 302-303.

Rapin, I. (2002). Diagnotistic dilemmas in developmental disabilities: Fuzzy margins at the edges of normality. An essay prompted by Thomas Sowell's new book: The Einstein Syndrome. *Journal of Autism and Developmental Disorders, 32*(1), 49-57.

Shore, S. (2000). *Beyond the wall: Personal experiences with autism and Asperger Syndrome, 2nd ed.* Shawnee Mission, KS: Autism Asperger Publishing Company.

Susman, E. (1996). How to tell Asperger's from autism. *Brown University Child and Adolescent Behavior Letter, 12*(1), 1-2.

Szatmari, P., Bartolucci, G., & Bremner, R. (1998). Asperger's Syndrome and autism: Comparison of early history and outcome. *Developmental Medicine and Child Neurology, 31*, 709-720.

Szatmari, P., et al. (1995). Asperger's Syndrome and autism: Differences in behavior, cognition, and adaptive functioning. *Journal of the American Academy of Child and Adolescent Psychiatry, 34*(12), 1662-1671.

Szatmari, P., et al. (2002). Two-year outcome of preschool children with autism or asperger's syndrome. *The American Journal of Psychiatry, 157*(12), 1980-1987.

Volkmar, F. R., Klin, A., Schultz, R. T., Rubin, E., & Bronen, R. (2000). Clinical case conference: Asperger's disorder. *American Journal of Psychiatry, 157*(2), 262-267.

Willey, L. H. (2001). *Asperger Syndrome in the family: Redefining normal.* London & Philadelphia: Jessica Kingsley Publications.

Willey, L. H. (1999). *Pretending to be normal: Living with Asperger's Syndrome.* London & Philadelphia: Jessica Kingsley Publications.

Williams, D. (1994). *Nobody nowhere: The extraordinary autobiography of an autistic.* New York: HarperCollins Publishers.

Wing, L. (1998). Asperger's syndrome: A clinical account. *Psychological Medicine, 11,* 115-129.

REFERENCES FOR SPECIFIC CHAPTERS

Chapter 1: Coping With Sensory Issues

Ahearn, W. H., Castine, T., Nault, K., & Green, G. (2001). An assessment of food acceptance in children with autism or pervasive developmental disorder-not otherwise specified. *Journal of Autism and Developmental Disorders, 31*(5), 505-511.

Dunn, W., Saiter, J., & Rinner, L. (2002). Asperger Syndrome and sensory processing: A conceptual model and guidance for intervention planning. *Focus on Autism and Other Developmental Disabilities, 17*(3), 172-185.

Green, D., et al. (2002). The severity and nature of motor impairment in Asperger's syndrome: A comparison with specific developmental disorder of motor function. *Journal of Child Psychology and Psychiatry, 43*(5), 655-668.

Legge, B. (2002). *Can't eat won't eat: dietary difficulties and autism spectrum disorders*. London & Philadelphia: Jessica Kingsley Publishers.

Myles, B. S., Cook, K. T., Miller, N. E., Rinner, L., & Robbins, L. A. (2000). *Asperger Syndrome and sensory issues: Practical solutions for making sense of the world*. Shawnee Mission, KS: Autism Asperger Publishing Company.

Ropar, D., & Mitchell, P. (1999). Are individuals with autism and asperger's syndrome susceptible to visual illusions? *Journal of Child Psychology and Psychiatry, 40*(8), 1283-1293.

Chapter 2: Maintaining a Home

McClannahan, L. E., & Krantz, P. (1999). *Activity schedules for children with autism: Teaching independent behavior*. Bethesda, MD: Woodbine House.

Chapter 4: Shopping

Clark, P. (2002, June). *Sensibilities and sensitivities – Food issues for people who are autistic* (note: includes information about food shopping). Workshop presented at Autreat 2002: Exploring Our Paths, Brantingham, NY.

Chapter 6: Health Care

Evens, K., & Dubowski, J. (2001). *Art therapy with children on the autistic spectrum: Beyond words*. London & Philadelphia: Jessica Kingsley Publishers.

Jacobsen, P. (2003). *Asperger Syndrome and psychotherapy: Understanding Asperger perspectives*. London & Philadelphia: Jessica Kingsley Publications.

Lainhart, J. E. (1999). Psychiatric problems in individuals with autism, their parents and siblings (note: includes information about physical illnesses and inability to perceive and/or report pain). *International Review of Psychiatry, 11*(4), 278-299.

Marshall, M. C. (2002). Asperger's Syndrome: Implications for nursing practice. *Issues in Mental Health Nursing, 23*(6), 605-616.

Ruberman, L. (2002). Psychotherapy of children with pervasive developmental disorders. *American Journal of Psychotherapy, 56*(2), 262-273.

Chapter 7: Vocational Challenges

Fast, Y. (2004). *Employment for individuals with Asperger Syndrome or non-verbal learning disability*. London & Philadelphia: Jessica Kingsley Publishers.

Grandin, T., & Duffy, K. (2004). *Developing talents: Careers for individuals with Asperger Syndrome and high-functioning autism*. Shawnee Mission, KS: Autism Asperger Publishing Company.

Hawkins, G. (2004). *How to find work that works for people with Asperger Syndrome.* London & Philadelphia: Jessica Kingsley Publishers.

Johnson, M. (2005). *Managing with Asperger Syndrome.* London & Philadelphia: Jessica Kingsley Publishers.

Smith, M. D., Belcher, R. G., & Juhrs, P. D. (1995). *A guide to successful employment for individuals with autism.* Baltimore: Paul H. Brookes Publishing Company.

Chapter 8: Dating on the Spectrum

Henault, I. (2005). *AS and sexuality: From adolescence through adulthood.* London & Philadelphia: Jessica Kingsley Publications.

Myles, B. S., & Simpson, R. L. (2005). Understanding the hidden curriculum: An essential social skill for children and youth with Asperger Syndrome. *Intervention in School and Clinic, 36*(5), 279-287.

Ouseley, O., & Mesibov, G. (1991). Sexual attitudes and knowledge of high-functioning adolescents and adults with autism. *Journal of Autism and Developmental Disorders, 21,* 471-481.

Stokes, M. A., & Kaur, A. (2005). High-functioning autism and sexuality – A parental perspective. *Autism, 9*(3), 266-289.

Chapter 9: Spectrum/Non-Spectrum Relationships – A New Perspective on Making It Work

Aston, M. C. (2003). *Aspergers in love: Couple relationships and family affairs.* London & Philadelphia: Jessica Kingsley Publications.

Aston, M. C. (2002). *The other half of Asperger Syndrome – A guide to living in an intimate relationship with a partner who has Asperger Syndrome.* Shawnee Mission, KS: Autism Asperger Publishing Company.

Buron, K. D., & Curtis, M. (2003). *The incredible 5-point scale – assisting students with autism spectrum disorders in understanding social interactions and controlling their emotional responses.* Shawnee Mission, KS: Autism Asperger Publishing Company.

Myles, B. S., & Southwick, J. (2005). *Asperger Syndrome and difficult moments: Practical solutions for tantrums, rage, and meltdowns.* Shawnee Mission, KS: Autism Asperger Publishing Company

Njiokiktjien, C., et al. (2001). Disordered recognition of facial identity and emotions in three Asperger type autistics. *European Child & Adolescent Psychiatry, 10,* 79-90.

Slater-Walker, G., & Slater-Walker, C. (2002). *An Asperger marriage.* London & Philadelphia: Jessica Kingsley Publishers.

Stanford, A. (2003). *Asperger Syndrome and long-term relationships.* London & Philadelphia: Jessica Kingsley Publishers.

Chapter 10: Keeping Ourselves Safe

Bock, M. A. (2001). SODA strategy: Enhancing the social interaction skills of youngsters with Asperger Syndrome. *Intervention in School and Clinic, 36*(5), 272-279.

Davis, B., & Schunick, W. G. (2002). *Dangerous encounters: Avoiding perilous situations with autism.* London & Philadelphia: Jessica Kingsley Publishers.

Debbaudt, D. (2001). *Autism, advocates, and law enforcement professionals: Recognizing and reducing risk situations for people with autism spectrum disorders.* London & Philadelphia: Jessica Kingsley Publishers.

Gagnon, E., & Robbins, L. (2001). Ensure success for the child with Asperger Syndrome. *Intervention in School and Clinic, 36*(5), 306-307.

Keating, K. A. (1998). Sexual abuse of persons with disabilities. *Advances in Special Education, 11,* 279-289.

Little, L. (2002). Middle-class mothers' perceptions of peer and sibling victimization among children with Asperger's Syndrome and nonverbal learning disorders. *Issues in Comprehensive Pediatric Nursing, 25*, 43-57.

Nadel, J., et al. (2000). Do children with autism have expectancies about the social behaviour of unfamiliar people? A pilot study using the still face paradigm. *Autism, 4*(2), 133-145.

Pietz, J., Ebinger, F., & Rating, D. (2003). Prosopagnosia in a preschool child with Asperger syndrome. *Developmental Medicine and Child Neurology, 45*, 55-57.

Rogers, M. F., & Myles, B. S.. (2001). Using social stories and comic strip conversations to interpret social situations for an adolescent with Asperger Syndrome. *Intervention in School and Clinic, 36*(5), 310-314.

Chapter 11: Gender Issues on the Spectrum

Atwood, T. (1999, September). *The Pattern of abilities and development of girls with Asperger's Syndrome.* Published by FAAAS at http://www.faaas.org/articles4.html.

Baron-Cohen, S. (2004). *The essential difference: Male and female brains and the truth about autism.* New York: Basic Books.

Biederman, J., et al. (2002). Influence of gender on attention deficit hyperactivity disorder in children referred to a psychiatric clinic. *American Journal of Psychiatry, 159*, 36-42.

Biederman, J., Faraone, S. V., & Monuteux, M. C. (2002). Differential effect of environmental adversity by gender: Rutter's Index of Adversity in a group of boys and girls with and without ADHD. *American Journal of Psychiatry, 159*, 1556-1562.

Constantino, J. N., & Todd, R. D. (2003). Autistic traits in the general population: A twin study. *Archives of General Psychiatry, 60*, 524-530.

Fausto-Sterling, A. (1992). *Myths of gender: Biological theories about women and men.* New York: Perseus Publishing.

Gilligan, C. (1983). *In a different voice: Psychological theory and women's development*. Cambridge, MA: Harvard University Press.

Gray, D. E. (2003). Gender and coping: the parents of children with high functioning autism. *Social Science and Medicine, 56*(3), 631-643.

Kindlon, D., Thompson, M., & Barker, T. (2000). *Raising Cain: Protecting the emotional life of boys.* New York: Random House, Inc.

Mead, M. (2001). *Coming of age in Samoa: A psychological study of primitive youth for western civilisation.* New York: Harper Perennial Modern Classics, a division of HarperCollins Publishers.

Miller, J. K. (Ed.). (2003). *Women from another planet? Our lives in the universe of autism.* Bloomington, IN: Authorhouse.

Chapter 12: Friendship

Adreon, D., & Stella, J. (2001). Transition to middle and high school: Increasing the success of students with Asperger syndrome. *Intervention in School and Clinic, 36*(5), 266-272.

Carrington, S., Templeton, E., & Papinczak, T. (2003). Adolescents with Asperger syndrome and perceptions of friendship. *Focus on Autism and Other Developmental Disabilities, 18*(4), 211-219.

Gutstein, S. E., & Whitney, T. (2002). Asperger Syndrome and the development of social competence. *Focus on Autism and Other Developmental Disabilities, 17*(3), 161-171.

Chapter 13: Disclosing Your Diagnosis

Attwood, T. (n.d.). Should you explain the diagnosis to the child? In T. Atwood (n.d.), *Diagnosis of Asperger Syndrome.* http://www.nas.org.uk/content/1/c4/78/22/tonyattwood.pdf, 10.

See, C. (Sept./Oct. 2004). George's place: autism swept him off to a secret world. Could his grandmother find a way to meet him halfway? *American Association of Retired Persons Magazine,* 40-44.

Shore, S. (Ed.). (2005). *Ask and tell: Self-advocacy and disclosure for people on the autism spectrum.* Shawnee Mission, KS: Autism Asperger Publishing Company.

Chapter 14: Invisibility and Self-Esteem in the Autistic Community

Barnhill, G. P. (2001). Social attributions and depression in adolescents with Asperger Syndrome. *Focus on Autism and Other Developmental Disabilities, 16*(1), 46-54.

Baron-Cohen, S. (2002). Is Asperger Syndrome necessarily viewed as a disability? *Focus on Autism and Other Developmental Disabilities, 17*(3), 186-192.

Gillott, A., Furniss, F., & Walter, A. (2001). Anxiety in high-functioning children with autism. *Autism, 5*(3), 277-286.

Henley, D. (2001). Annihilation anxiety and fantasy in the art of children with Asperger's Syndrome and others on the autistic spectrum. *American Journal of Art Therapy, 39*(4), 113-129.

Kim, J. A., et al. (2000). The prevalence of anxiety and mood problems among children with autism and Asperger syndrome. *Autism,* 4(2), 117-132.

Schwarz, P. (2004). Building alliances: community identity and the role of allies in autistic self-advocacy. In S. M. Shore (Ed.), Ask and tell: Self-advocacy and disclosure for people on the autism spectrum (pp. 143-176). Shawnee Mission, KS: Autism Asperger Publishing Company.

Sinclair, J. (1993). Don't mourn for us. *Our Voice, the Newsletter of Autism Network International, 1*(3), http://ani.autistics.org/dont_mourn.html.

Tantam, D. (1988). Lifelong eccentricity and social isolation: I. Psychiatric, social, and forensic aspects. *Journal of Psychiatry, 153,* 777-782.

Tantam, D. (1988). Lifelong eccentricity and social isolation: II. Asperger's Syndrome or schizoid personality disorder? *Journal of Psychiatry, 153,* 783-791.

Ward, M. J., & Meyer, R. N. (1999). Self-determination for people with developmental disabilities and autism: Two self-advocates' perspectives. *Focus on Autism and Other Developmental Disabilities, 14*(3), 133-140.

RESOURCES

Below is a list of resources that have helped me. They may also help you. Always use your own discretion, though. I can't endorse any products, goods, or services, I can only state my opinions.

RESOURCES FOR SENSORY ISSUES

Filters

My favorite brand of filter is Respro; my favorite model is the Respro City Mask. The company's website is: http://www.respro.com. This is a British company, though, so you have to find a U.S. supplier, which can be tricky. The Respro website recommends Street and Competition, a New York motorcycle supply store, which sells the City Mask I like at http://www.streetandcomp.com.You can also check bicycle shops in your area. People will most likely stare at you like you are crazy if you wear one, but when you hop into a cab and can't breathe because of the air freshener tree or when someone drenched in perfume plops down next to you at the movies and you can't find another seat in the dark, these masks can be a lifesaver.

Noise Cancelation Headphones

Bose has a very expensive version that does filters out most noises. In addition, you can use the headphones with a walkman or stereo. The only drawback is that you might feel like you are under water. You can see them at http://www.bose.com. Other companies make cheaper ones, but I haven't tried them.

Ear Plugs

My favorite brand is Mack's Aqua Block Swim Plugs. Designed for swimmers (that's how I discovered them), they work great out of the water, too, and are very comfortable. Again, do an Internet search to find a store that has them.

Sunglasses

The best pair of sunglasses I have ever owned are manufactured by Mine Safety Appliances Company, or MSA for short. The company carries several styles typically used in industrial settings. I like these sunglasses because they cover the whole eye area, not just the eye socket, so virtually no excess light seeps in from the top or sides. Also, they are virtually indestructible. You can't buy them directly from MSA, but you can call (800) MSA-2222 or visit their website at http://www.msasafetyworks.com for a list of distributors in your area. (Note: MSA also carries a variety of ear protection products that might help if you have auditory issues, but I've never tried any.)

Irlen Lenses

Irlen glasses are like sunglasses, but use a variety of colors for the lenses. As of press time, I have not tried Irlen lenses nor investigated their usage, but Dr. Temple Grandin recommended them to me because of my severe sensitivity to bright lights and suggested I mention them in my list of resources. Find out more on the Irlen Institute's website at http://www.irlen.com/index_autism.html.

Full-Spectrum Light Bulbs

Unlike regular bulbs, full-spectrum bulbs reflect the whole rainbow spectrum of light, potentially relieving eye fatigue and eye pain. If indoor lights bother you, give full spectrum bulbs a try. Even though they cost more, they are worth every penny if it means no more eye strain and, depending on the brand, they usually last longer anyway. Health food stores carry them. You can also do an Internet search for "full spectrum bulbs" – you may find them cheaper online.

ZoomCaps Keyboard Stickers

If you experience a lot of eyestrain staring at your computer screen, try sticking ZoomCaps keyboard stickers on your keyboard. ZoomCaps are large, heavily contrasted letters and numbers that you stick over the regular keys. Since the ZoomCaps characters are much bigger and bolder, it takes some processing load off of your eyes as you type. You can buy them from Therapro at http://www.theraproducts.com – do a keyword search for "zoomcap" on the Therapro website (Note: This company sells other adaptive and sensory equipment you may find useful).

USEFUL BOOKS

Social Tips

Packer, A. J. (1997). *How rude! The teenager's guide to good manners, proper behavior, and not grossing people out*. Minneapolis, MN: Free Spirit Publishing, Inc.

This serves as a great social "guide book" for everyone, but is especially useful for those of us on the spectrum. The book covers appropriate behavior, including what to say, for almost every social situation you can think of.

Dealing With Feelings

Madison, L. (2002). *The feelings book: The care and keeping of your emotions*. Middleton, WI: Pleasant Company Publications.

Even though it was written for teenage girls, this book contains much useful information for anyone of any age – men as well as women – about emotions and expressing them.

Cover Letters, Resumes, and Job Advice

Richardson, B. G. (1995). *Jobsmarts for twentysomethings*. New York: Vintage Books, a Division of Random House, Inc.

Yate, M. (2004). *Cover letters that knock 'em dead, sixth edition.* Holbrook, MA: Adams Media Corporation.

Yate, M. (2004). *Resumes that knock 'em dead, sixth edition.* Holbrook, MA: Adams Media Corporation.

Use these books at your own discretion. I found valuable information in them when job hunting (despite the strange titles of the last two). Concerning the first title, you don't have to be in your 20s to benefit from reading it. If you have trouble finding these books, check Amazon.com or your local library.

INDEX

T

V

W

Z

About the Author

Zosia Zaks has Asperger Syndrome. Although she completed her master's degree in technical journalism from Polytechnic University in 200 and held a variety of writing and editing jobs, it was various vocational and social challenges that led to her diagnosis at age 31. Now, with a clearer understanding of autism and how it impacts her life, Zosia has managed to face these challenges with creative ideas and innovative compromises. She now works as a heavy equipment operator in the International Union of Operating Engineers Local 825. This type of work allows her to go from project to project and is concrete in nature. She also runs www.intelligirl.com, a website that allows visitors to customize jewelry. Additionally, she lectures and conducts workshops nationally on issues of importance to the autistic community; consults with families, couples , and adults on the spectrum to find ways to meet challenges based on autistic strengths; and serves on the Advisory Board of GRASP, the Global and Regional Asperger Syndrome Partnership. She is married to her partner Gena. They live just outside New York City with their fifteen-month-old twin daughters, Ruby and Eislyn, and their cat, Zero.

APC

Autism Asperger Publishing Co.
P.O. Box 23173
Shawnee Mission, Kansas 66283-0173
www.asperger.net